FRAGMENTATION AND THE EUROPEAN PATENT SYSTEM

This book provides an in-depth study on current perceptions of, and responses to, fragmentation in the European patent system (EPS). For decades, attempts have been made to address this fragmentation by introducing a unitary patent system. The most recent attempt, the EU unitary patent system, will be the first of its kind. It is expected to significantly change the EPS. However, rather than reducing existing fragmentation, it will likely add to it.

Based on an analysis of the current and forthcoming systems, the book argues that the inherent nature of fragmentation within the EPS needs to be recognised and suggests that a multi-faceted approach is required to respond to it. Uniquely, it draws on work regarding fragmentation outside of the patent and intellectual property regimes, gaining insights from both European law-making and the international legal system.

These insights are used to investigate current responses to fragmentation in the EPS. Interpretations of substantive patent law are examined, including claim construction (*Actavis v Eli Lily*), exceptions to patentability related to uses of human embryos for industrial or commercial purposes (*WARF, Brüstle, ISCC*) and products resulting from essentially biological processes (*'Tomatoes II' and 'Broccoli II', G3/19*). Attempts towards convergence in these areas have had mixed results and in some instances fragmentation may be necessary. However, similar techniques to those applied in the international legal system to respond to fragmentation are being used in the EPS, and, where this is seen, it has been to good effect. It is argued that these methods should be recognised, structured and promoted to make our response to fragmentation more effective.

Fragmentation and the European Patent System will be of interest to academics, students and practitioners looking for a new perspective on the European patent system.

Fragmentation and the European Patent System

Karen Walsh

•HART•
OXFORD • LONDON • NEW YORK • NEW DELHI • SYDNEY

HART PUBLISHING

Bloomsbury Publishing Plc

Kemp House, Chawley Park, Cumnor Hill, Oxford, OX2 9PH, UK

1385 Broadway, New York, NY 10018, USA

29 Earlsfort Terrace, Dublin 2, Ireland

HART PUBLISHING, the Hart/Stag logo, BLOOMSBURY and the Diana logo are trademarks of Bloomsbury Publishing Plc

First published in Great Britain 2022

A catalogue record for this book is available from the British Library.

A catalogue record for this book is available from the Library of Congress.

ISBN: HB: 978-1-50993-931-2
ePDF: 978-1-50993-933-6
ePub: 978-1-50993-932-9

Typeset by Compuscript Ltd, Shannon

To Mom, Dad and Jason

ACKNOWLEDGEMENTS

Without the support of others, this book would not have been possible. I have many people whom I want to thank individually, but to everyone who helped in any way, you have my sincere gratitude.

This book is a revised and updated version of my D.Phil thesis, which was submitted to the University of Oxford in 2016. My first set of acknowledgements go to those who helped to shape that unforgettable journey.

First, I am immensely grateful to my supervisor, Justine Pila. During the D.Phil, she was an unrivalled source of knowledge and has taught me how to explore, define and refine the questions I consider in my research. Thank you for the constant encouragement and for always providing excellent advice, feedback and guidance, both during and beyond the D.Phil.

My sincere gratitude to my examiners and advisers while at Oxford, Stefan Enchelmaier, Simon Gardner, Angus Johnston, Stefan Luginbuehl, Duncan Matthews and Christopher Wadlow. Thank you for excellent discussions and feedback at various stages of the D.Phil. My thanks to Bríd Ní Ghráinne, Aisling McMahon and Kate Conneely for their feedback on the thesis in its final stages. Thanks also to Lincoln College and the University of Oxford Faculty of Law for funding my attendance at conferences and for various scholarships along the way.

While completing my D.Phil, I also spent a summer working with the Legal Research Service of the Boards of Appeal at the European Patent Office. My thanks to everyone there for welcoming me as part of the team and for all the fascinating discussions.

To my friends who made the D.Phil experience what it was – thank you for all the good times!

My second set of acknowledgements are for those who provided support while I was writing this book. In 2016, I was offered a lectureship at the University of Exeter. It was here that I started and finished that process. To all my friends and colleagues at Exeter, especially those in the SCuLE Research Centre, thank you for providing such a wonderful space for academic development.

I am extremely grateful to all who provided advice, feedback and insightful comments on various aspects of this book, particularly Naomi Hawkins, Aisling McMahon, Stefan Luginbuehl, Mathilde Pavis, Joasia Luzak, Kubo Mačák, Charlie Anderson, Alexandra Mogyoros, Anne Barlow, Bríd Ní Ghráinne, and Natalie Ohana. Any remaining errors or omissions are, of course, my own.

Parts of this research have previously been published and presented at numerous conferences and workshops. For the feedback received from these experiences I am very appreciative to all involved. I would also like to recognise that some of the suggestions in this book have been informed by ongoing research, currently supported by the British Academy, Department for Business, Energy and Industrial Strategy (Reference number SRG1819\190316).

My thanks to the reviewers, editors and designers at Hart Publishing for all the work that went into the production of this book behind the scenes.

Finally, my deepest thanks go to all my family and friends. This entire process could not have been completed without their unwavering support. Some people in particular deserve a special thank you: my parents, Brendan and Imelda, for their endless love and support; my brother Gar, for all his encouragement; my Granny Kay, for all her prayers; Kate, Ailís and Aoife, for their wonderful friendship; and my partner Jason, for always being there for me, through everything – *ó cheartlár mo chroí, míle buíochas*!

CONTENTS

Acknowledgements .... *vii*
Abbreviations .... *xiii*
Table of Cases .... *xv*
Table of Legislation .... *xxi*

Introduction 1
I. Background 3
II. The European Patent System 5
III. Terminology 7
IV. Perspectives on Fragmentation 12
V. Outline 13

PART I
FRAGMENTATION AND THE EUROPEAN PATENT SYSTEM TODAY

1. Existing Routes to Patent Protection in Europe 19
I. National Patent Systems 19
II. The European (EPC) Patent System 27
III. The International Patent Application 31
IV. Existing Fragmentation 34

2. Forthcoming Route to EU Unitary Patent Protection 36
I. Background to the Unitary Patent Package 37
II. The Unitary Patent Package 42
III. Concerns Related to the Unitary Patent Package 45
A. Substantive Issues 45
B. Territorial Fragmentation 49
i. Ratification and Membership of the UPCA 50
ii. Participation in the Unitary Patent 54
iii. Users of the UPP 59
C. Institutional Fragmentation 63
i. Internal Structure of the UPC 64
ii. Jurisdiction and Competence of the UPC and the Transitional Period 67
iii. Bifurcation 68
IV. Further Fragmentation 69

PART II
ALTERNATIVE PERCEPTIONS OF FRAGMENTATION

3. Fragmentation in European Law-Making 73
   I. Constructing Europe and the European Patent System....74
      A. Council of Europe – Longchambon Proposal 74
      B. European Coal and Steel Community....75
      C. Council of Europe – Strasbourg Patent Convention 78
      D. European Economic Community, the EPC and the CPC....79
      E. Shifting Perspectives and Objectives 81
   II. The Impact of Expansion 82
      A. Impact on the Patent System....85
   III. Fragmentation as a Means of Integration 88

4. Fragmentation in the International Legal System 90
   I. Fragmentation in the International Legal System 91
      A. Analysis of Fragmentation 94
      B. Responses to Fragmentation....95
      C. Judicial Dialogue and Cooperation....99
      D. From Fear to Acceptance....101
   II. Application to the European Patent System 102
   III. Fragmentation as an Inherent Aspect of a Legal System 105

PART III
FRAGMENTATION AND SUBSTANTIVE PATENT LAW

5. Responding to Fragmentation as an Inherent Aspect of the European Patent System....109
   I. Areas of Divergence....110
      A. Implementation of the EPC 111
      B. Approaches to Patentability 111
         i. Inventive Step....113
         ii. Patentable Subject Matter 114
   II. Towards Convergence – Judicial Dialogue and Cooperation 117
      A. Decision-making....118
         i. National Courts Considering Board of Appeal Decisions....118
         ii. National Courts Considering Other National Court Decisions....119
         iii. EPO Interpretation and Consideration of National Court Decisions 123
         iv. Boards of Appeal Considering CJEU Decisions and the CJEU Considering Board of Appeal Decisions....124
         v. Referrals by National Courts....125

B. Case Study in Cooperation – Claim Construction 126
i. Background 126
ii. Impact of the EPC....................128
iii. Divergence....................132
iv. Convergence....................133
v. Impact 136
vi. Post-*Actavis v Eli Lilly* 137
C. Judicial Meetings and Appointments....................137
D. Impact of the Unitary Patent Package 139
E. Limitations of Judicial Dialogue and Cooperation 140
III. Fragmentation as an Inherent Aspect of the European Patent System....................142

6. Accepting Fragmentation as a Necessary Aspect of the European Patent System....................144
I. The Impact of the Biotech Directive....................145
A. Legislative Harmonisation 146
B. Institutional Addition 148
II. Interpretations of the Exceptions to Patentability 149
A. Uses of Human Embryos for Industrial or Commercial Purposes 149
i. *WARF* 150
ii. *Brüstle*....................151
iii. *ISCC*....................152
iv. Evaluation 152
a. Convergence Overextended 153
b. Generalist v Specialist Decision-making....................156
c. Institutional Interactions 157
d. Conclusion....................159
B. Essentially Biological Processes....................160
i. G2/13 and G2/12 *(Broccoli II and Tomatoes II)* 160
ii. T1063/18 *Extreme Dark Green, Blocky Peppers* 161
iii. G3/19 *Pepper (follow-up to 'Tomatoes II' and 'Broccoli II')* 162
iv. Evaluation 162
a. Institutional Interactions and Convergence Overreach....................162
b. Specialist Institution Perspective 164
c. Conclusion....................164
III. Impact of the Unitary Patent Package 165
IV. Considering Diversity and Value Pluralism when Responding to Fragmentation....................168

Conclusion: Fragmentation and the European Patent System 169

Bibliography *177*
Index *189*

ABBREVIATIONS

CJEU	Court of Justice of the European Union
CPA	Community Patent Agreement
CPC	Community Patent Convention
EC	European Community
ECSC	European Coal and Steel Community
EEA	European Economic Area
EEC	European Economic Community
EIPR	European Intellectual Property Review
EPC	European Patent Convention
EPLA	European Patent Litigation Agreement
EPO	European Patent Office
EPOrg	European Patent Organisation
EPUE	European Patent with Unitary Effect
EU	European Union
ICJ	International Court of Justice
ICLQ	International and Comparative Law Quarterly
IIC	International Review of Intellectual Property and Competition Law
ILC	International Law Commission
IPQ	Intellectual Property Quarterly
ISA	International Search Authority
JIPLP	Journal of Intellectual Property Law and Practice
MLR	Modern Law Review
PCT	Patent Cooperation Treaty
SMEs	Small/Medium-Sized Enterprises
SPC	Supplementary Protection Certificate
TEU	Treaty on European Union

TFEU	Treaty on the Functioning of the European Union
TRIPS	Agreement on Trade-Related Aspects of Intellectual Property
UK	United Kingdom
UKIPO	United Kingdom Intellectual Property Office
UPC	Unified Patent Court
UPCA	Agreement on a Unified Patent Court
UPP	Unitary Patent Package
US	United States
VCLT	Vienna Convention on the Law of Treaties
WIPO	World Intellectual Property Office
WTO	World Trade Organization

TABLE OF CASES

United Kingdom

Actavis UK Ltd v Novartis AG [2010] EWCA Civ 82......114
Actavis v Eli Lilly [2014] EWHC 1511 (Pat)......134
Actavis v Eli Lilly [2015] EWCA Civ 555......134
Actavis v Eli Lilly [2017] UKSC 48......121, 133–36
Actavis v ICOS [2017] EWCA Civ 1671......137
Aerotel Ltd v Telco Holdings Ltd & Macrossan's Patent Application [2006] EWCA Civ 1371......116, 125, 158
Biogen Inc v Medeva [1996] UKHL 18......119
Bose Corporation v Freebit [2018] EWHC 889 (Pat)......137
Catnic v Hill & Smith Limited [1978] FSR 405......127
Catnic v Hill & Smith Limited [1979] FSR 619 (CA)......127
Catnic v Hill & Smith Limited [1982] RPC 183......127, 134
Document Security Systems v European Central Bank [2007] EWHC 600 (Pat)......31, 112
European Central Bank v Document Security Systems Inc [2007] EWHC 600 (Pat)......68
Fisher & Paykel v Resmed [2017] EWHC 2748 (Pat)......137
Fujitsu's Application [1997] RPC 608......115
Gale's Application [1991] RPC 305......115
Genentech Inc's Patent [1989] RPC 147......115, 118
Generics (UK) Ltd and others v Yeda Research and Development Company and others [2017] EWHC 2629 (Pat)......133
Generics (UK) Ltd v Daiichi Pharmaceutical Co Ltd [2009] EWCA Civ 646......114
Generics (UK) Ltd v Lundbeck A/S [2009] UKHL 12......119
Grimme Maschinenfabrik GmbH & Co KG v Derek Scott (t/a Scotts Potato Machinery) [2010] EWCA Civ 1110......111, 120
Human Genome Sciences Inc (HGS) v Eli Lilly [2011] UKSC 51......119
Icescape Limited v Ice-World International BV & Ors [2018] EWCA Civ 2219......137
Illumina v Premaitha [2017] EWHC 2930 (Pat)......137
Improver Corp v Remington Consumer Product Ltd [1990] FSR 181......31, 112, 128, 132, 170

International Stem Cell Corporation v Comptroller General of Patents [2013] EWHC 807 (Ch) 152
Kirin-Amgen Inc & Ors v Hoechst Marion Roussel Ltd & Ors [2004] UKHL 46 .... 129–32, 134–35
Kirin-Amgen v Transkaryotic Therapies [2002] RPC 2 135
L'Oréal Société Anonyme v RN Ventures [2018] EWHC 173 (Pat) 137
Liqwd Inc and Olaplex LLC v L'Oréal SA [2018] EWHC 1394 (Pat) 137
Merrell Dow Pharmaceutical Inc v Norton & Co Ltd [1996] RPC 76....118
Merrill Lynch's Application [1989] RPC 561 115
Novartis AG and Cibavision AG v Johnson & Johnson Medical Ltd and others [2009] EWHC 1671 (Pat).... 31, 112
Pozzoli SPA v BDMO SA [2007] EWCA Civ 588 112–14
Re Symbian's Application [2009] RPC 1 116
Schütz v Werit [2013] UKSC 16....121
Smith Kline and French Laboratories Ltd v RD Harbottle (Mercantile) Ltd [1980] RPC 363 111
Symbian Ltd v Comptroller General of Patents, Designs and Trademarks [2008] EWCA Civ 1066....116
Warner-Lambert Company LLC v Generics (UK) Ltd t/a Mylan and another [2018] UKSC 56....121
Wheatly v Drillsafe [2001] RPC 133....129
Windsurfing International Inc v Tabur Marine (Great Britain) Ltd [1985] RPC 59....113

Germany

Decision of the Bundesgerichtshof, 27 March 1969 – X ZB 15/67 '*Rote Taube (Red Dove)*'....115
Decision of the Bundesgerichtshof, 29 April 1986 – X ZR 28/85 '*Formstein (Moulded Curbstone)*' 130
Decision of the Bundesgerichtshof, 5 May 1998 – X ZR 57/96 '*Zahnkranzfräser (Gear rim mill)*' 121
Decision of the Bundesgerichtshof, 17 December 2009 – Xa ZR 58/07 '*Neurale Vorläuferzellen (Neural precursor cells)*' 151
Decision of the Bundesgerichtshof, 15 April 2010 – Xa ZB 10/09 '*Walzenformgebungsmaschine (Roller-forming-machine)*'....122
Decision of the BVerfG, Order of the Second Senate of 13 February 2020 – 2 BvR 739/17 52
Decision of the BVerfG, Order of the Second Senate of 23 June 2021 – 2 BvR 2216/20 and 2 BvR 2217/20....53
Decision of the Oberlandesgericht Düsseldorf, 21 November 1991 – 2 U 27/89 '*Improver*'.... 112, 132

France

Cour d'Appel de Montpellier, Civil division section 2, 17 September 2015 (13/05047), *MVF 3 APS v Intelligent Insect Control*....122
Tribunal de Grande Instance de Paris, 13 October 2015 (15/58725), *Warner-Lambert v Sandoz*....122
Tribunal de Grande Instance de Paris, 25 March 2009 (07/13504), *Novartis AG and Cibavision AG v Johnson & Johnson Medical Ltd and others*....31
Tribunal de Grande Instance de Paris, 3rd chamber 3rd section, 27 September 2012 (12/13507), *Akzo Nobel v Teva Sante*....122
Tribunal de Grande Instance de Paris, 23 September 2014 (14/58023), *Lilly France v Sanofi*....122
Tribunal de Grande Instance de Paris, 3rd chamber 3rd section, 1 July 2016 (15/05880), *AstraZeneca v Mylan*....122

Netherlands

District Court of The Hague, 11 February 2009, HA ZA 07-3547 *Novartis AG and Cibavision AG v Johnson & Johnson Medical Ltd and others*....31
District Court of The Hague, 19 June 2019, C/09/541424/ HA ZA 17-1097 *Eli Lilly v Fresenius Kabi Nederland BV* ECLI:NL:RBDHA:2019:6107....137

Hungary

Decision 9/2018 (VII. 9.) AB on the interpretation of Article E) paragraphs (2) and (4), Article Q) paragraph (3) and Article 25 of the Fundamental Law....53

Court of Justice of the European Union

Case 15/74 *Centrafarm BV and Adriaan de Peijper v Sterling Drug Inc* ECLI:EU:C:1974:114....21
Joined Cases C-584/10 P, C-593/10 P and C-595/10 P *Commission and Others v Kadi* ECLI:EU:C:2013:518....90
Case 78/70 *Deutsche Grammophon Gesellschaft mbH v Metro-SB-Grossmärkte GmbH & Co KG* ECLI:EU:C:1971:59....21
Joined Cases 56 and 58-64 *Établissements Consten S.à.R.L. and Grundig-Verkaufs-GmbH v Commission of the European Economic Community* ECLI:EU:C:1966:41....21
Case C-4/03 *Gesellschaft für Antriebstechnik mbH & Co KG v Lamellen und Kupplungsbau Beteiligungs KG* ECLI:EU:C:2006:457....25

Case C-364/13 *International Stem Cell Corporation v Comptroller General of Patents, Designs and Trade Marks* ECLI:EU:C:2014:2451 .... 125, 152–53, 155, 174
Case C-147/13 *Kingdom of Spain v Council of the European Union* ECLI:EU:C:2015:299 .... 40, 46–47, 49, 57–58, 87
Case C-146/13 *Kingdom of Spain v European Parliament and the Council of the European Union* ECLI:EU:C:2015:298 .... 40, 47, 87
Joined Cases C-274 and 295/11 *Kingdom of Spain and Italian Republic v Council of the European Union* [2013] ECLI:EU:C:2013:240 .... 39, 87
Case C-377/98 *Netherlands v European Parliament and Council of the European Union* ECLI:EU:C:2001:523 146
Case C-34/10 *Oliver Brüstle v Greenpeace eV* ECLI:EU:C:2011:669 .... 125, 145, 151, 174
Case C-36/02 *Omega Spielhallen- und Automatenaufstellungs-GmbH v Oberbürgermeisterin der Bundesstadt Bonn* ECLI:EU:C:2004:614 .... 83, 154
Case 24/67 *Parke, Davis & Co v Probel, Reese, Beintema-Interpharm and Centrafarm* ECLI:EU:C:1968:11 21
Case C-539/03 *Roche Nederland BV v Frederick Primus* ECLI:EU:C:2006:458 25
Case C-616/10 *Solvay SA v Honeywell Florine Products Europe BV and Others* ECLI:EU:C:2012:445 25–26
Opinion 1/09 ECLI:EU:C:2011:123 .... 39–41, 151

Enlarged Board of Appeal of the European Patent Office

G1/08 *Tomatoes/STATE OF ISRAEL* of 09.12.10 .... 115, 160
G1/13 *Admissibility of referral* of 25.11.2014 124
G1/19 *Pedestrian simulation* of 10.3.21 .... 113, 116
G2/06 *Use of embryos/WARF* of 25.11.2008 150
G2/07 *Broccoli/PLANT BIOSCIENCE* of 09.12.10 .... 115, 160
G2/08 *Dosage regime/ABBOTT RESPITORY* of 19.2.2010 123
G2/12 of 25.03.15 160–61
G2/13 of 25.03.15 160–61
G3/08 *Programs for computers* of 12.5.2010 125
G3/19 *Pepper (follow-up to 'Tomatoes II' and 'Broccoli II')* of 14.05.20 .... 145, 162, 174
G5/83 *Second medical indication* of 05.12.1984 123–24

Boards of Appeal of the European Patent Office

T1/80 *Bayer/Carbonless copying paper* of 06.4.1981 113
T1063/18 *Extreme dark green, blocky peppers/SYNGENTA* of 05.12.2018 161–62

T1441/13 *Embryonic stem cells, disclaimer/ASTERIAS* of 09.09.2014 158
T154/04 *Estimating sales activity/DUNS LICENSING ASSOCIATES* of 15.11.2006 124
T208/84 *VICOM/Computer-related invention* of 15.7.1986 115
T2221/10 *Culturing stem cells/TECHNION* of 04.02.2014 .... 151, 158
T258/03 *HITACHI/Auction Method* of 21.4.2004 116
T424/03 *MICROSOFT/Data transfer with expanded clipboard formats* of 23.2.2006 116
T452/91 of 5.07.1995 124
T465/92 *Alcan/Aluminium alloys* of 14.10.1994 114
T522/04 *Stem Cells/CALIFORNIA* of 28.05.2009 151
T641/00 *Two identities/COMVIK* of 26.9.2002 117
T931/95 *PBS PARTNERSHIP/Controlling pension benefits system* of 08.9.2000 115–17

European Court of Human Rights

Evans v UK App no 6339/05 (ECtHR, 7 March 2006) 154
Vo v France App no 53924/00 (ECtHR 8 July 2004) 154

TABLE OF LEGISLATION

Agreement 89/695/EEC of 15 December 1989 relating to Community Patents [1989] OJ L 401/1 (Community Patent Agreement) 20, 46, 48, 81

Agreement 2013/C on a Unified Patent Court [2013] OJ L 175/01 (UPCA) 6–7, 37, 41, 43–44, 46–47, 49–54, 59–69, 139, 166–67, 171, 175

Agreement on the application of Article 65 EPC (London Agreement) 2000 30

Agreement on Trade Related Aspects of Intellectual Property Rights (TRIPS) 1994 .... 4, 10, 13, 21–23, 97

Brussels Convention of 27 September 1968 on jurisdiction and the enforcement of judgments in civil and commercial matters [1972] OJ L 299 (Brussels Convention) 25

Charter of Fundamental Rights of the European Union [2000] OJ C 364/01 86

Consolidated Version of the Treaty on European Union (TEU) [2012] OJ C 326/13 .... 11, 39, 42, 55–56, 83–87

Consolidated Version of the Treaty on the Functioning of the European Union (TFEU) [2012] OJ C 326/47 .... 6, 11, 39, 42, 44–48, 55, 84–87, 125, 147–48

Convention for the European Patent for the Common Market (15 December 1975) (Community Patent Convention) 20–21, 46, 79–82, 103, 109, 111, 120–21

Convention for the Protection of Industrial Property 1883 (Paris Convention) 10, 13, 20–21, 24, 32–33, 102–03

Convention on jurisdiction and the recognition and enforcement of judgments in civil and commercial matters [2007] OJ L 339/3 (Lugano Convention) 45, 67

Convention on the Grant of European Patents 1973/2000 (European Patent Convention) 1, 3, 6–8, 10, 14–15, 19–20, 23, 27–35, 37–38, 40, 42–45, 47–49, 51, 59–60, 62–63, 67, 75, 79–82, 86, 91, 103–04, 109–18, 120–21, 123–34, 136, 139, 142, 144–45, 147–48, 150, 158–64, 170–72, 174–75

Convention on the Unification of Certain Points of Substantive Law on Patents for Invention 1963 (Strasbourg Patent Convention) 10, 15, 20–21, 28, 78–80, 82, 103, 109

Directive 2015/2436 of the European Parliament and of the Council of 16 December 2015 to approximate the laws of the Member States relating to trade marks [2015] OJ L 336/1 9

Directive 2001/29/EC of the European Parliament and of the Council of 22 May 2001 on the harmonisation of certain aspects of copyright and related rights in the information society [2001] OJ L 167/10 (InfoSoc Directive) 9

Directive 2004/48/EC of the European Parliament and of the Council of 29 April 2004 on the enforcement of intellectual property rights [2004] OJ L 195/16 (Enforcement Directive) 9, 87

Directive 2014/26/EU of the European Parliament and of the Council of 26 February 2014 on collective management of copyright and related rights and multi-territorial licensing of rights in musical works for online use in the internal market [2014] OJ L 84/72 (CRM Directive) 9

Directive 2019/790 of the European Parliament and of the Council of 17 April 2019 on copyright and related rights in the Digital Single Market [2019] OJ L 130/92 (DSM Directive) 9

Directive 96/9/EC of the European Parliament and of the Council of 11 March 1996 on the legal protection of databases [1996] OJ L 77/20 (Database Directive) 9

Directive 98/44/EC of the European Parliament and of the Council of 6 July 1998 on the legal protection of biotechnological inventions [1998] OJ L 213/13 (Biotech Directive) 5, 8–9, 15–16, 22–23, 87, 103–04, 109, 125, 145–54, 160, 163–64, 170–72

Directive 98/71/EC of the European Parliament and of the Council of 13 October 1998 on the legal protection of designs [1998] OJ L 289/98 9

Implementing Regulations to the Convention on the Grant of European Patents 2006 23

Patent Cooperation Treaty (PCT) 1970 .... 1, 6, 10, 19, 31–35, 170

Patentgesetz in der Fassung der Bekanntmachung vom 16. Dezember 1980 (BGBI. 1981 I S. 1), das durch Artikel 1 des Gesetzes vom 30. August 2021 (BGBI. I S. 4074) geändert worden ist (German Patents Act) 19, 130, 170

Patents Act 1977 (UK) 3, 19, 34, 103, 111, 113–15, 118, 128, 130, 170, 173

Preliminary set of provisions for the Rules of Procedure of the Unified Patent Court, 18th draft, 19 October 2015 (Rules of Procedure) 6, 44, 61–62, 69

Regulation (EC) 1610/96 of the European Parliament and of the Council of 23 July 1996 concerning the creation of a supplementary protection certificate for plant protection products [1996] OJ L 198/30 ....8–9, 22, 86
Regulation (EC) 6/2002 of 12 December 2001 on Community designs [2002] OJ L 3/1 9
Regulation (EC) 469/2009 of the European Parliament and of the Council of 6 May 2009 concerning the supplementary protection certificate for medicinal products (codified version) [2009] OJ L 152/1Regulation (EU) 1215/2012 of 12 December 2012 on jurisdiction and the recognition and enforcement of judgments in civil and commercial matters [2012] OJ L 351/1 (Brussels I Regulation)...............8, 22, 26, 45, 86
Regulation (EU) 1257/2012 of the European Parliament and of the Council of 17 December 2012 implementing enhanced cooperation in the area of the creation of unitary patent protection [2012] OJ L 361/1 (Regulation 1257) 6, 36, 42, 45–48, 59, 67, 171
Regulation (EU) 1260/2012 of the European Parliament and of the Council of 17 December 2012 implementing enhanced cooperation in the area of the creation of unitary patent protection with regard to the applicable translation arrangements [2012] OJ L 361/89 (Regulation 1260) 6, 36, 42–43, 55, 57, 59–61, 171
Regulation 1215/2012 of the European Parliament and of the Council of 12 December 2012 on jurisdiction and the recognition and enforcement of judgments in civil and commercial matters (Recast) [2012] OJ L 351/1 (Brussels I Regulation (Recast))............... 25, 67
Regulation 2017/1001/EU on the European Union trade mark [2017] OJ L 154/1 9
Single European Act 1986 82–83
Treaty establishing the European Atomic Energy Community (EURATOM) 1957............... 77, 79, 83
Treaty establishing the European Community 1993 83–84
Treaty establishing the European Economic Coal and Steel Community 1951 (Treaty of Paris)...............75
Treaty establishing the European Economic Community (EEC) 1957 (Treaty of Rome) 77–78, 83
Treaty of Brussels (Merger Treaty) [1965] OJ 152/2...............79
Treaty of Lisbon amending the Treaty on European Union and the Treaty Establishing the European Community [2007] C 306/01............... 38, 85
Vienna Convention on the Law of Treaties (Vienna, 23 May 1969, 1155 UNTS 331) (Vienna Convention) 51, 95–96, 123, 142, 173, 175

Introduction

Fragmentation implies that something has been broken into pieces. The European patent system was never a single unit, but it has been increasingly referred to as fragmented given the repeated attempts that have been made towards its unification. In that sense, it is and always has been fragmented. Moreover, it likely always will be.

Legislative attempts to unify the system at both European and European Union (EU) level have been plentiful. The introduction of a unitary patent system has been seen as vital to overcoming the obstacle of fragmentation and improving the European patent system. However, there has been such a significant focus on responding to fragmentation in this way that we have not paused to comprehensively consider the concept itself, whether it can be classified as 'good' or 'bad', whether it can or should be removed, and how.

Fragmentation can take many forms and it is not easily responded to, let alone removed. With or without a unitary patent system, it is likely to remain. Recognising and accepting this is necessary so that we can respond to fragmentation in the most appropriate manner. The aim of this book is to fill a critical gap by providing an in-depth study on fragmentation and the European patent system. It also suggests additional responses to fragmentation that can recognise its inherent nature.

The European patent system is made up of many layers and includes countries expanding beyond the EU. There are currently three routes to patent protection in Europe. The first is through the national patent systems, implemented by individual national patent offices. Second, the European Patent Convention (EPC) established the European (EPC) route to patent protection.[1] This is implemented by the European Patent Office (EPO) and the Administrative Council of the European Patent Organisation (EPOrg). It provides a streamlined patent grant procedure in 38 Contracting States. The third route is through an international application to the World Intellectual Property Office (WIPO), introduced by the Patent Cooperation Treaty (PCT).[2] Opting for this route results in an international filing date, which can then be used when entering the national or regional (EPC) phase. Each applies different procedures and is governed by different institutions. The result of each route to protection is effectively a national patent, validated and

[1] Convention on the Grant of European Patents of 5 October 1973 (European Patent Convention) (EPC), amended in 2000.

[2] Patent Cooperation Treaty 1970 (PCT).

enforced at a national level. This can lead, and has led, to divergence in the grant of patents and their enforcement, as well as in the interpretation of substantive patent law.[3]

Fragmentation in the European patent system is often understood to mean territorial fragmentation. Territorial fragmentation exists because it is not currently possible to have a single patent granted that covers all countries in Europe. Therefore, the same invention is being protected by a similar, but separate, patent in several territories. However, fragmentation can take many forms in a legal system. For example, it can also be substantive, institutional and procedural. These forms of fragmentation are apparent in the European patent system. Substantive fragmentation relates to self-contained regimes existing and operating in a vacuum, interpreting similar concepts in different ways. This is possible in the European patent system because patent law issues overlap with other areas such as competition law, human rights law and contract law, to name a few. Substantive fragmentation is often referred to on a more local level in the European patent system because of the multiple and overlapping sources from which patent law derives its substance. Given that each institution involved has its own rules and practices, it can operate as a self-contained regime. That being said, substantive patent law is essentially harmonised across Europe, and so, despite differences in implementation, each law is based on the same international conventions. Institutional fragmentation can occur because patents are still mostly enforced at the national level, where offices and courts can come to divergent decisions on validity and infringement, despite examining the same invention or interpreting the same legal concepts. This is not limited to divergence in parallel proceedings, but is rather a more widespread matter relating to the interpretation of substantive patent law generally. Procedural fragmentation can occur because patent offices and courts throughout Europe operate with different procedural norms, which can have an impact on decision-making.

Fragmentation, coupled with the cost associated with the current systems, are the main reasons for the repeated and long-standing attempts towards creating a unitary system. The existence of and potential for fragmentation in the European patent system are generally perceived in a negative light, evidenced by criticisms of the current and forthcoming systems and the number of attempts that have been made towards a unitary patent system. Indeed, fragmentation can have serious negative consequences on legal certainty, and the risks associated with it must be responded to.

Even with the introduction of a unitary patent system, fragmentation will remain. It will not replace previous systems. It will exist alongside them. Therefore,

[3] See SJH Graham and N Van Zeebroeck, 'Comparing Patent Litigation Across Europe: A First Look' (2014) 17 *Stanford Technical Law Review* 655, 708. This evidence has been confirmed in another more recent study published in 2016: K Cremers, M Ernicke, F Gaessler, D Harhoff, C Helmers, L McDonagh, P Schliessler and N van Zeebroeck, 'Patent Litigation in Europe' (2016) 44 *European Journal of Law and Economics* available at http://link.springer.com/article/10.1007/s10657-016-9529-0.

these forms of fragmentation will continue to exist but in a more complex fashion. Having one system where fragmentation has been taken away will not remove it from the bigger picture. Multiple patents will still exist for the same invention, and multiple institutions will still rule on similar legal concepts in different ways. Fragmentation can never be fully removed without a single unified patent system that covers all of Europe, which has never been seen as achievable, even if it were considered desirable. The possibility of substantive fragmentation will also remain due to the overlapping nature of patent law with other areas of law.

This book examines the European patent system from a broad perspective using the concept of fragmentation as experienced elsewhere to offer fresh insights for the patent system. Specifically, these insights emerge by investigating the development of European law-making processes, and perspectives of fragmentation in the international legal system. It transpires that allowing for the introduction of differing laws between Member States in the EU was required for integration to move forward post-expansion, and that fragmentation is seen by many as an inherent part of the international legal system with effective methods being used to reduce the risks associated with it. Considering how substantive patent law is currently being interpreted in this fragmented European patent system, it is seen that these methods are already being used, albeit informally and irregularly. Reflecting on these findings, this book argues that our current response to fragmentation in the European patent system can be improved. Overall, if we change our perception of fragmentation and accept its existence as something that is inherent, we can shift our focus onto developing additional mechanisms to respond to it with a view to improving the system as a whole.

I. Background

A patent is an exclusive right, granted by the state to the patentee for a limited term of protection in exchange for the disclosure of the protected invention to the public. The subject matter must be an invention that is new, involves an inventive step and has industrial application.[4] The commercialisation of the invention cannot be contrary to *ordre public* and/or morality.[5] Patents will not be granted for certain inventions for public policy reasons, for example methods of medical treatment, plant and animal varieties, and essentially biological processes.[6] Details on how to make the invention work must be disclosed in a manner that would allow a person skilled in the relevant art to make the invention work.[7] If granted, a patent confers on the patentee an exclusive right to prevent a third party from

[4] Section 1(1) Patents Act 1977 (UK) and Articles 54, 56 and 57 EPC.
[5] Section 1(3) Patents Act 1977 (UK) and Article 53 EPC.
[6] Section 4A and Schedule A2 Patents Act 1977 (UK) and Article 53 EPC.
[7] Section 14(3) Patents Act 1977 (UK) and Article 83 EPC.

making, using, offering for sale, selling, or importing the protected invention.[8] Once the term of protection has expired, 20 years after the filing date of the patent application, the public will be free to use the invention in any way.

Patents are said to incentivise innovation and promote the disclosure of technological developments resulting in benefits to society.[9] By granting patentees a 20-year exclusive right, they are given the opportunity to generate income that will support both recouping the investment required for the research and development of the successful invention, as well as previous failures, and provide the means to improve the invention or incentivise additional developments. The justification for granting these exclusive rights is based on the resulting societal benefit of increased innovation and technological development. It is said that without the patent system, inventions would be kept secret for as long as possible to avoid copying from competitors, which in turn would hinder technological developments for society. Thus, the system ostensibly rests on a balance between protecting the inventor and making technological developments available to society. However, evidence is lacking to prove that a patent system sufficiently incentivises innovation.[10] Further, it has been argued that there are other factors that can promote technological development, such as prizes and alternative sources of funding.[11] Despite these valid arguments, there is no indication that patent systems will be abandoned. The often-quoted conclusions of Fritz Machlup that it would be irresponsible to implement the system that we have knowing what we know, but also irresponsible to remove it now that we have it, leaves us with the task of making this system more responsible.[12] Although this statement was in reference to the US patent system in 1958, it rings true for the European patent system today. Without an appropriate alternative, it is important to ensure that the

[8] As required by Article 28 of the Agreement on Trade-Related Aspects of Intellectual Property Rights 1994 (TRIPS), which sets out the minimum standards for the protection of intellectual property for the Members of the World Trade Organization (WTO).

[9] For discussions on rationales for patent protection, see J Pila, *The Subject Matter of Intellectual Property* (Oxford University Press 2017); R Tushnet, 'Intellectual Property as a Public Interest Mechanism' in RC Dreyfuss and J Pila (eds), *The Oxford Handbook of Intellectual Property Law* (Oxford University Press 2017); R Merges, *Justifying Intellectual Property* (Harvard University Press 2011).

[10] See S Thambisetty, 'Liza's Bucket: Intellectual Property and the Metamodern Impulse' [2020] *LSE Law, Society and Economy Working Papers* 19/2020 available at https://papers.ssrn.com/sol3/papers.cfm?abstract_id=3743217.

[11] These debates have been summarised in RC Dreyfuss, 'In Praise of an Incentive-Based Theory' in RC Dreyfuss and ES-K Ng (eds) *Framing Intellectual Property Law in the 21st Century: Integrating Incentives, Trade, Development, Culture, and Human Rights* (Cambridge University Press 2018) 3–11. See also, for example, M Boldrin and DK Levine, 'The Case Against Patents' (2013) 27(1) *Journal of Economic Perspectives* 3; D Baker, A Jayadev and J Stiglitz, 'Innovation, Intellectual Property and Development: A Better Set of Approaches for the 21st Century' [2017] *Access IBSA: Innovation & Access to Medicines in India, Brazil & South Africa* available at http://ip-unit.org/wp-content/uploads/2017/07/IP-for-21st-Century-EN.pdf; B Wright, 'The Economics of Invention Incentives: Patents, Prizes, and Research Contracts' (1983) 73(4) *The American Economic Review* 691; J Love and T Hubbard, 'Prizes for Innovation of New Medicines and Vaccines' (2009) 18 *Annals of Health Law* 155.

[12] F Machlup, 'An Economic Review of the Patent System' [1958] Study of the Subcommittee of Patents, Trademarks and Copyrights of the Committee on the Judiciary, 80.

current system operates as effectively and equitably as possible, and that ongoing steps are taken to make this a reality.

Reform in the field of patent law is often focused on economic perspectives, with less attention on the importance of societal considerations.[13] However, these considerations are highly significant because patent law does not exist in a vacuum. As stated by Justine Pila, 'patent law does not belong exclusively to the worlds of commerce, industry, and technology, but rather has other social and cultural dimensions which must be considered by the legislature and courts when developing and applying it'.[14] Jens Schovsbo also argues that

> [t]he challenge is to create a system which not only benefits innovation but can also deal with the sensitive issues involving morality and does so in a way which is at the same time effective and centralized and respects … cultural and legal diversities.[15]

The societal and moral issues that arise when dealing with the protection of inventions and the diversity that exists within the field cannot be ignored and are a key consideration in this book. Cultural, legal and procedural diversity is what makes the European patent system fragmented. Using the term 'fragmentation' rather than 'diversity' in relation to the European patent system reflects the reality that this is widely perceived as a problem; diversity does not have the same negative connotation. While the European patent system is fragmented, it is important to also see it as diverse. When responding to fragmentation this needs to be considered and it must be recognised that in certain situations fragmentation should persist unless consensus can be built in an appropriate and considered way. A more nuanced framing of fragmentation would allow us to respond to it in a more effective manner.

II. The European Patent System

In the context of the European patent system, as has been outlined above, fragmentation takes many forms and is the result of differences in grant, interpretation, enforcement and procedure. The existence and impact of such differences is why fragmentation is perceived in a negative light, which has led to an expansive desire to create a unitary patent system.[16]

[13] A significant exception is Council Directive 98/44/EC of the European Parliament and of the Council of 6 July 1998 on the legal protection of biotechnological inventions [1998] OJ L 213/13 (Biotech Directive).

[14] J Pila, 'A Constitutionalized Doctrine of Precedent and the *Marleasing* Principle as Bases for a European Legal Methodology' in A Ohly and J Pila (eds), *The Europeanization of Intellectual Property Law: Towards a European Legal Methodology* (Oxford University Press 2013) 228.

[15] J Schovsbo, 'Constructing an Efficient and Balanced European Patent System: "Muddling Through"' in C Geiger (ed), *Constructing European Intellectual Property: Achievements and New Perspectives* (Edward Elgar 2013) 230.

[16] As outlined in Chapters 1 and 2.

As noted previously, there are currently three routes to patent protection in Europe – national, European (EPC), and international (PCT). If successful, the result of each route is essentially a national patent. Discussions concerning the creation of a unitary patent system in Europe can be traced back as far as 1949, when a French senator, Henri Longchambon, proposed the idea. Although preliminary in nature, this set the agenda for the following 70 (plus) years of negotiations, which have been circuitous, tortuous, long and convoluted. Numerous attempts have been made.[17]

In 2012 and 2013, the Unitary Patent Package (UPP) was finalised, which will establish the EU unitary patent system.[18] It consists of two EU Regulations, one introducing a European patent with unitary effect and the other introducing a new language regime, as well as an international Agreement establishing a Unified Patent Court (UPCA). Although the Regulations of the UPP have a legal basis in Article 118 of the Treaty on the Functioning of the European Union (TFEU) and create European intellectual property rights, the result will not be uniform throughout the EU. Unanimous agreement could not be achieved in relation to the language regime. Therefore, the Regulations were implemented using the enhanced cooperation procedure.

Both Regulations have been implemented and have entered into force, yet their application is dependent on the ratification of the UPCA. The UPCA will establish a common patent court, the Unified Patent Court (UPC), with cross-border jurisdiction throughout all participating EU Member States for both unitary and European (EPC) patents. To enter into force, it must be ratified by at least 13 Member States. This includes, according to Article 89 UPCA, the ratification of the 'three Member States in which the highest number of European patents had effect in the year preceding the year in which the Agreement was signed'. Prior to Brexit, this denoted France, Germany and the United Kingdom (UK). However, Italy will now take the place of the UK, due to the decision of the UK to withdraw its ratification of the UPCA. A number of participating Member States also had to agree to be bound by the Protocol on Privileges and Immunities of the UPC and by the Protocol on the Provisional Application of the UPCA. The entry into force of the latter has allowed the provisional application of certain provisions of the UPCA, for example, the adoption of secondary legislation, such as the Rules of Procedure of the UPC, the adoption of the first budget of the Court, and the appointment of judges. This provisional period will ensure that the Court is operational as of day one of the entry into force of the UPCA. At the time of writing,

[17] See Chapter 3.

[18] The UPP consists of Regulation (EU) 1257/2012 of the European Parliament and of the Council of 17 December 2012 implementing enhanced cooperation in the area of the creation of unitary patent protection [2012] OJ L 361/1 (Regulation 1257); Regulation (EU) 1260/2012 of the European Parliament and of the Council of 17 December 2012 implementing enhanced cooperation in the area of the creation of unitary patent protection with regard to the applicable translation arrangements [2012] OJ L 361/89 (Regulation 1260); and Agreement 2013/C on a Unified Patent Court [2013] OJ L 175/01 (UPCA).

16 Member States, including France and Italy, have ratified the UPCA. Germany is in a position to do so once the provisional period is close to completion.

The UPP can be expected to significantly change the European patent system. Although its aims are laudable and the UPP has numerous beneficial aspects, it can also be expected to increase rather than decrease the existing fragmentation of the European patent system. The impact of this is a key issue moving forward when considering how we perceive and respond to fragmentation.

III. Terminology

Notably, when referring to the European patent system, this book is not referring to a specific system, but rather the field as a whole, which includes countries beyond the EU, in particular the Contracting States to the EPC which are not Member States of the EU.[19] It is important to base our considerations from this perspective because not doing so would lead to exclusion. When referring to specific systems and the patents resulting therefrom, this book will make reference to, for example, the European (EPC) patent/patent system or specific national patents/patent systems. There is also a distinction between a unitary patent system in general and the forthcoming EU unitary patent system, which will be established by the UPP and includes participating EU Member States only. As such, while there will be some focus on EU law and law-making, observations made within this book are to cover the European patent system more broadly.

The European patent system and the aims of its attempted reforms have been described as efforts to *unify*, *harmonise* and *integrate* the European patent field.[20] It has also been said that the system is currently *fragmented* and *flexible*, an example of *pluralism* and *differentiation*.[21] Before embarking on an analysis of fragmentation and the European patent system, it is necessary to define these terms and discuss how they may be distinguished from one another in the context of this book. These terms are discussed generally in reference to the European patent

[19] Those countries are Albania, Iceland, Liechtenstein, Macedonia, Monaco, Norway, San Marino, Serbia, Switzerland, Turkey and the UK.

[20] In general, see C Wadlow, 'Strasbourg, the Forgotten Patent Convention, and the Origins of the European Patents Jurisdiction' (2010) 41(2) *IIC* 123; J Pila, 'The European Patent: An Old and Vexing Problem' (2013) 62(4) *ICLQ* 917; M LaFlame Jr, 'The European Patent System: An Overview and Critique' (2010) 32 *Houston Journal of International Law* 605; H Ullrich, 'Patent Protection in Europe: Integrating Europe into the Community or the Community into Europe?' (2002) 8(4) *European Law Journal* 433.

[21] In general, see B Van Pottelsberghe, 'Lost Property: The European Patent System and Why It Doesn't Work' (2009) IX *Bruegel Blueprint Series* available at http://bruegel.org/2009/06/lost-property-the-european-patent-system-and-why-it-doesnt-work/. For a European perspective on Merges, *Justifying Intellectual Property* (2011) see J Pila, 'Pluralism, Principles and Proportionality in Intellectual Property' (2014) 34(1) *Oxford Journal of Legal Studies* 181. On harmonisation versus differentiation, see N Thumm, *Intellectual Property Rights – National Systems and Harmonisation in Europe* (Springer Verlag 2000) chapter 5.

system; however, some also have a separate and particular meaning in the EU context.

In the efforts to further develop the European patent system, considerable focus has been placed on partial unification. Unification can be described as the process of introducing a single patent title and patent system for Europe, to the exclusion of all other national and European systems. Unification would involve the replacement of all patent systems in Europe with a single European patent system that would deal with all aspects of substantive European patent law and enforcement.[22] In practice, this would mean that rather than having 38 national patent laws implementing and enforcing the EPC, itself incorporating the central EU Directive concerning patent law matters,[23] one law would exist for all of Europe, not solely the EU. It would be necessary for all European states, including non-EU states, to abide by this law and to implement and interpret it accordingly.

As noted above, the European patent system is not unified. Numerous patent systems exist, and the patentee has an option as to which route to take to protection. A unified system would remove the risk of differing examination standards and divergent outcomes in patent litigation, thereby ensuring efficiency and legal certainty. However, it would not consider the social, economic or cultural diversity that exists between states. It can be argued that it is for this reason, namely the impact of a unified patent system on the sovereignty and diversity of European states, that a unified patent system has not been successful.[24] Consequently, the European patent system has come to be harmonised rather than unified, even for the 27 Member States of the EU.

Harmonisation, for the purpose of this book, is the approximation rather than the assimilation of laws.[25] Harmonisation is understood as the process of creating common standards in the laws of various states through various agreements and having national courts interpret these provisions in a consistent manner, sometimes with the support of a supranational tribunal. The result is minimum standards that also consider varying national cultures and values. If harmonisation is taken far enough, unification may result.

The field of intellectual property law is familiar with the concept of harmonisation. For example, the protection of trade marks and designs has been substantially

[22] This view is shared by authors such as RH Graveson, 'The International Unification of Law' (1968) 16(1) *The American Journal of Comparative Law* 4.

[23] Biotech Directive; *cf* Regulation (EC) 469/2009 of the European Parliament and of the Council of 6 May 2009 concerning the supplementary protection certificate for medicinal products (codified version) [2009] OJ L 152/1 and Regulation (EC) 1610/96 of the European Parliament and of the Council of 23 July 1996 concerning the creation of a supplementary protection certificate for plant protection products [1996] OJ L 198/30 (SPC Regulations).

[24] See Chapter 3.

[25] This view is shared by authors such as W Van Gerven, 'Harmonisation Within and Beyond' in M van Empel (ed), *'From Paris to Nice': Fifty Years of Legal Integration in Europe* (Kluwer Law International 2003); and W Kamba, 'Comparative Law: A Theoretical Framework' (1974) 23(3) *ICLQ* 485, 501.

harmonised across the EU, and unitary rights are available.[26] Numerous Directives have also been put into place by the EU with the aim of bringing together the domestic laws of Member States to have a consistent and coherent copyright law among them.[27]

In the context of the European patent system, the situation is similar. However, there is one important difference. In the realm of trade mark, design and copyright law, most harmonisation measures have taken place under the auspices of the EU. In the European patent field, however, harmonisation has been achieved through international treaties and conventions, with the addition of a few EU Directives and Regulations.

The main piece of EU legislation relevant to substantive patent law is the Biotech Directive.[28] Additionally, two Regulations on supplementary protection certificates apply to certain inventions once patent protection lapses: one for medicinal products and one for plant products.[29] These certificates grant a similar protection, to make up for delays relating to marketing authorisation. Finally, the Enforcement Directive is relevant to all intellectual property laws, including patents.[30] The EU also attempted to introduce a Directive on the patentability of computer-implemented inventions, but this initiative failed.[31]

[26] Trade marks: Directive (EU) 2015/2436 of the European Parliament and of the Council of 16 December 2015 to approximate the laws of the Member States relating to trade marks [2015] OJ L 336/1; Regulation 2017/1001/EU on the European Union trade mark [2017] OJ L 154/1. Designs: Directive 98/71/EC of the European Parliament and of the Council of 13 October 1998 on the legal protection of designs [1998] OJ L 289/98; and Regulation (EC) 6/2002 of 12 December 2001 on Community designs [2002] OJ L 3/1. For a discussion of criticisms relating to the EU trade mark, see GB Dinwoodie, 'The Europeanization of Trade Mark Law' in A Ohly and J Pila (eds), *The Europeanization of Intellectual Property Law: Towards a European Legal Methodology* (Oxford University Press 2013) 76.

[27] To name a few: Directive 96/9/EC of the European Parliament and of the Council of 11 March 1996 on the legal protection of databases [1996] OJ L 77/20 (Database Directive); Directive 2001/29/EC of the European Parliament and of the Council of 22 May 2001 on the harmonisation of certain aspects of copyright and related rights in the information society [2001] OJ L 167/10 (InfoSoc Directive); Directive 2014/26/EU of the European Parliament and of the Council of 26 February 2014 on collective management of copyright and related rights and multi-territorial licensing of rights in musical works for online use in the internal market [2014] OJ L 84/72 (CRM Directive); and Directive 2019/790 of the European Parliament and of the Council of 17 April 2019 on copyright and related rights in the Digital Single Market [2019] OJ L 130/92 (DSM Directive). Interestingly, arguments have emerged calling for the unification of these laws to promote legal certainty. Bernt Hugenholtz claims that the Directives implemented in the European copyright field have 'created a measure of uniformity' between the laws of Member States. However, he argues that despite extensive harmonisation, copyright law will remain fragmented until a unified European copyright law is introduced – one that consolidates the existing body of harmonised copyright law: B Hugenholtz, 'Harmonisation or Unification of European Union Copyright Law' (2012) 38(1) *Monash University Law Review* 4.

[28] Biotech Directive.

[29] SPC Regulations.

[30] Directive 2004/48/EC of the European Parliament and of the Council of 29 April 2004 on the enforcement of intellectual property rights [2004] OJ L 195/16 (Enforcement Directive).

[31] Proposal for a Directive of the European Parliament and of the Council on the patentability of computer-implemented inventions (COM (2002) 92 final) [2002] OJ C 151 E/129.

It has been suggested that one of the reasons for the lack of further EU harmonisation in patent law is due to international initiatives such as the Paris Convention, the Strasbourg Patent Convention, the EPC, the PCT and the Agreement on Trade-Related Aspects of Intellectual Property Rights (TRIPS).[32] One of the most important examples of a non-EU harmonisation measure is the EPC. Its provisions apply to all 38 current Contracting States, who are to apply this law in a consistent manner to ensure certain minimum standards across Europe. However, the EPC does not cover all aspects of patent law, and Contracting States retain their autonomy, giving priority to national law. For example, issues on post-grant matters, including validity and infringement, are for national systems to decide.[33] As mentioned previously, it is important when considering the harmonisation of the European patent system that all European countries are included. The involvement of EU and non-EU states in the existing European patent system immediately creates an issue for any EU-based harmonisation or unification initiatives.

Many reforms of the European patent system, both attempted and successful, have had the aim of promoting integration. For the purpose of this book, integration is broadly understood as the process of cooperating and compromising among European nations (not only EU nations) on certain policies and laws. In the context of the EU, integration is a distinct legal process. It concerns the development of a closer Union, which is achieved through the harmonisation and unification of national Member State laws.[34] Its aim is more specifically to promote the internal market, free movement and fundamental rights protection, as well as the other aims of the EU outlined in its Treaties.[35] Integration on the EU level has been achieved not only by the Treaties and EU legislation, but also by the Court of Justice of the European Union (CJEU) in its interpretation of them.[36] However, as Karen Alter has pointed out, it is 'not simply the issuing of legal decisions which create new doctrine, but more importantly the acceptance of this jurisprudence within national legal systems and by national politicians'.[37]

Unification and harmonisation are general tools that can be used to reach goals of European integration. Nonetheless, they are not the only methods. Although

[32] Convention for the Protection of Industrial Property 1883 (Paris Convention); Convention on the Unification of Certain Points of Substantive Law on Patents for Invention 1963 (Strasbourg Patent Convention); EPC; PCT; TRIPS. See C Seville, *EU Intellectual Property Law and Policy* (Edward Elgar 2009) 70.

[33] Noting the possibility of an opposition action being taken to the European Patent Office (EPO) within nine months of grant for central revocation of the patent.

[34] D Dinan, *Ever Closer Union* (4th edn, Palgrave Macmillan 2010).

[35] For more on European integration see ibid; K Alter, 'Explaining National Court Acceptance of European Court Jurisprudence: A Critical Evaluation of Theories of Legal Integration' in A-M Slaughter, A Stone Sweet and JHH Weiler (eds), *The European Courts and National Courts – Doctrine and Jurisprudence* (Hart Publishing 1998).

[36] A-M Burley and W Mattli, 'Europe before the Court: A Political Theory of Legal Integration' (1993) 47(1) *International Organization* 41.

[37] Alter, 'Explaining National Court Acceptance' 229.

often conceived as having aims opposite to that of unification and harmonisation,[38] methods such as differentiation (also known as flexibility measures, multi-speed Europe etc) can also promote integration, albeit in a different manner.

Differentiation, in the context of this book, is understood as a further potential mechanism of integration. During the legislative process, it allows differences between nations for the purpose of achieving deeper integration among a participating group, with the expectation that those non-participating states will eventually align their laws to the common framework. This has also been called differentiated integration. In the EU context, some commentators, such as Deidre Curtin, believe this process undermines the 'cohesiveness and unity' of the Community order.[39] However, others, such as Bruno de Witte, Dominik Hanf and Ellen Vos, see differentiation as 'the facilitation or accommodation of a degree of difference between Member States or regions in relation to what would otherwise be common Community or Union policies'.[40] They go on to say that although this method would not lead to uniformity, it could 'actually strengthen European *unity*'.[41] This latter perspective allows for more flexibility and for progress towards integration to be made, albeit gradually.

For example, the use of the EU enhanced cooperation procedure is a method of differentiated integration.[42] This procedure allows nine or more EU Member States to join in specific policy areas to advance the objectives of the EU and to progress with deeper integration when other Member States are unwilling or unable to do so at that time. This gives rise to a degree of flexibility for Member States to join the integration process when they are able and willing to do so. Differentiation allows for flexibility, which in turn facilitates substantial progress towards integration being achieved, relative to the stagnation that would otherwise occur. This is the reason that differentiation has been described as 'integration by parts'.[43]

Another distinct concept that has emerged as a possible justification for the European patent system is that of pluralism. In general terms, legal pluralism may be described as 'the presence in a social field of more than one legal order in which law and legal institutions are not subsumable within one system but have various sources';[44] or, as a system that 'contains inconsistent rules of recognition that cannot be legally resolved from within the system'.[45] These descriptions could be,

[38] D Curtin, 'The Constitutional Structure of the Union: A Europe of Bits and Pieces' (1993) 30 *Common Market Law Review* 17.

[39] ibid 67.

[40] B de Witte, D Hanf and E Vos, 'Introduction' in B de Witte, D Hanf and E Vos (eds), *The Many Faces of Differentiation in EU Law* (Intersentia 2001) xii.

[41] ibid.

[42] Contained in Article 20 of the Treaty on European Union (TEU) and Articles 326–34 of the Treaty on the Functioning of the European Union.

[43] De Witte, Hanf and Vos, 'Introduction'.

[44] J Griffiths, 'What Is Legal Pluralism?' (1986) 24(1) *Journal of Legal Pluralism* 55, 1.

[45] N Barber, 'Legal Pluralism and the European Union' (2006) 12(3) *European Law Journal* 306, 306.

and have been, applied to the European patent system.[46] If the European patent system is accepted and supported as a pluralist legal system, it must be conceded that it never will be a unified system. As such, any divergence that exists will be an inherent and intended feature of the system. However, this is not the predominant view that is taken of the European patent system currently. Instead, the system is largely described as fragmented, and treated as such.

IV. Perspectives on Fragmentation

This book investigates current perceptions of and responses to fragmentation in the European patent system. It argues that the inherent nature of fragmentation needs to be recognised and accepted. It challenges the view that fragmentation is best responded to through the introduction of a unitary patent system and suggests that instead, a multifaceted approach is required. Crucially, it uniquely draws on the work regarding fragmentation that has been done outside of the patent and intellectual property regimes. It applies insights from an examination of fragmentation in both European law-making and in the international legal system, to the European patent system.

As Europe has developed and expanded, so too have law-making methods. In the EU particularly, the introduction of enhanced cooperation suggests that fragmentation does not go against the vision of European unity – its inevitability was predicted. As a result, there are areas where fragmentation will persist, while progress towards integration is made elsewhere. As long as such processes are not used to exclude Member States, they can be used to make progress towards harmonisation, but not at the expense of national diversity. Perceiving fragmentation as such allows for much-needed flexibility in supranational efforts towards harmonisation.

Fragmentation has also been a key focus in scholarship on the international legal system. The initial fear surrounding fragmentation in international law has dissipated. Conversations are now more focused on convergence and how to respond to fragmentation in the most effective manner. This is not to imply that fragmentation has been 'solved' or that it has disappeared but, instead, that it is not as significant a concern as it was initially. This is because it is now seen as an inherent part of the international legal system, which has tools to mitigate the risks associated with it. The word convergence implies that something is approaching the same point. It is not an end, but an action. Based on an investigation into fragmentation in international law, the attitude towards fragmentation in the field has changed, and there is now also a focus on, and appreciation of,

[46] For more on a pluralistic approach to intellectual property, see Merges, *Justifying Intellectual Property*; D Resnik, 'A Pluralistic Account of Intellectual Property' (2003) 46(4) *Journal of Business Ethics* 319; and Pila, 'Pluralism, Principles and Proportionality'.

diversity and its corresponding benefits. In the introduction to *A Farewell to Fragmentation*, Mads Andenas and Eirik Bjorge state that 'We regard fragmentation more as a part of a dynamic legal system, and fragmentation may be a fruitful perspective by which to study almost any legal system or sub-system'.[47]

Graeme B Dinwoodie has reflected on the 'multiplication of sources and institutions playing in the [international] intellectual property space' and the commonalities shared with discussions of fragmentation in the international legal system.[48] Henning Grosse Ruse-Khan has examined this in detail in relation to the protection of intellectual property law in international law.[49] Some of these similarities are also apparent on a regional level in the European patent system. Responses to institutional fragmentation are particularly influential and bear much-needed consideration. Such scholarship on fragmentation in international law can and should be tailored to the European patent system and its internal interactions.

This book argues that the European patent system can learn from these perceptions and approaches and use similar mechanisms when dealing with the fragmentation experienced within. Additionally, there could and should be a similar change in attitude towards fragmentation. Such a change could see discussions focus more on how to respond to fragmentation in more inclusive ways, and how to harness it in the future. Fragmentation will never be removed from the European patent system entirely. It is an inherent aspect of the system, and it should be treated as such. Moving forward, we need to move beyond attempting to eliminate it altogether, and rather accept it is a feature that is here to stay and, as such, develop additional and more appropriate ways to respond to it.

V. Outline

This book proceeds in three parts, with a total of six chapters. Part I examines the current and future European patent system with a view to uncovering the fragmentation that exists and will continue to exist.

[47] M Andenas and E Bjorge (eds), *A Farewell to Fragmentation: Reassertion and Convergence in International Law* (Cambridge University Press 2015).

[48] GB Dinwoodie, 'Diversifying Perspectives of the International Intellectual Property System' in C Geiger (ed), *The Intellectual Property System in a Time of Change: European and International Perspectives* (Lexis Nexis 2016) 224. Additional literature on the nature of international intellectual property law is plentiful, for example, on the impact of international Conventions with a global reach, such as the Paris Convention, the Berne Convention, and TRIPS. For a few more examples in a rich field of scholarship, see G Dutfield and U Suthersanen, *Dutfield and Suthersanen on Global Intellectual Property Law* (2nd edn, Edward Elgar 2020); D Gervais, *The TRIPS Agreement; Drafting History and Analysis* (5th edn, Sweet & Maxwell 2021); and RL Okejidi and MA Bagley (eds), *Patent Law in Global Perspective* (Oxford University Press 2014).

[49] H Grosse Ruse-Khan, *The Protection of Intellectual Property in International Law* (Oxford University Press 2016).

Chapter 1 examines the European patent system as it is today. As mentioned above, there are currently three routes to patent protection in Europe. Although multiple routes to protection exist, the result of each process, if ultimately successful, is a national patent, restricted territorially. This chapter outlines the purpose, legal basis, procedural and enforcement aspects of each system, as well as their perceived advantages and disadvantages. It examines how one of the main problems associated with the present European patent system is that of fragmentation – because patents remain territorially restricted, divergence in grant and enforcement can result.

Following on from this outline of the European patent system today, Chapter 2 discusses the purpose, legal basis, procedural and enforcement aspects of the forthcoming EU unitary patent system. The relevant Regulations introduce a new title of patent for Europe that is to have unitary effect throughout the participating Member States of the UPP. This new system will be administered by the EPO and the UPC. The Court will have (subject to a transitional period) exclusive competence over both European patents with unitary effect and European (EPC) patents, with the capacity to deliver cross-border judgments on infringement and validity.

Although numerous advantages have been predicted, including lower costs and less frequent divergence in proceedings across Europe, the EU unitary patent system has also been fiercely criticised. One of the main aims of this system is to promote integration amid the fragmentation of the current European patent system identified in Chapter 1, that is, to address the problems that arise as a result of the existence of numerous patents, laws and courts that deal with patent law matters, particularly in relation to cost. It has attracted an enormous amount of discussion and warranted criticism in the field of European patent law, more generally in intellectual property law, as well as in EU law. The problems outlined are diverse in nature, including legal, political, procedural and institutional issues. As will be shown, underpinning many of these criticisms is a concern that the UPP will increase rather than decrease existing fragmentation in the European patent system.

From an investigation of these systems, it is clear that fragmentation is generally seen as a negative feature of the European patent system. To respond to it, attempt after attempt has been made to introduce a unitary patent system. However, as will be argued, such a response to fragmentation may indeed be limited and ensuing responses need to be tailored accordingly.

Part II examines alternative perspectives on fragmentation. Chapter 3 investigates the aims and motivations of the European and EU legal systems, as well as those of the European patent system. It is shown that fragmentation does not run contrary to European objectives of an integrated community and that it is not necessarily a negative aspect of a legal system. Even in the EU, new methods of integration, including enhanced cooperation, allow for national diversity and show an appreciation of value pluralism. The way in which the system has developed has allowed for fragmentation to take these values into account if, and where, necessary.

The aim of Chapter 4 is to study fragmentation as it has been experienced in the international legal system, with a view to understanding its potential significance for the European patent system. It is shown that while previously feared in international law, fragmentation has more recently been accepted as an inherent feature of the international legal system, and even embraced as a means of protecting diversity and flexibility. Various methods have been used to respond to fragmentation in an effective manner, particularly judicial dialogue and cooperation; that is, judges considering or discussing relevant decisions and interpretations of other courts. Applying the insights gained therefrom, it is asked whether, in a field such as patent law, it is useful or even possible to see the fragmentation that currently exists as an inherent and/or constructive element, and whether it is likewise possible to implement similar mechanisms to assist in changing that perspective.

Part III seeks to test this suggestion with a study of the development of the European patent system to date, current interpretations of substantive patent law, and institutional responses to fragmentation. Much of the fragmentation in the European patent system relates to how substantive patent law is interpreted, for 'it is only with experience of how courts and tribunals interpret such law and apply it that one can start to appreciate its true scope and effect'.[50] Many examples are taken from case law across Europe, but the jurisdictional focus is predominantly on the UK, the EPO and the CJEU.

Prior to the introduction of the Strasbourg Patent Convention and the EPC, the patent field in Europe was based purely on national patent law and its interpretation by national offices and courts. Subsequently, the patent landscape changed into one with the purpose of an integrated European approach to substantive patent law. The EPC also introduced the Boards of Appeal, responsible for the interpretation of the EPC in relation to European (EPC) patent applications. However, substantive patent law is also still interpreted by national courts. Although these specialist tribunals were introduced at a European level, there is no formal route for national courts to refer questions on interpretation to these bodies. As shown in Chapter 5, while this results in considerable potential for institutional fragmentation, in practice informal attempts are being made to keep this in check by various judicial methods, which are akin to those used in the international legal system seen in Chapter 4. However, it is argued that these methods should be recognised, harnessed and promoted further to make our response to fragmentation more effective.

Chapter 6 expands on this argument. It shows that responding to fragmentation in relation to the exceptions to patentability is more complicated because in these areas, diverse views on matters of social and constitutional importance exist. This requires careful consideration. The impact of EU law in this area is analysed, including particularly the Biotech Directive. For the first time, following the introduction of this Directive, national courts could, and in some cases were required

[50] T Cook (ed), *The Patent Litigation Law Review* (2nd edn, Law Business Research 2018) Preface.

to, refer questions on the interpretation of substantive patent law to the CJEU to ensure consistency in its interpretation.

One of the stated aims of the Biotech Directive is to ensure that the application of patent law by EU Member States takes sufficient account of the requirements of fundamental rights, including, in particular, human dignity. A discussion of case law involving the Directive shows how its interpretation has resulted in a unitary understanding of those requirements for all EU Member States, where one does not exist. In this attempt towards convergence, adequate consideration of value pluralism and substantive fragmentation was lacking, resulting in a problematic outcome. In an inherently fragmented system, allowing a level of fragmentation or discretion may be required. It is also shown that attempts towards convergence on a supranational level can sometimes result in the use of problematic practices which also ought to be prevented. Importantly, allowing a level of fragmentation to persist in these areas will not prevent progress towards integration entirely – progress towards consensus can still be encouraged where possible and beneficial through judicial dialogue and cooperation. It is argued that the desire to remove fragmentation should not disengage institutions from important substantive and procedural considerations. Fragmentation may be necessary unless consensus can be achieved in an appropriate manner.

As will be made clear, responding to fragmentation in the European patent system is complex and requires a multifaceted approach. The fragmentation that exists and is likely to remain as a feature of the European patent system can and should be regarded as an inherent aspect of the system. As it will remain a feature of the European patent system, with or without an EU unitary patent system, we need to focus on developing additional mechanisms to respond to fragmentation, which will also allow for considerations of value pluralism and the wider impact of patent law on society.

PART I

Fragmentation and the European Patent System Today

Before embarking on an analysis of fragmentation more generally, it is pertinent to discuss its presence in the European patent system today, including how it is perceived. Part I will discuss the current and forthcoming patent systems in Europe and the various routes to patent protection. This will include their historical development and legal basis, and the procedures a patent applicant must follow on their chosen route to patent protection. The advantages and disadvantages of each system will be considered from the perspective of various stakeholders. It will be seen that many of the perceived disadvantages that relate to the core of these systems concern the fact that they are either fragmented or will increase fragmentation.

1

Existing Routes to Patent Protection in Europe

Currently, there are three routes to patent protection in Europe. Each involves a complex series of pre- and post-grant procedures. First, a national patent can be granted by applying to a national patent office operating within its national patent system.[1] Second, the EPO, which applies the EPC, can grant a European (EPC) patent, which is, in reality, a bundle of national patents.[2] Third, an international patent application can be submitted to WIPO under the PCT, which gives the applicant an international priority date and opinion on patentability. This can be used when entering the national or regional phase, possibly resulting in a number of national patents worldwide.[3] If applications are eventually successful, a single invention may have multiple associated patents – one for each territory. Post-grant opposition, invalidity or revocation proceedings, as well as claims of infringement, will mainly be taken at national level but some actions can be taken at regional level depending on the circumstances. Each office and court operates according to its own procedure.

In order to highlight the existing fragmentation within the European patent system this initial chapter will provide an overview of the current routes to patent protection in Europe, including their purpose, legal basis, procedural and enforcement aspects, as well as their individual and combined strengths and weaknesses.

I. National Patent Systems

Historically, patents were created as monopoly rights intended to promote competition and boost national economies.[4] These rights became proprietary over time

[1] For example, Patents Act 1977 (UK); Patentgesetz in der Fassung der Bekanntmachung vom 16. Dezember 1980 (BGBI. 1981 I S. 1), das zuletzt durch Artikel 1 des Gesetzes vom 30. August 2021 (BGBI. I S. 4074) geändert worden ist (Germany).

[2] Convention on the Grant of European Patents of 5 October 1973, amended in 2000.

[3] Patent Cooperation Treaty 1970.

[4] A brief history of patents can be found in books such as A Brown, S Kheria, J Cornwell and M Iljadica, *Contemporary Intellectual Property* (5th edn, Oxford University Press 2019); L Bently, B Sherman, D Gangjee and P Johnson, *Intellectual Property Law* (5th edn, Oxford University Press 2018). See also C Seville, 'The Emergence and Development of Intellectual Property Law in Western Europe' in RC Dreyfuss and J Pila (eds), *The Oxford Handbook of Intellectual Property Law* (Oxford University Press 2017).

and requirements were increasingly introduced to improve the systems. Reflecting associated rationales, the aim of national patent systems was to protect inventions and incentivise innovation within a certain territory.

National patent rights are territorial. Each country originally designed its patent laws and system to benefit its own economy, resulting in a multitude of national laws intended to 'meet the perceived commercial and moral needs of its inhabitants'.[5] The success of national patent systems in boosting innovation in particular states (as well as boosting innovation in general) has been debated.[6] Nevertheless, they remain a key aspect of the patent landscape in Europe.

Over time, the general purpose of national patents has not radically changed; the protection of inventions and the promotion of innovation remain central.[7] However, the context in which a patent is granted today is starkly different. Due to the advent and continuing development of emerging technologies, changes in the economy, Europeanisation and globalisation, new challenges have arisen for national patent systems.

A number of international and regional developments have required amendments to national patent laws. The initiation of European cooperation, especially, (both EU and non-EU) required many changes, particularly relating to territoriality. The inherently fragmented nature of national patent systems in Europe was seen as an issue that needed to be resolved.

The earliest international development in this area was the Paris Convention for the Protection of Industrial Property of 1883.[8] It established a union for the protection of industrial property through equal national treatment and the creation of a priority right. National treatment requires Contracting States to give the same treatment to nationals of other states as it does to nationals of its own state. The priority right allows patentees to use their first filing date as the priority date for patent applications in other participating states for 12 months.

Substantive patent law in Europe has also been largely harmonised by international conventions. This began with the Strasbourg Patent Convention of 1963, created by the Council of Europe and responsible for unifying substantive law on the requirements for patentability in participating nations.[9] The EPC of 1973, which will be discussed in detail below, incorporated the substantive law provisions of the Strasbourg Patent Convention and additionally introduced a streamlined procedure for patent applications throughout Europe. Despite never being ratified, the Community Patent Convention/Agreement of 1975/1989 (CPC/CPA)

[5] H Laddie, 'National IP Rights: A Moribund Anachronism in a Federal Europe?' (2001) 23(9) *EIPR* 402, 403.

[6] See, for example, D Guellec and B Van Pottelsberghe de la Potterie, *The Economics of the European Patent System* (Oxford University Press 2007); and M Boldrin and DK Levine, 'The Case Against Patents' (2013) 27(1) *Journal of Economic Perspectives* 3.

[7] However, note the discussion on the disagreement in literature around whether patents incentivise innovation in the Introduction.

[8] The Paris Convention is currently administered by WIPO and has 177 contracting parties.

[9] Convention on the Unification of Certain Points of Substantive Law on Patents for Invention 1963.

also had an impact on the standardisation of national laws.[10] Its provisions on scope of protection and infringement, also stemming from the Strasbourg Patent Convention, were implemented into many national laws in preparation for ratification, and remain despite its failure.[11]

Another significant global development was the TRIPS Agreement of 1994. TRIPS sets out minimum standards of protection for intellectual property in the 164 members of the WTO. The provisions of the Paris Convention have been incorporated into TRIPS and further provisions were developed and included. Signatories have the option to implement a higher standard of protection but must meet its minimum requirements.[12]

On the creation of what is now the EU, specific provisions were required to deal with the tension that arose between national intellectual property rights and the creation of the internal market removing barriers to trade between Member States. To manage this strain, the CJEU introduced the doctrine of exhaustion.[13] The doctrine of exhaustion provides an intellectual property rightsholder the right to first marketing of the product in the European Economic Area (EEA). Once first marketing has occurred under the conditions developed by the CJEU, the right is exhausted, meaning that particular product, or those particular products, can be resold within the EEA without permission. By introducing the doctrine of exhaustion to deal with the first marketing of products protected by intellectual property law, national rights, including patents, can remain subject to national laws. Due to the differences between national intellectual property systems, their abolishment was regarded as unfeasible and undesirable.[14] Instead, the intention was to balance the rights of the intellectual property right owner and the need to achieve an internal market in the EU.[15]

[10] Convention for the European Patent for the Common Market (15 December 1975) (Community Patent Convention; CPC); although the Community Patent Convention/Agreement of 1975/1989 never entered into force, some Member States changed their patent laws in preparation for its implementation.

[11] See J Pila, 'The European Patent: An Old and Vexing Problem' (2013) 62 *ICLQ* 917.

[12] For a commentary on TRIPS, see CM Correa, *Trade Related Aspects of Intellectual Property Rights: A Commentary on the TRIPS Agreement* (2nd edn, Oxford University Press 2020).

[13] The steps leading up to this point can be seen through case law, including, but not limited to: Joined Cases 56 and 58-64 *Établissements Consten S.à.R.L. and Grundig-Verkaufs-GmbH v Commission of the European Economic Community* ECLI:EU:C:1966:41; Case 24/67 *Parke, Davis & Co v Probel, Reese, Beintema-Interpharm and Centrafarm* ECLI:EU:C:1968:11; Case 78/70 *Deutsche Grammophon Gesellschaft mbH v Metro-SB-Grossmärkte GmbH & Co KG* ECLI:EU:C:1971:59; and Case 15/74 *Centrafarm BV and Adriaan de Peijper v Sterling Drug Inc.* ECLI:EU:C:1974:114.

[14] J Pila, 'A Constitutionalized Doctrine of Precedent and the *Marleasing* Principle as Bases for a European Legal Methodology' in A Ohly and J Pila (eds), *The Europeanization of Intellectual Property Law: Towards a European Legal Methodology* (Oxford University Press 2013) 242.

[15] R Davis, T St Quintin and G Tritton, *Tritton on Intellectual Property in Europe* (5th edn, Sweet & Maxwell 2020) 7-026; A Strowel and H-E Kim, 'The Balancing Impact of General EU Law on European Intellectual Property Jurisprudence' in A Ohly and J Pila (eds), *The Europeanization of Intellectual Property Law: Towards a European Legal Methodology* (Oxford University Press 2013) 130.

This has not been the EU's only involvement in European patent law. The EU also implemented a number of Directives and Regulations relevant to patent law.[16] The first were the Supplementary Protection Certificate (SPC) Regulations.[17] An SPC is a *sui generis* right that extends the protection afforded to medicinal products and plant protection products in certain circumstances for up to five years.[18] It is distinct from a patent. It was deemed necessary by the EU to implement a uniform solution to compensate for the time lost between filing an application and receiving market authorisation, and to avoid different approaches in Member States that might create obstacles to free movement.[19] However, the interpretation of the Regulations by the CJEU, especially regarding medicinal products, has been the subject of considerable controversy.[20]

The EU also aimed to enter the patent field in the area of computer-implemented inventions. After much debate as well as fierce criticism from anti-patent software groups, the proposed Directive on the patentability of computer-implemented inventions failed.[21] Its objective was to clarify the existing law and to resolve some inconsistencies in the approach of national laws. The proposal was rejected by the Council of Ministers and returned to the European Parliament, but rather than attempting to amend the proposal further, it was rejected. In this case, the compromise that could have been reached on certain issues would have resulted in the implementation of provisions that were so broad that, in practice, they would change nothing.

The most significant example of EU involvement in substantive patent law is the Biotech Directive.[22] The aim of the Biotech Directive is to encourage a strong biotechnology industry in Europe by introducing effective and harmonised protection for biotechnological inventions throughout the EU.[23] This was seen as essential to maintain investment in the field.[24] However, it was also introduced to

[16] It is also worth noting that the EU has taken a regional position on intellectual property law issues in the context of TRIPS, for example opting out of Article 31bis as importer countries and with regard to the TRIPS waiver in relation to COVID-19. Additional protections by the EU elsewhere can also impact intellectual property rights, such as data and market exclusivity protection impacting the use of compulsory licensing.

[17] Regulation (EC) 469/2009 of the European Parliament and of the Council of 6 May 2009 concerning the supplementary protection certificate for medicinal products (codified version) [2009] OJ L 152/1; Regulation (EC) 1610/96 of the European Parliament and of the Council of 23 July 1996 concerning the creation of a supplementary protection certificate for plant protection products [1996] OJ L 198/30.

[18] Article 13 Regulation 469/2009.

[19] Recital 4 Regulation 469/2009.

[20] For more, see K Walsh, 'The Unitary Patent Package, the Court of Justice of the European Union, and Brexit: (Ir)reconcilable?' (2019) 2 *IPQ* 91, 99–101; D Smyth, 'Two Gaps Instead of One: The CJEU's Effect on Supplementary Protection Certificate Jurisprudence' (2014) 9(6) *JIPLP* 445.

[21] Proposal for a Directive of the European Parliament and of the Council on the patentability of computer-implemented inventions (COM (2002) 92 final) [2002] OJ C 151 E/129.

[22] Council Directive 98/44/EC of the European Parliament and of the Council of 6 July 1998 on the legal protection of biotechnological inventions [1998] OJ L 213/13.

[23] Recital 3, Biotech Directive.

[24] ibid.

protect fundamental rights, such as human dignity. The Biotech Directive has had a profound impact on national patent systems, which will be discussed in detail in Chapter 6. However, for the purpose of this chapter, it sets out and harmonises the conditions and exceptions for the patentability of biotechnological inventions. The Contracting States to the EPC also take the provisions of the Biotech Directive into account because some have been directly incorporated into the Implementing Regulations to the EPC and the Directive is also used as a supplementary means of interpretation.[25]

Despite the significant steps made towards standardising national patent systems, especially with regard to the unifying role of international conventions and regional legislation on substantive patent law, procedures and interpretations can and do still differ between countries. Ultimately, national patents are dealt with on a national level, national court systems are used to defend the validity of patents, and relief, in the form of injunctions or damages, is also decided on a national level. The protection of inventions across Europe remains fragmented.

The procedure for obtaining a national patent also depends on the country in which patent protection is sought.[26] Once an application is sent to a national patent office, a search for prior art and an examination of the patent application is undertaken according to local procedures and approaches to patentability. The type of search and examination varies across Europe. Some offices have an examination system, whereas others have a registration system.[27] Furthermore, some countries have been found to have more stringent search authorities, whereas others have been found to be more permissive.[28] If granted, the patent is enforceable but will only have effect in that territory. At this point, validity is not guaranteed. A national patent can be opposed or subject to revocation proceedings in the patent office or national court of the granting state until it has been declared valid.

There are a number of advantages and disadvantages to national patent systems, which can have an impact on users, attorneys, patent offices and courts, law-makers and society.

From a user perspective, an applicant may favour the national route to protection if their invention is suited to smaller geographic areas, their funds are limited or their operations are exclusively in the national market.[29] For some applicants, especially individual inventors and small/medium-sized enterprises (SMEs), it can make economic sense to file for national protection in one or a small number of European countries rather than throughout Europe. This approach is particularly advantageous because of the patent priority system. As mentioned, if an applicant files in a national patent office for the first time, their filing date becomes their

[25] Implementing Regulations to the Convention on the Grant of European Patents 2006 (as amended).

[26] The TRIPS Agreement provides for some minimum standards regarding procedure.

[27] For details on each country, see www.epo.org/applying/national.html.

[28] Guellec and Van Pottelsberghe de la Potterie, *The Economics of the European Patent System* 29; D Harhoff, 'Research Paper: Challenges Affecting the Use and Enforcement of Intellectual Property Rights' [2009] *Economic Value of Intellectual Property*, 9.

[29] Guellec and Van Pottelsberghe de la Potterie, *The Economics of the European Patent System* 157.

priority date. The applicant then has one year to file applications in other national patent offices, claiming priority from the original application.[30]

Despite these advantages, national patent applicants must comply with the differing procedural requirements in each country and undergo further search and examination with each application.[31] As a result of this procedural fragmentation, an applicant seeking protection for the same invention in more than one country may receive different outcomes depending on the scope of that search and examination.

A major disadvantage is the potential cost of using national patent systems. If protection is only required in a small number of European countries the national patent system can be cost-effective. However, if patent protection is required throughout Europe, the cost increases significantly.[32] Territorial fragmentation plays a role here. The main reason for the significant cost of the national patent system is the requirement in many states that an application is received in its official language, coupled with the cost of hiring local patent attorneys and paying renewal fees in each country.

Applying for protection via the national patent system can offer the experienced applicant a number of tactical advantages, including (by filing in certain countries) a less stringent examination of their application and invention, a more suitable forum for enforcement, and lower costs, depending on the protection sought.[33] By avoiding patent offices with an abundance of applications, the applicant may also be able to minimise delays in securing a patent, or alternatively to maximise them, thereby keeping their competitors uncertain regarding the patentability of the invention for longer, potentially causing them to move into another area, leaving the applicant competition free. Fragmentation can therefore be used as part of a tactical filing strategy, which reinforces issues related to forum shopping.

In the context of national patent enforcement, there is less harmonisation in relation to interpretations of patent law. One of the most discussed aspects of national patent systems is the lack of cross-border enforcement and potential for institutional fragmentation.

In an EU-specific context, cross-border enforcement is only possible to a very limited extent.[34] The CJEU has had a significant impact on the scope of cross-border enforcement in relation to patent rights within the EU. Described by commentators as two 'unfortunate' judgments,[35] in *GAT v LUK* and *Roche v Primus*

[30] ibid 156. The priority grace period was introduced by the Paris Convention and applies to signatories of the Paris Convention.

[31] Laddie, 'National IP Rights' 403.

[32] See European Commission Memo, 'Patent reform Package – frequently asked questions' available at http://europa.eu/rapid/press-release_MEMO-12-970_en.htm?locale=en.

[33] O Bossung, 'The Return of European Patent Law to the European Union' (1996) 27(3) *IIC* 287, 289 and 296.

[34] J Brinkhof and A Ohly, 'Towards a Unified Patent Court in Europe' in J Pila and A Ohly (eds), *The Europeanization of Intellectual Property Law: Towards a Legal Methodology* (Oxford University Press 2013).

[35] ibid 208.

the CJEU restricted the circumstances in which a national court could make a cross-border decision for EU Member States.[36]

In *GAT v LUK*, the Court of Appeal in Düsseldorf referred a question on the scope of the exclusive jurisdiction provided to national courts in relation to proceedings concerning the registration or validity of patents under Article 16(4) of the Brussels Convention.[37] Under this provision, national courts have exclusive jurisdiction to determine the validity of a patent granted in that state. There was uncertainty as to whether this provision implied that the exclusive jurisdiction conferred only applied if proceedings were brought to declare the patent invalid by way of an action, or if it included all proceedings regarding the registration or validity of a patent, irrespective of whether the question was raised by way of an action or as a defence/counterclaim to infringement.[38]

The CJEU maintained that the exclusive jurisdiction provided by Article 16(4) of the Brussels Convention covered all cases where grounds for invalidity are raised as an action and as a defence.[39] It was ultimately decided that only national courts can rule on the validity of patents granted in that jurisdiction – if the matter of validity is raised, be it as an attack or defence, cross-border enforcement is not possible. Therefore, a national court can make a cross-border decision on infringement, but only in the rare circumstances where validity is not raised as a defence. Considering that validity is the most common form of defence in an infringement action, in practice, this has little impact and increases the difficulty for a patentee to enforce a patent simultaneously in several countries.[40]

In the second 'unfortunate' judgment of *Roche v Primus*,[41] the Supreme Court of the Netherlands had referred a question to the CJEU relating to the consolidation of patent infringement proceedings under Article 6(1) of the Brussels Convention.[42] Proceedings can be consolidated and an infringer domiciled in another jurisdiction 'can be added as an additional defendant to infringement proceedings conducted outside its "home" state if there is a sufficient connection

[36] Case C-4/03 *Gesellschaft für Antriebstechnik mbH & Co KG v Lamellen und Kupplungsbau Beteiligungs KG* ECLI:EU:C:2006:457 (*GAT v LUK*) and Case C-539/03 *Roche Nederland BV v Frederick Primus* ECLI:EU:C:2006:458 (*Roche v Primus*). For more detail on cross-border enforcement of patents and intellectual property more generally, see E-J Min and JC Wichard, 'Cross-border Intellectual Property Enforcement' in RC Dreyfuss and J Pila (eds), *The Oxford Handbook of Intellectual Property Law* (Oxford University Press 2017).

[37] Brussels Convention of 27 September 1968 on jurisdiction and the enforcement of judgments in civil and commercial matters [1972] OJ L 299 (Brussels Convention) – also now contained in Article 24(4) of Regulation 1215/2012 of the European Parliament and of the Council of 12 December 2012 on jurisdiction and the recognition and enforcement of judgments in civil and commercial matters (Recast) [2012] OJ L 351/1 (Brussels I Regulation (Recast)).

[38] *GAT v LUK*, paras 12–13.

[39] ibid para 32. See also Brinkhof and Ohly, 'Towards a Unified Patent Court' 208.

[40] M Trimble, '*GAT*, *Solvay*, and the Centralization of Patent Litigation in Europe' (2012) 26 *Emory International Law Review* 515.

[41] *Roche v Primus*.

[42] This provision is also now contained in Article 8(1) Brussels I Regulation (Recast).

between the infringements in the two territories and a need to avoid the risk of irreconcilable judgments'.[43]

Primus had sued Roche Netherlands, and eight other Roche companies based in various Member States. The Dutch jurisdiction was contested. On the same day as *GAT v LUK*, the CJEU decided that consolidation of infringement proceedings against affiliated companies in different Member States was not possible, even if they were acting according to common policy.[44] The Court was of the opinion that the same situation of fact could not be inferred and that infringement actions had to be examined based on the relevant national law.[45] A sufficient connection could not be established and the Court saw no risk of irreconcilable judgments. Essentially, this judgment limits the scope for consolidating proceedings and makes the possibility of numerous proceedings on the same patent and/or issue in various Member States, with the risk of divergent outcomes, more likely.

In these cases, the CJEU was attempting to reduce the possibility of forum shopping and torpedoes,[46] but the decisions were criticised for 'failing to eliminate the possibility of undesirable litigation practices'.[47] The overall result is that the CJEU has significantly restricted the possibility of cross-border enforcement in the EU. Some slight allowances were made in the more recent case of *Solvay* where the CJEU allowed cross-border injunctions, but only as provisional measures under Article 31 of the Brussels I Regulation.[48]

Although this case law is EU specific, the lack of cross-border enforcement impacts Europe more generally. Without the possibility of effective cross-border enforcement, divergent decisions on the same inventions can occur in Europe. Institutional fragmentation can result in inefficiency and legal uncertainty for users and society.[49] However, at the same time, there are a number of possible reasons for divergent decisions. Additionally, a degree of security remains for the patentee, who may lose their patent in one country but retain it in another, allowing them to partly continue with their business.

It must also be noted that divergence in interpretations of substantive patent law by different national courts can result in additional forum shopping. Forum

[43] S Warner and S Middlemiss, 'Patent Litigation in Multiple Jurisdictions: An End to Cross Border Relief in Europe?' (2006) 28(11) *EIPR* 580, 581.

[44] *Roche v Primus*, para 41. See also Brinkhof and Ohly, 'Towards a Unified Patent Court' 208.

[45] *Roche v Primus*, paras 27 and 30.

[46] Torpedoes are a patent litigation strategy where a declaratory action is filed in a slower jurisdiction when threatened with patent infringement to slow down potential infringement proceedings in faster jurisdictions. *Lis pendens* requires the latter Court to stay proceedings until jurisdiction is established by the first.

[47] Trimble, '*GAT*, *Solvay*, and the Centralization of Patent Litigation' 520.

[48] Case C-616/10 *Solvay SA v Honeywell Florine Products Europe BV and Others* ECLI:EU:C:2012:445 (*Solvay*).

[49] For example, a patent on a biotechnological invention could be opposed at the EPO or challenged before numerous national courts, one of which could refer a question on the matter to the CJEU. The length of time taken to resolve these issues would likely have a significant impact on the commercialisation of the invention, which could be to the detriment of the patentee and the public.

shopping occurs in this context when enforcement proceedings are strategically taken in courts that are well known for being, for example, pro-patentee, and thus more likely to find infringement in certain types of cases than the courts of other states.

Divergences in the procedures of national courts can also have an impact. One such difference is whether courts bifurcate proceedings.[50] In a bifurcated system, two courts exercise independent jurisdiction, one addressing validity and the other addressing infringement. For example, in Germany, where infringement proceedings progress much faster than elsewhere in Europe, if the validity of a patent is contested, the court will stay the infringement proceedings if it is likely that the patent will be revoked on the balance of probabilities.[51] The revocation claim will be referred to the relevant court. The result of bifurcation is that until a decision is made on validity, which can take longer than infringement proceedings, competitors are left unaware as to the definite result of the case and must then wait for the matter to be decided before taking further action. Furthermore, if an infringement action does go ahead without a decision on validity, the decision on infringement may need to be amended if a patent, which has been declared infringed, is later found to be invalid. This has an impact on legal certainty for patentees, litigators, competitors and society.

Although national patent systems have many advantages, particularly for SMEs, focus remains on the effects of fragmentation. The territorial nature of patent protection and lack of cross-border enforcement creates a situation in which divergence can flourish. Thus, various types of fragmentation are generally perceived as one of the main problems associated with national patent systems.

II. The European (EPC) Patent System

The need for a European patent system arose from the expansion of markets, a move towards Europeanisation, and the difficulties faced by patentees using national patent systems to apply and enforce multiple patents throughout Europe. These difficulties related to the burden of filing numerous applications, onerous translation requirements, cost and the lack of cross-border enforcement. Societal concerns regarding the dissemination of information and the quality of granted patents also played a role.

Following years of negotiations, the European (EPC) patent system was created. It is governed by the EPC, which was signed at a diplomatic conference in Munich in 1973 and came into force four years later. This is a supranational agreement by a

[50] Patent proceedings are bifurcated in, for example, Austria, Poland and Germany.

[51] For more detailed information on bifurcation in Germany, see M Haedicke and H Timmann, *Patent Law: A Handbook* (CH Beck 2013) 835–47.

group of EU and non-EU Contracting States. Concluding and then implementing the EPC was not a simple accomplishment, as stated by Bob van Bentham:

> That this detailed preparation took so long is due precisely to the overcoming of national attitudes: the latest views and developments had to be taken into account on a practical level, while at the same time refashioning traditional national attitudes into supra-national, European attitudes and expanding national consciousness into a European consciousness.[52]

To reach agreement on the provisions of the EPC required a compromise. The legislative basis of the system that now exists under the EPC is made up of various aspects of national laws taken directly or partly and brought together alongside some entirely new provisions.[53] It built upon previous international unifying conventions, especially the substantive provisions of the Strasbourg Patent Convention.[54]

The aim of the EPC was to introduce a new system of granting patents that would not abolish national systems, outlined above, but would allow the applicant to apply for a patent in a number of countries by means of one application, though without granting a unitary right. It is concerned with 'providing a less wasteful, but nonetheless substantial examination of patent applications'.[55]

The EPOrg was set up in response to the EPC. It consists of two bodies: the Administrative Council and the EPO. The Administrative Council is made up of representatives of Contracting States. The EPO is the body responsible for granting European (EPC) patents. It established a means of applying for patent protection in a number of national states through one application and a system for the grant of European (EPC) patents in the form of a bundle of national patents. Post-grant matters, with the exception of oppositions within nine months of grant and relevant appeals, remain under the control of individual states.

Although an application for a European (EPC) patent includes a significant number of procedural requirements, it is relatively simple. The applicant is obliged by Article 14(6) EPC to submit their application in one of the three official languages of the EPO (English, French or German).[56] European (EPC) patent applications must contain: a request for the grant of a European patent; a description of the invention; one or more claims; any drawings referred to in the description or the claims; and an abstract.[57] Once received, EPO examiners

[52] P Griset, *The European Patent: A Success Story for Innovation* (Kösel Burch Altusried-Kuugzell 2013) 90.

[53] G Paterson, *The European Patent System: The Law and Practice of the European Patent Convention* (2nd edn, Sweet & Maxwell 2001) 4.

[54] J Pila, 'Article 53(b) EPC: A Challenge to the *Novartis* Theory of European Patent History' (2009) 72 *MLR* 436, 437; C Wadlow, 'Strasbourg, the Forgotten Patent Convention, and the Origins of the European Patents Jurisdiction' (2010) 41(2) *IIC* 123.

[55] D Llewelyn and T Aplin, *Cornish Llewelyn & Aplin; Intellectual Property: Patents, Copyright, Trade Marks and Allied Rights* (9th edn, Sweet & Maxwell 2019) 132.

[56] Article 14(6) EPC.

[57] Article 78 EPC.

conduct the search and examination against the state of the art to ensure that the application fulfils the criteria for patentability.

If successful, a European (EPC) patent is granted, which must then be validated by the relevant Contracting States. At this stage, a translation of the application into the national language is required in some states.[58] Article 2 EPC confirms that 'a European patent shall confer on its proprietor, in each Contracting State in respect of which it is granted, the same rights as would be conferred by a national patent granted in that State'. It is not a cross-border right and therefore patents remain territorially fragmented.

Post-grant, a European (EPC) patent is only treated as a whole during appeal or opposition proceedings. If an application to the EPO initially fails, applicants have the option to appeal the Examining Division decision to the Boards of Appeal of the EPO. The decisions of the Boards of Appeal are only bound by the EPC.[59] A notice of appeal must be filed within two months of the notification of the contested decision along with a fee. The Board will then decide if the appeal is admissible.[60] If so, the Board may exercise any power within the competence of the department responsible for the decision that has been appealed or remit the case for further examination.[61]

Opposition proceedings can be brought by any member of the public within nine months of grant. Under Article 100 EPC, an opposition action can be filed if the subject matter was not patentable, if the invention was not sufficiently disclosed, or if improper amendments have been made to the original application. It must be filed in writing along with an opposition fee. If permitted, the grounds on which it was filed are examined and the patentee has the chance to reply. Depending on the outcome, the patent can be maintained as granted, maintained with amendments or revoked. If revoked, it is as if the patent never existed.[62] This is currently the only opportunity for third parties to have a European (EPC) patent revoked centrally. Otherwise, they are enforced through national courts.

The EPC has been widely regarded as successful in achieving its aims. The establishment of the EPC, and in turn the EPO, has given applicants the option of a centralised patent application system, reducing procedural fragmentation by

[58] European Patent Office, *National Law Relating to the EPC* (20th edn, European Patent Office 2019) IV.

[59] There are currently 28 Technical Boards of Appeal, as well as the Legal Board of Appeal, the Enlarged Board of Appeal, and the Disciplinary Board of Appeal. The Technical Boards of Appeal and the Legal Board of Appeal examine appeals from the decisions of the Examining, Legal and Opposition Divisions of the Office (Article 21 EPC). To ensure uniform application of the law, a matter may be referred to the Enlarged Board of Appeal of the EPO (Article 22 EPC). The Enlarged Board of Appeal can also issue decisions when the case law of the Boards of Appeal becomes inconsistent and opinions when it is referred a question from the President of the EPO (Article 22 EPC). The Disciplinary Board of Appeal hears appeals against decisions of the Disciplinary Committee and the Disciplinary Board of the EPO on infringement of the rules of conduct for professional representatives before the EPO.

[60] Article 110 EPC.

[61] Article 111 EPC.

[62] Article 68 EPC.

reducing the number of separate national applications required for protection in multiple Contracting States, which also lowers costs and inefficiencies. The EPC has also balanced the standard of search and examination.[63]

Compared to national patent systems, some applicants will find this route to protection more appealing. An applicant will most likely choose this route if patent protection is required throughout a number of European countries, as the initial filing procedure is less cumbersome than applying for numerous national patents individually.

However, the cost of protection across Europe remains relatively high. According to the European Commission, in 2012 a European (EPC) patent validated in 27 EU Member States would cost €36,000.[64] In 2017 the cost for a patent validated in 25 Member States was €32,119.[65] This can be compared to the cost of a patent in the United States (approx. €2,000), and in China (approx. €600).[66] The majority of fees are used for translations and other costs linked to validation, such as fees of local patent offices and costs for local patent attorneys.[67] These fees, clearly linked to territorial fragmentation, are one of the major disadvantages of seeking patent protection across Europe.

Some steps have been taken to reduce costs around translations. For example, the London Agreement 2000 provides that once granted, translation of the whole application (as distinct from the claims) into an official language of a participating state will not be necessary once the application is in one of the three official languages of the EPO. For example, France would not require the translation of an application granted in German or English. Many Contracting States have signed up to this agreement.[68]

For national patent offices, the European (EPC) patent system can mean less examination work, which may have an impact on employment. Once a patent is granted, renewal fees are paid nationally. For patent attorneys, a more streamlined process may bring benefits when filing applications; however, to stand before the EPO an attorney must qualify as a European patent attorney. This is in addition to qualifications required nationally. The EPO search and examination can bring benefits to society. Search and examination are streamlined across Europe, which results in more certainty, and information on inventions can be accessed through the EPO database, Espacenet.

One of the most important considerations of the European (EPC) patent system relates to enforcement. A successful EPO application results in a bundle

[63] Guellec and Van Pottelsberghe de la Potterie, *The Economics of the European Patent System* 29.

[64] Given the timing of this report, these figures include the UK and exclude Croatia.

[65] As seen from the figures compiled by the European Commission, available at www.bristowsupc.com/assets/files/UPC%20Comm%20Slides2.pdf.

[66] European Commission Memo, 'Patent reform Package – frequently asked questions' (11 December 2011) available at http://europa.eu/rapid/press-release_MEMO-12-970_en.htm?locale=en.

[67] ibid.

[68] Agreement on the application of Article 65 EPC (London Agreement) 2000. European Patent Office, *National Law Relating to the EPC*, IV.

of national patents rather than a single unitary patent. Similar advantages and disadvantages raised relating to the fragmentation of national patent systems are therefore also applicable in the European (EPC) context. This is particularly so in relation to the potential for institutional fragmentation at the national level because there are currently limited means for the cross-border enforcement of patents, as mentioned previously. For example, if a case is brought before a number of national courts relating to the same invention it is still possible that a court in the UK will come to a different conclusion to that of a court in Germany. This was the outcome in the well-known case of *Improver v Remington*.[69] When the *Improver* case was litigated, the court in the United Kingdom reached the opposite conclusion to that of the German court (among others) on the matter of infringement. *Improver* could happen and has happened again on numerous occasions.[70]

Most infringement and all validity claims (nine months post-grant) related to a European (EPC) patent are dealt with at national level. Other important issues that arise during enforcement such as entitlement, the rights conferred and exceptions to infringement also remain matters for national law. This has an impact on all relevant stakeholders.

III. The International Patent Application

As well as European expansion, markets were also developing internationally. In response, patent law was discussed on the international level. Depending on the size of their market, a patentee may need to apply for protection in countries across the world. Furthermore, as mentioned previously, countries in Europe have different procedures and standards of examination. The same is true globally. The extremes of either situation can have a negative impact on the quality of granted patents and legal certainty.

It was seen as necessary to introduce an international procedure that could rectify these issues by providing a streamlined international search and examination. The expectation was that this would allow patentees to apply for international protection centrally and to ensure that those offices that had been overly stringent or flexible would benefit from an efficient, smooth-running system with fewer discrepancies in search and examination standards.[71]

[69] *Improver Corp v Remington Consumer Product Ltd* [1990] FSR 181 (*Improver*).

[70] For more, see S Luginbuehl, *European Patent Law: Towards a Uniform Interpretation* (Edward Elgar 2011), where the following are identified: *Novartis AG and Cibavision AG v Johnson & Johnson Medical Ltd and others*, EP 0819258 – High Court of the United Kingdom [2009] EWHC 1671 (Pat), Tribunal de Grande Instance de Paris, March 25, 2009 (07/13504), and District Court of The Hague, 11 February 2009, HA ZA 07-3547; *Document Security Systems v European Central Bank*, EP 0455750, [2007] EWHC 600 (Pat) – the patent in question was upheld in Germany, the Netherlands and Spain and invalidated in the UK, Austria, Belgium and France. See also K Cremers, M Ernicke, F Gaessler, D Harhoff, C Helmers, L McDonagh, P Schliessler and N Van Zeebroeck, 'Patent Litigation in Europe' (2016) 44 *European Journal of Law and Economics* 1.

[71] For more on the PCT, see www.wipo.int/pct/en/faqs/faqs.html.

In 1970, the PCT was signed and came into force as a special agreement under the Paris Convention. It aims to simplify the filing, search and examination of patent applications when protection is sought in multiple countries to make this more cost-effective, to increase the disclosure of technical information and to foster economic development.[72] It has created an international application procedure that is administered by WIPO and available to all Contracting States of the Paris Convention. Today, there are over 150 Contracting States.[73] It is important to note from the outset that WIPO does not grant patents of any kind but gives applicants another route to eventual patent protection.

The procedure is quite similar to that of the European (EPC) patent application, but on a larger scale. An international application may be filed by those who are nationals or residents of a Contracting State through a Receiving Office (national patent office or the EPO) or directly to the International Bureau of WIPO.[74] The application must contain a request, a description, one or more claims, one or more drawings (where required), and an abstract.[75] The request automatically designates all Contracting States.[76] The application must be filed in one of the prescribed languages of the PCT.[77]

The Receiving Office checks the application for formalities and copies are provided to the International Bureau and the International Search Authority (ISA). It also records the international filing date of the application.[78] If this is the first patent application filed in relation to an invention this date will also be the international priority date giving the applicant 30/31 months to enter the national or regional phase.[79]

The application launches a search of prior art known as an international search, which is carried out by the prescribed ISA.[80] Once the international search has been completed, a report and written opinion is sent to the International Bureau, and is then published. If requested by the applicant, a supplementary search of additional prior art can be undertaken by a second ISA. The applicant can also request an international preliminary examination on an updated application. The objective of the search and examination is to formulate a preliminary, non-binding opinion on the patentability of the claimed invention.[81]

[72] PCT Preamble.

[73] According to www.wipo.int/pct/en/pct_contracting_states.html.

[74] Article 9(1) PCT.

[75] Article 3(2) PCT.

[76] Prior to PCT amendments in 2004, the request required a designation of the countries in which protection was sought.

[77] Article 10 PCT.

[78] Article 11 PCT.

[79] The time limit depends on the relevant patent office. See www.wipo.int/pct/en/texts/time_limits.html.

[80] International Search Authorities are patent offices appointed by the PCT Assembly to carry out an extensive inspection and examination of prior art. See www.wipo.int/pct/en/access/isa_ipea_agreements.html.

[81] Article 33 PCT.

Reports are sent to the applicant and the International Bureau. If the opinion is positive, the applicant may decide to enter the national phase in any relevant territory. At this stage, the applicant must pay national fees, appoint local agents or attorneys, and file translations where required. Assisted by the PCT reports, the national patent office(s) will then determine if a patent will be granted. The applicant could also, or alternatively, choose to send their reports to a regional patent office, such as the EPO.[82] If successful in the national or regional phase, numerous national patents may be granted. As mentioned, the international application does not result in an international patent.

The PCT gives patent applicants a number of advantages that benefit them in their pursuit for patent protection. One major advantage is the international priority filing date, which, as mentioned, gives an applicant 30/31 months from the original filing date to enter the national or regional phase. An initial application through the PCT procedure allows the patentee to subsequently proceed with an application for patent protection either through the national patent systems, or regional systems (for example, the European (EPC) patent system), using their priority filing date from the PCT procedure. The length of priority is significantly longer than the period granted under the Paris Convention. By having this extra time, the patentee has more opportunity to assess whether their invention will be successful in different markets, and subsequently, whether to continue on the path to patent protection, which comes at a significant cost.[83]

Moreover, as the international search and examination reports are sent to the applicant, they will have an idea as to whether their invention is patentable in the first place. If the report shows a significant amount of anticipatory prior art, continuing to the national or regional phase may not be worth the expense. Having this information before having to pay additional application and translation costs is advantageous to the patent applicant, who can then decide whether to pursue the patent at national or regional level.

Furthermore, with search and examination completed, and a designated priority date, the next stage of procedure (gaining protection in individual countries) is much quicker.[84] This reduces the burden on national patent offices and is a highly beneficial starting point for those entering a competitive international market.

Following a period of 18 months from the priority date, the application and report is published on PATENTSCOPE. This database includes all applications and reports and is a key resource for potential applicants informally searching for prior art. It also allows the public to view and gain knowledge from this information and

[82] In fact, for the last 10 years at least, the majority of applications to the EPO have been subsequent filings from the PCT procedure. Statistics available at www.epo.org/about-us/annual-reports-statistics/statistics.html.

[83] Bently, Sherman, Gangjee and Johnson, *Intellectual Property Law*.

[84] B Van Pottelsberghe, 'Lost Property: The European Patent System and Why It Doesn't Work' (2009) IX *Bruegel Blueprint Series* available at http://bruegel.org/2009/06/lost-property-the-european-patent-system-and-why-it-doesnt-work/, 4.

to use it in research (albeit only to a certain extent).[85] This has the effect of widely disseminating information that will often benefit society.

However, this route to protection also has some disadvantages that may dissuade applicants. The main concern is the cost. The average cost per PCT application is €4,000–€5,000, excluding the cost of drafting the application and entry into the national or regional stage.[86] This raises a barrier for many potential applicants. Some ISAs have reduced search fees for SMEs and applicants from low/middle-income countries, but the financial investment remains significant and out of reach for many.[87]

Finally, the enforcement of any patent granted remains at national level. Each country in which the patentee decides to protect their invention will deal with matters relating to validity, revocation, infringement and remedies. Therefore, the advantages and disadvantages relating to the enforcement of national and European (EPC) patents are also relevant when considering the PCT route to patent protection. Patent rights remain territorially, procedurally and possibly institutionally fragmented.

IV. Existing Fragmentation

The nature of a patent has significantly progressed, evolving from unchecked privileges to enormously valuable property rights. The purpose of patents has remained largely unchanged. They grant the patentee an exclusive right in return for the disclosure of their invention. However, there has been a significant change over time in the scope of market operations. Initially concerned with promoting innovation and boosting the economy in individual countries, a progression towards European and international harmonisation has advanced discussions and developments in this area towards promoting a patent system that will advance integration, Europeanisation and globalisation.

The patent system has adapted and expanded to take these developments into account, and it will likely continue to do so. It is important to ensure that inventions are afforded fair protection, especially considering the enormous changes that have occurred in technology to date and that will, without doubt, continue. However, it is imperative that this is done while ensuring that those who continue to operate in smaller markets are not left behind, that over-protection is curtailed, and that patented technologies (particularly in the health context) are accessible

[85] In some jurisdictions, an exemption to infringement exists for certain uses in research. For example, section 60(5)(b) Patents Act (UK) 1977 allows for acts 'done for experimental purposes relating to the subject matter of the invention'.

[86] See www.wipo.int/export/sites/www/pct/en/fees.pdf.

[87] See, for example, www.wipo.int/pct/en/fees/oepm_fee_reduction.html; http://documents.epo.org/projects/babylon/eponet.nsf/0/D712DD08A7CEF1F2C12574FF003A99DA/$File/low_income_states_en.pdf.

downstream. The attempted balance between exclusivity and access within the patent system must be at the forefront of any developments.[88]

As elaborated upon above, three routes to obtaining patent protection exist in Europe today – the national, European (EPC) and international (PCT). Each is supported by its own separate but interconnecting system and exists for a different purpose and to serve a different community. Consistent with this, each has its own perceived strengths and weaknesses. However, the ultimate result of each route to protection is the grant of one or more national patents, the enforcement of which is predominantly restricted to the territory of the granting state. In other words, no matter which route is taken, territorial, procedural and institutional fragmentation exists.

Despite the introduction of the EPC and PCT, the territoriality of national patents remains. Although these initiatives have streamlined the application procedure for patents and balanced standards of search and examination, they have also added further legal, institutional and procedural layers to the existing field. This has created a number of overlapping laws of different scope and jurisdiction, as well as additional institutions to interpret those laws, resulting in complexity and legal uncertainty. Enforcement is also mostly dealt with on a national level. Differences in pre- and post-grant matters on the same inventions and interpretations of substantive patent law will remain.

The mere existence of these different systems and procedures has an impact on all parties concerned. For applicants, careful consideration is required before proceeding with an application by any route. For competitors inventing around a patented invention, multiple databases need to be investigated. For patent offices, judicial bodies and litigators, the existence of numerous routes to protection and numerous patents on a single invention often means that similar work is being done on multiple occasions, sometimes producing different results. For European patent law- and policy-makers, the benefits and shortcomings of each system must be at the centre of new initiatives in the European patent field. For society, the complexity surrounding patent protection in Europe can cause confusion and uncertainty.

From this overview of the current routes to patent protection, it is clear that the patent system in Europe is fragmented. Each patent on a single invention must be granted/validated and enforced in each country individually and according to local procedure, potentially resulting in divergence pre- and post-grant. This is one of the main problems associated with patent protection in Europe and it has been with a view to reducing fragmentation that the introduction of a unitary patent and unified patent court have been consistently debated.

[88] For a detailed discussion of this argument see K Walsh, 'Invoking the Public Interest in the European Patent System' in N Hawkins (ed), *Patenting Biotechnological Innovation: Eligibility, Ethics and Public Interest* (Edward Elgar 2022). See also K Murray, *A Politics of Patent Law: Crafting the Participatory Patent Bargain* (Routledge 2013).

2

Forthcoming Route to EU Unitary Patent Protection

The pursuit of a European unitary patent system has been long-standing, contentious and persistent. There have been many attempts to introduce a unitary patent system in Europe at both a European level and at an EU level.[1] Most proposals have involved the creation of a supranational patent and patent court. A supranational patent would create a right conferring uniform and unitary patent protection on inventions across Europe. The unitary effect of such a right would be entirely distinct compared to pre-existing rights, which remain subject to the territoriality of national laws. A European patent court would create a single jurisdiction for patents in Europe to provide cross-border, specialised judgments in patent disputes rather than multiple, individual and potentially diverse national decisions. The effect of such a court would be to reduce the risks and costs involved with duplicated litigation and divergent interpretations of substantive patent law.

The potential benefits of such an idealistic European unitary patent system would be plentiful; however, the success of such a system depends on the scope and standard of the legislation concerned, as well as who would reap the benefits. The coexistence of national systems must also be recognised in these debates because their abolishment has never been given serious consideration and they remain beneficial to a variety of stakeholders.

The latest attempt at a partial unification of the European patent system – the Unitary Patent Package – has been led by the EU. Following over 10 years of proposals and negotiations, in December 2012, two EU Regulations on unitary patent protection were approved.[2] In February and March 2013, 25 EU Member

[1] These attempts have been detailed in J Pila and C Wadlow (eds), *The Unitary EU Patent System* (Hart Publishing 2015) chapters 2 and 3.

[2] Regulation (EU) 1257/2012 of the European Parliament and of the Council of 17 December 2012 implementing enhanced cooperation in the area of the creation of unitary patent protection [2012] OJ L 361/1 (Regulation 1257) and Regulation (EU) 1260/2012 of the European Parliament and of the Council of 17 December 2012 implementing enhanced cooperation in the area of the creation of unitary patent protection with regard to the applicable translation arrangements [2012] OJ L 361/89 (Regulation 1260).

States signed an agreement to create a unified patent court to support an (almost) EU-wide unitary patent system.[3] Together, these three legal instruments form the UPP or the EU unitary patent system.

The UPP has the potential to significantly change the patent landscape in Europe. As with all previous attempts, the ambition of the UPP is to address the disadvantages associated with national patent systems. That is, to reduce costs and various instances of fragmentation. It is perceived that by doing so, the patent system in Europe will become more efficient and cost-effective, and result in more legal certainty. However, whether the UPP will effectively reduce fragmentation is questionable, and for whom the system will become more efficient, more cost-effective and more certain is a contentious issue.

Despite substantial concerns over its content and scope of protection, alongside significant political developments in the EU, the push for implementation of the UPP remains strong among its proponents. The Agreement awaits complete ratification; however at the time of writing, it is expected that this will soon occur. This chapter will examine the UPP in detail, including the lengthy process to finalisation, its purpose, legal basis, and procedural and enforcement aspects, as well as the main criticisms against it. It highlights the preoccupation of policy-makers in this area with reducing fragmentation and the paradoxical situation whereby, when implemented, this package will also increase fragmentation.

I. Background to the Unitary Patent Package[4]

In 2000, the latest initiative to create a unitary patent system began. A resurgence of negotiations at the time led to the European Council approving the creation of a unitary patent system.[5] On the basis of that decision, the European Commission prepared a proposal for a Community Patent Regulation.[6] The main aims of the proposal were to introduce a unitary patent right that would be granted by the EPO, reduce translation costs and introduce a specialised and centralised patent court that would operate alongside the CJEU. The European Community was to accede to the EPC[7] as a new contracting party and the EPO would grant Community Patents. This new system was to coexist with those already available.

[3] Agreement 2013/C on a Unified Patent Court [2013] OJ L 175/01. Signatories included the UK as this occurred pre Brexit.

[4] This section contains a summary of content that was previously published by Sweet & Maxwell in *Intellectual Property Quarterly*: K Walsh, 'The Unitary Patent Package, the Court of Justice of the European Union, and Brexit: (Ir)reconcilable?' (2019) 2 *IPQ* 91. It is reproduced by agreement with the publishers.

[5] This idea was based on Commission Paper (EU) on Promoting innovation through patents – Green Paper on the Community patent and the patent system in Europe [1997] COM (97) 314 final, and subsequent consultations.

[6] Proposal for a Council Regulation (EU) 2000/C 337 E/45 on the Community patent [2000] COM (2000) 412 final.

[7] Convention on the Grant of European Patents of 5 October 1973, amended in 2000.

Between 2000 and 2004, issues including the court system, language, cost, the role of national patent offices and the distribution of fees were extensively negotiated. A number of updated proposals were put forward, as well as proposals to establish a Community Patent Court and confer jurisdiction on the CJEU.[8] However, consensus could not be achieved on these proposals and a press release by the Commission indicated that the main reason for this related to the proposed translation regime.[9]

Over the next few years, the Commission undertook a public consultation, followed by several publications and proposals highlighting the need for a unitary patent and integrated judiciary for both unitary and European (EPC) patents, which included features of previous proposals including the European Patent Litigation Agreement (EPLA).[10]

In 2008, a draft agreement and statute on a European patent court (what became known as the European and Community/Union Patent Court (EEUPC)) was debated.[11] It was to be an international court including non-Community states with exclusive jurisdiction for Community/EU patents and European (EPC) patents in relation to revocation and infringement. Once again, consensus could not be achieved, and negotiations stagnated.

In 2009, the Lisbon Treaty entered into force, making significant changes to EU law.[12] This spurred EU law-makers into further action in relation to the creation of a unitary patent. An opinion was sought from the CJEU on the compatibility of the EEUPC with EU law and an approach was put forward in relation to

[8] Including Council Document (EU) 7159/03 of 7 March 2003 on the Community patent – Common political approach [2003] PI 24; Proposal for a Council Regulation (EU) 15086/03 of 21 November 2003 on the Community patent [2003] LIMITE PI 122; Proposal for a Council Decision (EU) 2003/0324 (CNS) establishing the Community Patent Court and concerning appeals before the Court of First Instance [2003] COM (2003) 828 final; and Proposal for a Council Decision (EU) 2003/0326 (CNS) conferring jurisdiction on the Court of Justice in disputes relating to the Community patent [2003] COM (2003) 827 final; Proposal for a Council Regulation (EU) 7119/04 on the Community patent [2004] LIMITE PI 28.

[9] European Commission Memo, 'Results of the Competitiveness Council of Ministers' (MEMO/04/58, 12 March 2004). For more detail on this period and the lead-up to the UPP, see H Dunlop, *European Unitary Patent and Unified Patent Court* (2nd edn, Chartered Institute of Patent Attorneys 2014); A Ilardi, *The New European Patent* (Hart Publishing 2015); Walsh, 'The Unitary Patent Package'.

[10] Communication from the Commission to the European Parliament and the Council (EU) on Enhancing the patent system in Europe [2007] COM (2007) 165 final; Council Document (EU) 11622/07 of 12 July 2007 Towards an Enhanced Patent Litigation System and a Community Patent – How to Take Discussions Further [2007] PI 35. The Draft Agreement on the establishment of a European patent litigation system 2004 or the European Patent Litigation Agreement was the result of a Working Party on Litigation, established by the Contracting States to the EPC, with the aim of drawing up an optional protocol to the EPC, committing signatories to an integrated judicial system.

[11] Council Document (EU) 9124/08 of 14 May 2008 on a Draft Agreement on the European Union Patent Judiciary [2008] PI 24 COUR 19.

[12] Treaty of Lisbon amending the Treaty on European Union and the Treaty Establishing the European Community [2007] C 306/01.

the proposed Regulation.[13] Following the changes made by the Lisbon Treaty, the Regulation would now have its legal basis in Article 118 TFEU.[14]

The translation regime remained a contentious issue. In 2010, a proposal for a separate regulation on the translation arrangements for the proposed EU patent was published but it was not possible to reach the unanimous agreement required by Article 118(2) TFEU.[15] The European Council decided that consensus could not be achieved within a reasonable time frame. Subsequently, the European Commission, at the request of 12 EU Member States (shortly followed by all but Spain and Italy), proposed that the process of enhanced cooperation be used to implement unitary patent protection.[16] Enhanced cooperation is a procedure that allows a minimum of nine EU Member States to cooperate in a certain area without the participation of all Member States.[17] The aim of this procedure is to overcome deadlock and it is to be used only as a last resort.

In February 2011 consent was granted by the European Parliament, and in March a Council Decision authorised the use of enhanced cooperation.[18] However, this decision was subsequently challenged by Spain and Italy,[19] and, two days before the Council Decision was adopted, the CJEU had issued Opinion 1/09 stating that the EEUPC was not compatible with EU law.[20] A case of one step forward, two steps back for the proposed unitary patent system.

The challenge raised by Spain and Italy arose once the Commission, following the Council Decision, adopted the two proposals implementing enhanced cooperation.[21] The action was taken to the CJEU against the Council, alleging that

[13] Council Conclusions (EU) 17229/09 on the Enhanced Patent System in Europe [2009] PI 141 COUR 87; Council General Approach (EU) 16113/09 ADD 1 on the Proposal for a Council Regulation on the Community patent [2009] PI 122.

[14] Article 118 TFEU: '(1) In the context of the establishment and functioning of the internal market, the European Parliament and the Council, acting in accordance with the ordinary legislative procedure, shall establish measures for the creation of European intellectual property rights to provide uniform protection of intellectual property rights throughout the Union and for the setting up of centralised Union-wide authorisation, coordination and supervision arrangements. (2) The Council, acting in accordance with a special legislative procedure, shall by means of regulations establish language arrangements for the European intellectual property rights. The Council shall act unanimously after consulting the European Parliament'.

[15] Proposal for a Council Regulation (EU) 2010/0198 (CNS) on the translation arrangements for the European Union patent [2010] COM (2010) 350 final.

[16] Proposal for a Council Decision (EU) 2010/0384 (NLE) authorising enhanced cooperation in the area of the creation of unitary patent protection [2010] COM (2010) 790 final.

[17] Article 20 of the Treaty on European Union (TEU) [2012] OJ C 326/13.

[18] Council Decision (EU) 2011/167/EU of 10 March 2011 authorising enhanced cooperation in the area of the creation of unitary patent protection [2011] OJ L 76/53.

[19] Joined Cases C-274 and 295/11 *Kingdom of Spain and Italian Republic v Council of the European Union* [2013] ECLI:EU:C:2013:240 (*Spain and Italy v Council* [2013]).

[20] Opinion 1/09 ECLI:EU:C:2011:123 (Opinion 1/09).

[21] Council General Approach (EU) 11328/11 on the Proposal for a Regulation of the Council and the European Parliament implementing enhanced cooperation in the area of the creation of unitary patent protection and on the Proposal for a Council Regulation implementing enhanced cooperation in the area of unitary patent protection with regard to the applicable translation arrangements [2011] PI 67 CODEC 995.

it had unlawfully authorised enhanced cooperation by circumventing the requirement for unanimity and unduly dismissing objections regarding the proposed translation regime.[22] Following the dismissal of this case, Spain brought two further actions to the CJEU, also challenging the legality of the Regulations. These were also dismissed.[23] Although unsuccessful, the arguments raised against the use of enhanced cooperation and legality of the Regulations persist in debates on the future of the EU unitary patent system and therefore require a more detailed examination below.

On the proposed EEUPC, the CJEU stated that removing the possibility for EU Member States to refer questions on the interpretation of EU law to the CJEU made it incompatible with the EU Treaties.[24] It was held that

> the envisaged agreement, by conferring on an international court which is outside the institutional and judicial framework of the European Union an exclusive jurisdiction to hear a significant number of actions brought by individuals in the field of the [European Union] patent and to interpret and apply European Union law in that field, would deprive courts of Member States of their powers in relation to the interpretation and application of European Union law and the Court of its powers to reply, by preliminary ruling, to questions referred by those courts and, consequently, would alter the essential character of the powers which the Treaties confer on the institutions of the European Union and on the Member States and which are indispensable to the preservation of the very nature of European Union law.[25]

As it could not be guaranteed that the EEUPC would refer relevant questions to the CJEU coupled with the lack of remedies available for individuals against breaches of EU law, it was decided that the agreement was inconsistent with the Treaties.[26] It has been suggested that it has now become much more difficult to implement a European patent court that extends beyond the EU due to the CJEU's protective attitude over the EU legal order.[27] Opinion 1/09 has been interpreted as meaning that a court including all EPC Contracting States making decisions on matters of EU law is not possible.[28] However, this limitation now excludes Contracting States to the EPC that are not members of the EU, adding another layer of fragmentation to the European patent system. Some commentators have found Opinion 1/09 to be 'unconvincing' in some respects and that it 'did not consider the possibility of

[22] *Spain and Italy v Council* [2013].

[23] Case C-146/13 *Kingdom of Spain v European Parliament and the Council of the European Union* ECLI:EU:C:2015:298 and Case C-147/13 *Kingdom of Spain v Council of the European Union* ECLI:EU:C:2015:299 (*Spain v Council* [2015]).

[24] Opinion 1/09, para 66.

[25] ibid para 89.

[26] ibid.

[27] T Lock, 'Taking National Courts More Seriously? Comment on Opinion 1/09' (2011) 36(4) *European Law Review* 576, 577.

[28] A Ohly, 'Concluding Remarks: Postmodernism and Beyond' in A Ohly and J Pila (eds), *The Europeanization of Intellectual Property Law: Towards a European Legal Methodology* (Oxford University Press 2013) 259.

finding member states collectively severally liable for any breaches of EU law by the proposed patent court', indicating that the Opinion could be circumvented.[29] However, legislators decided to pursue an option that only included EU Member States.

Potential solutions to the problems identified in Opinion 1/09 were published by the Commission, and a full amendment, including a name change to the Unified Patent Court, was put forward for discussion.[30] The CJEU had mentioned the differences between the EEUPC and the Benelux Court of Justice, which the Council noted, and then took an approach described as 'The EEUPC is dead, long live the EEUPC'.[31] Draft after draft of the updated UPC Agreement was released, each attempting to rectify issues including opposition to the translation arrangements, the role of the CJEU, the location of the UPC central division, and compatibility with Opinion 1/09.[32]

In December 2011, great strides were apparently being made towards an agreement on the UPP. However, interested parties were concerned about the political and potentially undemocratic nature of negotiations as they were proceeding *in camera*.[33] A press release was issued by the Parliament claiming that there had been political agreement on the UPP, and only the necessary approvals were required to progress.[34] However, a further 12 months of deliberations took place to resolve a dispute over the seat of the central division of the Court of First Instance of the UPC and the role of the CJEU in the proposed system.

In 2012/2013, the UPP, consisting of two EU Regulations and the international Agreement on a Unified Patent Court, was finalised and approved. In December 2012 the Regulations were adopted by 25 EU Member States. In February/March 2013 the UPCA was finalised and signed by a different combination of 25 EU Member States and the process of ratification began. Another 10 years later, or 22 years since the European Council first approved the creation of a unitary patent system, it has yet to be fully ratified. This delay can be pinned down to

[29] S Peers, 'The Constitutional Implications of the EU Patent' (2011) 7(2) *European Constitutional Law Review* 229, 247.

[30] Council Orientation Debate (EU) 10630/11 creating a Unified Patent Litigation System [2011] PI 54 COUR 28.

[31] T Jaeger, 'Back to Square One? An Assessment of the Latest Proposals for a Patent and Court for the Internal Market and Possible Alternatives' (2012) 43(3) *IIC* 286, 296.

[32] Presidency Text (EU) 11533/11 on a Draft agreement on a Unified Patent Court and draft Statute [2011] PI 68 COUR 32; Revised Presidency Text (EU) 13751/11 on a Draft agreement on a Unified Patent Court and draft Statute [2011] PI 108 COUR 48; Opinion of the Legal Service (EU) 15856/11 on the compatibility of the draft agreement with the Opinion 1/09 [2011] PI 138 COUR 61.

[33] These views were expressed in A Merelle Ward, 'Recap & Update: the Unitary Patent System and Unified Patent Court' (*IPKat*, 20 December 2011) available at http://ipkitten.blogspot.co.uk/2011/12/recap-update-unitary-patent-system-and.html. Since then, Ingve Björn Stjerna has published translations of meetings from the European Parliament and its Legal Affairs Committee. See IB Stjerna, *The Parliamentary History of the European 'Unitary Patent': Verbatim Protocol of Selected Meetings in the European Parliament and its Legal Affairs Committee* (Tredition 2015).

[34] European Parliament Press Release, 'Done deal on the EU patent?' (1 December 2011) available at www.europarl.europa.eu/pdfs/news/expert/infopress/20111201IPR33061/20111201IPR33061_en.pdf.

two major events – Brexit and multiple constitutional complaints to the German Constitutional Court (discussed below) – however, there is much more about the package that has been criticised.

The main aim of the EU unitary patent system is to promote integration, harmonisation and unification amid the fragmentation of the current European patent system that was identified in Chapter 1, that is, to address the perceived problems that arise because of the existence of numerous laws, courts and procedures that impact patent law matters. It has attracted an enormous amount of discussion and controversy in the field of European patent law, as well as more generally in intellectual property law and EU law.

Many problems have been identified. These are diverse in nature and include legal, political, procedural and institutional issues. The following sections will consider these criticisms and show that underpinning them is a concern that the UPP will likely increase the existing fragmentation in the European patent system.

II. The Unitary Patent Package

Regulations 1257 and 1260 both have a legal basis in Article 118 TFEU and were implemented through the enhanced cooperation procedure under Article 20 TEU.[35]

Regulation 1257 establishes the European patent with unitary effect (EPUE), which provides patent protection across all participating EU Member States. It outlines the main features of the patent, including its unitary effect, the uniform nature of the protection conferred, the EPUE as an object of property, and certain administrative aspects of the system, for example relating to fees. Being a European (EPC) patent with unitary effect, patentability is based on the provisions of the EPC, with post-grant matters being determined by the UPP.

Regulation 1260 establishes the applicable translation arrangements. According to its Preamble, translation arrangements for EPUEs ought to be simple and cost-effective. They should ensure legal certainty and stimulate innovation, as well as making access to the EPUE and the patent system easier, less costly, and legally secure.[36]

[35] As authorised by Council Decision 2011/167/EU of 10 March 2011 authorising enhanced cooperation in the area of the creation of unitary patent protection [2011] OJ L 76/53. Article 20 TEU: '(1) Member States which wish to establish enhanced cooperation between themselves within the framework of the Union's non-exclusive competences may make use of its institutions and exercise those competences by applying the relevant provisions of the Treaties, subject to the limits and in accordance with the detailed arrangements laid down in this Article and in Articles 326 to 334 of the Treaty on the Functioning of the European Union. Enhanced cooperation shall aim to further the objectives of the Union, protect its interests and reinforce its integration process. Such cooperation shall be open at any time to all Member States, in accordance with Article 328 of the Treaty on the Functioning of the European Union. (2) The decision authorising enhanced cooperation shall be adopted by the Council as a last resort, when it has established that the objectives of such cooperation cannot be attained within a reasonable period by the Union as a whole'.

[36] Regulation 1260, Preamble (4) and (5).

The procedure involved in applying for the EPUE is quite simple. Applicants must follow the procedure outlined in Chapter 1 for obtaining a European (EPC) patent by filing an application with the EPO. The translation regime is based on Article 14 EPC.[37] Precisely, a patent application must be filed in one of the official languages of the EPO (English, French or German). If the application is filed in another language, it must be translated into English, French or German. Before grant, the claims must also be translated into the two other official languages of the EPO.[38] For example, if a patent application is submitted in English, the claims must be translated into French and German before the patent is granted. However, if a patent application is submitted in Dutch, the entire application must be translated into either English, French or German as the language of proceedings, and the claims must be translated into the remaining languages for the purpose of Article 14(6) EPC. The language of proceedings is the official language of the EPO in which the application is filed or into which it is translated.[39] If filed correctly, the EPO will conduct the necessary search and examination and issue a decision. If successful, depending on the requirements of the Contracting States, the patent may need to be translated further.

For the EPUE, the patentee has one month after grant to submit a request for unitary effect. Additionally, during the transitional period, together with this request, if the language of proceedings is French or German a full translation of the application into English is required; or where the language of proceedings is English, a full translation of the specification into any other official language of the EU is required.[40] The transitional period ends once high-quality machine translations into all official languages of the EU are available, and no longer than 12 years from the date of application of the Regulation.[41] If the formal requirements are met, the EPUE will be registered by the EPO.

The UPCA is a supranational agreement that establishes the UPC, which has been devised (according to the Preamble of the UPCA) to ensure the cross-border enforcement of high-quality, expeditious judgments for patents throughout Europe in order to promote legal and institutional unity, in addition to legal certainty, that strikes a fair balance between the interests of right holders and other parties.[42] It is a specialised patent court common to the Member States of the EU for the

[37] Article 14(6) EPC: 'Specifications of European patents shall be published in the language of the proceedings and shall include a translation of the claims in the other two official languages of the European Patent Office'.

[38] Article 3 Regulation 1260: 'where the specification of a European patent, which benefits from unitary effect has been published in accordance with Article 14(6) of the EPC, no further translations shall be required'. Article 14(6) EPC: 'Specifications of European patents shall be published in the language of the proceedings (the language used to file the patent – English, French or German) and shall include a translation of the claims in the other two official languages of the European Patent Office'.

[39] Article 14(3) EPC.

[40] Article 6 Regulation 1260.

[41] Regulation 1260, Preamble (13).

[42] UPCA, Preamble.

settlement of disputes relating to EPUEs, European (EPC) patents, and supplementary protection certificates.

The UPCA contains provisions on substantive patent law, defining the rights of the proprietor of an EPUE or European (EPC) patent, to prevent the direct and indirect use of the invention.[43] This includes making, offering, placing on the market, or using a product which is the subject matter of the patent, or importing/storing the product for those purposes. It also includes using a process that is the subject matter of a patent and offering, placing on the market, or using a product obtained directly by a patented process, or importing/storing the product for those purposes. The rights defined by the UPCA also extend to indirect infringement.[44] They are subject to certain limitations, including the use of an invention for private and non-commercial purposes, prior use, and use for experimental purposes relating to the subject matter of the invention.[45] The doctrine of exhaustion also applies.[46]

The UPCA also contains provisions on the structure and procedure of the UPC, the judges of the court, as well as financial and transitional provisions. The Statute of the Unified Patent Court provides more detailed institutional and financial arrangements for the UPC.[47] Finally, the Rules of Procedure, currently in their 18th draft, outline all procedural aspects of the UPC.[48]

The UPC will comprise of a Court of First Instance, a Court of Appeal and a Registry.[49] It will be required to base its decisions on Union law, the UPCA, the EPC and other international agreements applicable to patents that are binding on all the participating Member States.[50] The Court can also apply the national law of a Member State, for example when dealing with rights of prior use or the EPUE as an object of property.[51] EU law shall have primacy[52] and the UPC must cooperate with the CJEU in properly interpreting Union law by relying on its jurisprudence and by requesting preliminary rulings in accordance with Article 267 TFEU.[53] Once the division of the Court appropriate to hear a case has been established, proceedings will then commence in the language of proceedings. Ultimately, the Court will make a decision that will be enforceable throughout the territories of all participating Member States.[54]

[43] Articles 25 and 26 UPCA.
[44] Articles 25 and 26 UPCA.
[45] Article 27 UPCA.
[46] Article 29 UPCA.
[47] UPCA, Annex I, Statute of the Unified Patent Court.
[48] Preliminary set of provisions for the Rules of Procedure of the Unified Patent Court, 18th draft, 19 October 2015 (Rules of Procedure).
[49] Article 6(1) UPCA.
[50] Article 24(1) UPCA.
[51] Article 24(2) UPCA.
[52] Article 20 UPCA.
[53] Article 21 UPCA.
[54] The court also has the power under Part III, Chapter IV UPCA to appoint experts during proceedings, protect confidential information, make orders to produce evidence, preserve evidence, inspect premises, make freezing orders, grant provisional and protective measures, permanent injunctions,

The UPP represents a significant achievement for European patent law reformers. After decades of attempts, a unitary patent and patent court will soon be established. For participating Member States, it will provide a new title of patent conferring unitary protection with less onerous requirements relating to validation and translation. It will also provide, for the first time, specialised patent law judgments that will be binding and applicable across the territories of participating Member States.

Its aims are laudable. In essence, it is an attempt to reduce the existing fragmentation in the European patent system and associated costs. However, there have been many aspects of the UPP that have been criticised and which point towards the opposite conclusion.

III. Concerns Related to the Unitary Patent Package

The criticisms of the UPP go to the core of the perceived legitimacy and functioning of the system and share a common overarching theme – that the UPP will add to the pre-existing fragmentation of the European patent system on several levels.

A. Substantive Issues

Prior to the finalisation of the UPP, there were some serious concerns over the substantive content of the package. These issues related to the legal basis of the Regulations and the applicable law for the EPUE as an object of property.

The concern raised in relation to the legal basis and substantive provisions of the Regulations was particularly in respect of Regulation 1257. The main substantive content of Regulation 1257 is in Articles 3 and 5.

Article 3 establishes the EPUE. It states that a European (EPC) patent, having the same claims in respect of all participating Member States, will benefit from unitary effect provided it has been registered for unitary patent protection on request of the European (EPC) patent holder.[55] The EPUE has unitary character, provides uniform protection and has equal effect in all participating Member States.[56] It can only be limited, transferred, revoked or lapse in respect of all participating Member States but can be licensed in respect of the whole or part of the same territory.

Article 5 guarantees uniform protection and prevents third parties from committing acts against which the patent provides protection throughout

corrective measures, make decisions on validity, order the communication of information, award damages and award legal costs. Decisions could also be enforceable beyond these territories due to the Brussels I Regulation, the Lugano Convention, and possible bilateral agreements.

[55] Article 3(1) Regulation 1257.

[56] Article 3(2) Regulation 1257.

participating Member States.[57] Article 5 also explicitly states that the scope of the right and its limitations will be uniform in all participating Member States.[58] Acts against which the patent provides protection are defined by the law applied to EPUEs in the participating Member States whose national law is applicable to the EPUE as an object of property.[59] Prohibited acts are therefore not included in Regulation 1257 and so it has been described as an 'empty shell'.[60] It has been argued that the Regulations contain no substantive patent law and thus do not create uniform rights to provide protection throughout the Union, as mandated by Article 118 TFEU.[61]

Prior to the finalisation of the Regulations, the unitary patent regulation did include substantive patent law to a greater extent. Articles 6–8 included provisions on prohibited acts, injunctions and limitations.[62] However, there was a fear among some Member States that this would provide the CJEU with a significant role in the interpretation of substantive patent law in relation to the UPP and this was not acceptable.[63] It was decided that Articles 6–8 would be deleted from Regulation 1257 and transferred into the UPCA (Articles 25–27).[64]

Article 5 confers uniform protection by referencing the national law of the Member State. This reference to national law could be said to directly undermine the unitary effect of the patent.[65] However, since the Regulations will only become applicable for Member States that have ratified the UPCA, and those States will be bound by the version of Articles 6–8 that now appear in Articles 25–27 of the UPCA,[66] the reference to 'national law' in Article 5 could be interpreted as a

[57] Article 5(1) Regulation 1257.

[58] Article 5(2) Regulation 1257.

[59] Article 5(3) Regulation 1257.

[60] A term used by Spain to refer to the Regulations in *Spain v Council* [2015].

[61] T Jaeger, 'What's in the Unitary Patent Package?' [2014] *Max Planck Institute for Intellectual Property & Competition Law Research Paper* No 14-08 available at http://papers.ssrn.com/sol3/papers.cfm?abstract_id=2435125, 7 and 14–15.

[62] Based on Articles 29–31 Convention for the European Patent for the Common Market (15 December 1975) or Articles 25–27 Council Agreement 89/695/EEC of 15 December 1989 relating to Community Patents [1989] OJ L 401/1 (Community Patent Agreement).

[63] For more on the role of the CJEU, see Walsh, 'The Unitary Patent Package'.

[64] European Parliament, 'Parliament approves EU unitary patent rules' (11 December 2012) available at www.europarl.europa.eu/news/en/news-room/20121210IPR04506/parliament-approves-eu-unitary-patent-rules.

[65] A Kaisi, 'Finally a Single European Right for the EU? An Analysis of the Substantive Provisions of the European Patent with Unitary Effect' (2014) 36(3) *EIPR* 170, 178 and 179.

[66] Article 25 UPCA – Right to prevent the direct use of the invention: 'A patent shall confer on its proprietor the right to prevent any third party not having the proprietor's consent from the following: (a) making, offering, placing on the market or using a product which is the subject matter of the patent, or importing or storing the product for those purposes; (b) using a process which is the subject matter of the patent or, where the third party knows, or should have known, that the use of the process is prohibited without the consent of the patent proprietor, offering the process for use within the territory of the Contracting Member States in which that patent has effect; (c) offering, placing on the market, using, or importing or storing for those purposes a product obtained directly by a process which is the subject matter of the patent'.

Article 26 UPCA – Right to prevent the indirect use of the invention: '(1) A patent shall confer on its proprietor the right to prevent any third party not having the proprietor's consent from supplying or offering to supply, within the territory of the Contracting Member States in which that patent has

reference to the UPCA.[67] Nonetheless, the fact remains that an EU patent derives its substantive content from a non-EU instrument.

Of relevance here is the opposition by Spain and Italy challenging the legality of the Regulations.[68] The legal basis of the Regulations and the possibility of increasing fragmentation in the European patent system were raised before the CJEU. However, the Court ruled that introducing a unitary patent would create more integration and that these claims were unfounded because uniform rights were being created within the territory of Member States, just not all of them.[69]

The CJEU validated the legal basis of the Regulation in these two initial cases; however, as mentioned, Spain subsequently brought two further actions.[70] Legal basis issues were raised once again and it was argued that no act of the EU existed and, in the alternative, that there was no introduction of measures guaranteeing uniform protection as required by Article 118 TFEU.[71] Advocate General Bot, whose opinion was followed by the CJEU, stated that Regulation 1257 is not an empty shell and that uniform protection is guaranteed: 'Each European patent will be subject to the national law of a single Member State and that legislation will apply throughout the territory of the participating Member States'.[72]

In an examination of the specific provisions of Regulation 1257, the CJEU found that there exists a 'guarantee that the designated national law will be applied in the territory of all participating Member States in which that patent has unitary effect' and therefore, the contested Regulation provides uniform protection within the meaning of Article 118 TFEU.[73]

This debate and decision have created a degree of legal uncertainty regarding the legal basis of the UPP. There is now a confusing patchwork of law from which the right is implemented and from which it derives its substance, including EU Regulations, EPC law, EU law more broadly, and international (UPCA) law.

effect, any person other than a party entitled to exploit the patented invention, with means, relating to an essential element of that invention, for putting it into effect therein, when the third party knows, or should have known, that those means are suitable and intended for putting that invention into effect. (2) Paragraph 1 shall not apply when the means are staple commercial products, except where the third party induces the person supplied to perform any of the acts prohibited by Article 25. (3) Persons performing the acts referred to in Article 27(a) to (e) shall not be considered to be parties entitled to exploit the invention within the meaning of paragraph 1'.

Article 27 UPCA – Limitations of the effects of a patent.

[67] See W Tilmann, 'The Compromise on the Uniform Protection for EU Patents' (2013) 8(1) *JIPLP* 78, 81.

[68] *Spain and Italy v Council* [2013].

[69] ibid para 68.

[70] *Spain v Council* [2015].

[71] ibid para 33.

[72] *Spain v Council* [2015], Opinion of AG Bot, para 93. Tilmann also raises the incorporating referral argument mentioned above in support of the legal basis of Regulation 1257. Accordingly, Articles 3 and 5 provide the unitary effect necessary and only part of the legal requirements for uniform protection is dealt with by an incorporating referral. See W Tilmann, 'Spain's Action Against the EU Patent Package – Arguments and Counter-arguments in Case C-146/13' (2014) 36(1) *EIPR* 4, 5.

[73] *Spain v Council* [2015], para 47.

Additionally, under Article 7, the EPUE as an object of property is treated as a national patent of the participating Member State in which that patent has unitary effect and where the applicant has either their residence, principal place of business, or place of business on the date of filing of the application for the European (EPC) patent.[74] The EPUE as an object of property concerns important areas such as the transfer of rights, enforcement proceedings, insolvency, licensing, applications for protective rights, rights *in rem*, the willingness to grant a licence, and compulsory licensing.[75] If the applicant has no residence, principal place of business, or place of business in a participating Member State at that time, the EPUE is treated as a national patent of the state in which the EPO has its headquarters (Germany).[76]

By having the EPUE as an object of property based on the national law of the principal place of business/residence of a specific patentee for a single patent throughout the participating Member States, a plethora of national property laws will apply to different patents. Users will find it difficult to decipher which national laws will apply to which patents. This will be especially apparent regarding compulsory licences.[77] The situation has even been described as contrary to the purpose of the Regulations in establishing unitary protection.[78] For example, Hanns Ullrich has noted the lack of harmonisation of the property aspects (as well as procedural and remedial aspects) of patent laws and argues that this lack of uniformity results in Article 7 Regulation 1257 failing to fulfil the purpose of Article 118 TFEU.[79]

It has also been argued that Article 7 could potentially go so far as to entail indirect discrimination on grounds of nationality. The national laws of countries not involved in the UPP would never be considered, impacting on patentees residing there,[80] whereas enterprises that are domiciled in countries participating in the UPP will have the benefit of their unitary patents being governed by their

[74] Article 7(1) Regulation 1257.

[75] For a detailed discussion of this aspect of the EPUE, see T Muller-Stoy and F Paschold, 'European Patent with Unitary Effect as a Property Right' (2014) 9(10) *JIPLP* 848, 856, with reference to previous Community Patent Agreements, the Community Trademark Regulation, and the Community Design Regulation; H Ullrich, 'The Property Aspects of the European Patent with Unitary Effect: A National Perspective for a European Prospect?' [2013] *Max Planck Institute for Intellectual Property and Competition Law Research Paper* No 13-17 available at http://papers.ssrn.com/sol3/papers.cfm?abstract_id=2347921.

[76] Article 7(3) Regulation 1257.

[77] H Ullrich, 'Harmonizing Patent Law: The Untamable Union Patent' [2012] *Max Planck Institute for Intellectual Property and Competition Law Research Paper* No 12-03 available at http://papers.ssrn.com/sol3/papers.cfm?abstract_id=2027920, 40.

[78] Ullrich, 'The Property Aspects' 15.

[79] ibid 10.

[80] Under Article 18 TFEU, as expressed in 'Spain takes Parliament and Council to Court over Unitary Patent Package' (*IPKat*, 27 March 2013) available at http://ipkitten.blogspot.co.uk/2013/03/spain-takes-parliament-and-council-to.html.

domestic law.[81] This problem arises because the EPUE as an object of property is not governed by a rule of uniform EU law.[82]

In an attempt to circumvent this criticism, Advocate General Bot stated that despite the application of national law to the EPUE as an object of property, the Regulation provides for uniform protection across the participating Member States because the national law applicable to a particular EPUE will be the same across all of the participating Member States.[83]

Although it will be in a uniform manner, by having a number of different national laws applying to a number of different unitary patents, fragmentation is almost guaranteed. Despite the concerns raised above being dismissed by the CJEU, the point remains that the compromise reached on the UPP is not ideal and raises serious issues of legal uncertainty. Questions over the substantive content and law applicable to the EPUE as an object of property also impact the perceived legitimacy of the UPP and may result in increased fragmentation owing to the patchwork of laws from which it derives its substance.

B. Territorial Fragmentation

Another serious concern that must be discussed is that the UPP will add to the pre-existing territorial fragmentation in the European patent system. By introducing a new patent and patent court, the UPP adds an additional layer to the European patent system.

Most important in this context is that the UPP will not replace previously existing systems. EPUEs will exist alongside national patents and European (EPC) patents, increasing fragmentation. Additionally, national patents, European (EPC) patents outside the UPP, European (EPC) patents inside the UPP, and EPUEs will all coexist and be treated separately, leading to further fragmentation and a lack of legal certainty for users.

Relatedly, the process of ratification for the UPCA and the limited membership of the UPP may result in EPUEs being granted for different groups of countries at different moments in time, and in some, not at all. Finally, the potential users of the system must also be considered. Some users, particularly SMEs, may not benefit from the UPP and may therefore keep their inventions within the national systems. Some will find that the system is not cost-effective. Others may choose to opt European (EPC) patents out of the jurisdiction of the UPC.[84] As a result, the territory of protection for individual patents and patent portfolios will become much more complicated and fragmented. Each of these concerns will now be discussed in turn.

[81] Ullrich, 'The Property Aspects' 12.

[82] ibid 13.

[83] *Spain v Council* [2015], Opinion of AG Bot, para 93.

[84] Article 83 UPCA.

i. Ratification and Membership of the UPCA

The first of these issues that must be addressed are those of UPCA ratification and membership.

The UPP is dependent on the entry into force of the UPCA. For this to happen, the UPCA is subject to ratification by a minimum of 13 participating Member States, including 'the three Member States in which the highest number of European patents had effect in the year preceding the year in which the signature of the Agreement takes place'.[85] A number of participating Member States also had to agree to be bound by the Protocol on Privileges and Immunities of the UPC and the Protocol on the Provisional Application of the UPCA. At the time of writing, 16 Member States have ratified the Agreement[86] and the provisional period has begun. The last remaining step is for Germany to ratify the UPCA once the provisional period is near complete.

Ratification has been a consistent obstacle for the implementation of a unitary patent system in Europe, and this has been no different for the UPCA. It is important to note from the outset that only 25 out of the then 28 EU Member States signed the UPCA. Spain refused to sign the UPCA as it disagreed with the UPP entirely. Croatia was not yet a Member State of the EU but has since indicated that it is not interested in accession.[87] Poland decided not to sign the UPCA based on an economic report indicating that the UPP would be disadvantageous to SMEs.[88] The reasons for not signing the UPCA are entirely legitimate but the effect of not having a full set of signatures already limits the membership of the UPC and could result in having to address some national courts separately.[89]

For those that had signed the Agreement, the next step was ratification. Following the finalisation of the UPP in 2012/2013, ratification became even more complex because of political and legal developments in the UK and Germany.

The first major complication was Brexit – the decision of the UK in 2016, by referendum, to leave the EU. As the UK was one of 'the three Member States in which the highest number of European patents had effect in the year preceding the year in which the signature of the Agreement takes place', its ratification was key to the entry into force of the UPP. Mixed signals on the UK's willingness to participate in the UPP were being received post-Brexit. Additionally, whether the UK *could* still participate in the UPP was also questioned.

[85] Article 89 UPCA.

[86] These Member States are Austria, Belgium, Bulgaria, Denmark, Estonia, France, Italy, Latvia, Lithuania, Luxembourg, Malta, the Netherlands, Portugal, Slovenia, Sweden and Finland.

[87] S Luginbuehl, 'An Institutional Perspective I: The Role of the EPO in the Unitary (EU) Patent System' in J Pila and C Wadlow (eds), *The Unitary EU Patent System* (Hart Publishing 2015) 46.

[88] Deloitte, 'Analysis of prospective economic effects related to the implementation of the system of unitary patent protection in Poland' (1 October 2012) available at www.uil-sipo.si/uploads/media/UPP-Analiza-PL.pdf.

[89] This is a concern that has also been highlighted in L McDonagh, 'Exploring Perspectives of the Unified Patent Court and Unitary Patent Within the Business and Legal Communities' (UKIPO, 2014), expanded on in L McDonagh, *European Patent Litigation in the Shadow of the Unified Patent Court* (Edward Elgar 2016).

In April 2018, almost two years after the referendum, the UK ratified the UPCA and agreed to be bound by the Protocol on Privileges and Immunities, indicating the possibility that the UPP could continue with the UK included. Many opinions from academia and industry were put forward: some believed the UK could participate in the UPP with some minor amendments;[90] others thought that this would not be possible;[91] and some, including this author, were of the opinion that regardless of whether this was possible, the opportunity should be taken to amend the UPP to address areas of concern and make the package more inclusive.[92]

Before these questions could be answered, in 2020, the British government announced that it would not continue to participate in the UPP as it was 'incompatible with [its] overall approach to future relations with the EU'.[93] The UK's staunch objection to the CJEU having any impact on the UK post-Brexit was likely the main reason for this. Subsequently, the UK notified EU institutions of their decision and withdrew ratification.[94]

This has wide implications for the UPP. First, the UK was one of the Member States whose ratification was required for the entry into force of the UPP. Without UK participation, Italy was the Member State with the third-highest number of European (EPC) patents in effect in 2012. Italy has already ratified the UPCA. However, amendments to the legislation and protocols will be required to remove any reference to the UK or London, which could be a lengthy process.[95]

[90] R Gordon and T Pascoe, 'Re The Effect of "Brexit" on the Unitary Patent Regulation and The Unified Patent Court Agreement' [2016] *Opinion* available at www.bristowsupc.com/assets/files/counsel_s%20opinion%20on%20effect%20of%20brexit%20on%20upc,%2012%20sept%202016.pdf; A Ohly and R Streinz, 'Can the UK Stay in the UPC System after Brexit?' (2017) 12(3) *JIPLP* 245.

[91] M Lamping and H Ullrich, 'The Impact of Brexit on Unitary Patent Protection and its Court' [2018] *Max Planck Institute for Innovation and Competition Research Paper Series* available at https://papers.ssrn.com/sol3/papers.cfm?abstract_id=3232627. For an anonymous response to this paper, see http://eplaw.org/wp-content/uploads/2018/10/2018-10-05_Reply_to_Lamping_Ullrich_Brexit_UP_UPCA.pdf.

[92] T Jaeger, 'Reset and Go: The Unitary Patent System Post-Brexit' (2017) 48(3) *IIC* 254; MA Gandía Sellens, 'The Viability of the Unitary Patent Package After the UK's Ratification of the Agreement on a Unified Patent Court' (2018) 49 *IIC* 136; A McMahon, 'Brexit and the Unitary Patent Package: A Further Compromised Future?' (2018) 15(2) *SCRIPTed* 175; Walsh, 'The Unitary Patent Package'.

[93] This was confirmed in A Soloway, Reply to the House of Lords EU Justice Sub-Committee, 'Unified Patent Court' (24 March 2020) available at https://committees.parliament.uk/publications/446/documents/1739/default/.

[94] There are some questions over whether this was legal as there are no provisions in the UPCA on withdrawal (Article 25 Vienna Convention on the Law of Treaties (VCLT)).

[95] In an attempt to circumvent an amendment to the Protocol on the Provisional Application, the Preparatory Committee of the UPC prepared a declaration indicating that, despite the reference to the UK, Article 3 should be interpreted as mirroring Article 89 UPCA (which mentions the three Member States in which the highest number of European patents had effect in the year preceding the signature of the UPCA) – Report of the Preparatory Committee Meeting (27 October 2021) available at www.unified-patent-court.org/news/report-preparatory-committee-meeting-held-27-october-2021. This has not been received well. For an initial commentary, see 'Member States will sign Declaration to clear way for preparatory phase Unified Patent Court' (*Kluwer Patent Blog*, 28 October 2021) available at http://patentblog.kluweriplaw.com/2021/10/28/member-states-will-sign-declaration-to-clear-way-for-preparatory-phase-unified-patent-court/.

Second, a seat of the central division of the UPC Court of First Instance was to be established in London. In fact, the building was ready to open.[96] Now, this branch of the central division needs to be relocated. Most recently, Milan had entered an official bid to take over the seat.[97] The central division had been split because of a dispute between France, Germany and the UK as to which country it should be situated in. Ideally, the opportunity would be taken to re-combine the central division, although this is highly unlikely.

Finally, there have been questions over whether the UPP is as appealing without the inclusion of the UK. This is because the extensive experience of UK judges in patent law will no longer inform the UPP, litigation will have to be taken separately to UK courts (which are notoriously expensive), and the requirement of maintaining a patent portfolio in the UK, the UPP, other Member States outside the UPP, and countries outside the EU, adds additional complications for patent attorneys and patentees.

The second major complication arose on the attempted ratification of the UPCA in Germany. In March 2017, Germany passed a law to ratify the UPCA. However, before the Federal President signed off on the ratification a constitutional complaint was filed with the German Constitutional Court. The complaint argued that the Agreement was in violation of EU law, it was not compatible with the German Constitution and that a quorum had not been achieved when the vote in the German Parliament took place.[98]

Almost two years later the German Constitutional Court ruled that the required two-thirds majority vote had not been achieved with the required quorum and the complaint was upheld on that basis.[99] On the other more substantive issues raised in relation to the compatibility of the UPCA with the German Constitution, the Court was silent.

Shortly after, the German Federal Minister of Justice and Consumer Protection made a statement to the press that every effort was being made to provide innovative industry in Europe with a unitary patent and court.[100] In June 2020, only a few months after the decision, a new draft Bill was presented with the hope of a quick consultation, vote and subsequent ratification of the UPCA. The draft opened for

[96] As reported here: A Merelle Ward, 'UPC-ing is Believing: Preview of London's UPC location' (*IPKat*, 22 September 2015) available at https://ipkitten.blogspot.com/2015/09/upc-ing-is-believing-preview-of-londons.html.

[97] As reported here: A Sandys, 'Italian Government officially fields Milan for UPC central division' (*Juve Patent*, 11 September 2020) available at www.juve-patent.com/news-and-stories/people-and-business/italian-government-officially-fields-milan-for-upc-central-division/.

[98] Details of the complaint are detailed in the decision of the Court: Decision of the BVerfG, Order of the Second Senate of 13 February 2020 – 2 BvR 739/17.

[99] ibid.

[100] German Federal Ministry of Justice and Consumer Protection Press Release, 'European patent reform is to be continued' (26 March 2020) available at www.bmjv.de/SharedDocs/Pressemitteilungen/DE/2020/032620_Patentreform.html.

consultation and received mixed opinions and the possibility of further constitutional complaints was flagged.[101]

Towards the end of 2020 the Bill was making its way through the chambers of the German Parliament. This time, it was approved by the required two-thirds majority (with quorum) in the Bundestag. Next, on 18 December 2020, the Bundesrat voted in favour of the UPC. However, on the same day, two new constitutional complaints were filed.[102] An interim injunction against the ratification of the UPCA was requested.

It was expected at the time that a decision on these complaints would also take years. There are multiple pending complaints before the German Constitutional Court against the EPO and it also hears all constitutional complaints, not only those related to patent law.[103] However, a decision was announced in June 2021. The Second Senate of the German Federal Constitutional Court rejected the actions against the UPC. The Court found that the requests were inadmissible as the complainants had failed to adequately substantiate that the fundamental rights of citizens would be violated.[104] As a result, the ratification law was endorsed by the Federal President, and Germany has since deposited the ratification instrument concerning the Protocol on the Provisional Application. Germany is now in a position to ratify the UPCA once the provisional period is near complete.

Doubts over the compatibility of the UPCA with domestic Constitutions and obstacles to ratification have not been limited to the UK and Germany. The European Software Market Association and others in Belgium challenged the ratification of the UPCA before the Belgian Constitutional Court.[105] This appeal was deemed to be inadmissible due to the non-observance of time limits rather than a disagreement with the arguments raised against the ratification of the Agreement.[106] Although the appeal was never heard, and the UPCA was ratified in Belgium, the fact that the case was taken displays further hesitance towards the implementation of the UPCA.

A challenge was also taken to the Constitutional Court in Hungary.[107] The Court found that the UPCA ratification procedure was not compatible with

[101] As reported here: 'FFII preparing constitutional complaint against Unified Patent Court Agreement' (*Kluwer Patent Blog*, 23 October 2020) available at http://patentblog.kluweriplaw.com/2020/10/23/ffii-preparing-constitutional-complaint-against-unified-patent-court-agreement/.

[102] Cases 2 BvR 2216/20 and 2 BvR 2217/20.

[103] Cases include 2 BvR 2480/10, 2 BvR 421/13, 2 BvR 756/16, 2 BvR 786/16, and 2 BvR 561/18.

[104] Decision of the BVerfG, Order of the Second Senate of 23 June 2021 – 2 BvR 2216/20 and 2 BvR 2217/20.

[105] ESOMA, 'Unitary Patent Challenged at the Belgian Constitutional Court' (*ESOMA*, 2015) available at www.esoma.org/forum/t-1162188/unitary-patent-challenged-at-the-belgian-constitutional-cour.html.

[106] Bristows, 'Belgian UPC Case Dropped' (*Bristows*, 27 May 2015) available at www.bristowsupc.com/latest-news/Belgian-UPC-case-dropped/.

[107] Decision 9/2018 (VII. 9.) AB on the interpretation of Article E) paragraphs (2) and (4), Article Q) paragraph (3) and Article 25 of the Fundamental Law available at https://hunconcourt.hu/uploads/sites/3/2018/07/dec-on-unified-patent-court.pdf.

its Fundamental Law. As a result, the Hungarian Constitution would have to be amended before Hungary could ratify the UPCA.

Another potential hurdle facing the full ratification of the UPC is the requirement of a referendum in Ireland for the UPCA to be ratified (notwithstanding the success of the Danish referendum). The UPCA had been part of the Irish legislative programme for government (2016–21) but given developments in the UK and Germany, this has not been a priority for some time.[108] Additionally, it has been suggested that if national parliaments are not satisfied with the contents of the UPCA the only option available to them is to ratify it or to refuse it in its entirety because it cannot be amended by them, nor can they have any formal input into its content.[109] These instances of hesitation and complication may have an impact on the ratification process elsewhere.

Additionally, the ratification process of the UPCA itself may increase fragmentation in the European patent system. Under Article 89 UPCA, only 13 Member States need to ratify the UPCA for it to enter into force and membership may be limited as a result. A situation could arise whereby the UPCA is ratified and only applicable in a limited number of Member States. Membership may increase over time, however if this is a stagnated process, some EPUEs will exist for one group of Member States, some for a larger group of Member States, and so on. Additionally, the ability of Member States to individually decide when they will become bound by the UPP increases the fragmented nature of the system by making the community of participating Member States difficult to identify at any one point. Different laws will be applicable in different Member States, with limited membership, causing fragmentation.

Although wider interest in the package had been waning,[110] staunch proponents of the UPP kept pushing it forward. At the time of writing, it is now increasingly likely that the UPCA will be ratified by Germany in the near future, and enter into force. If so, these concerns, among others, will have to be addressed.

ii. Participation in the Unitary Patent

The scope of the UPP has also been limited because of the way in which the Regulations have been implemented. Not all EU Member States are currently participating in the system.

Translation requirements have been a main reason for disagreement over proposals for a unitary patent system since attempts first began. The EPUE was

[108] 'A Programme for Partnership Government' [2016] available at https://merrionstreet.ie/merrionstreet/en/imagelibrary/programme_for_partnership_government.pdf.

[109] H Ullrich, 'The European Patent and Its Courts: An Uncertain Prospect and an Unfinished Agenda' (2015) 46(1) *IIC* 1, 4. Ullrich discusses what he sees as a democratic deficit in the UPC.

[110] A Sandys, 'IP community losing appetite for Unified Patent Court' (*Juve Patent*, 17 April 2020) available at www.juve-patent.com/news-and-stories/people-and-business/patent-community-losing-appetite-for-unified-patent-court/.

no different. Reaching a compromise on translation arrangements was the most difficult aspect of the negotiations concerning the EU unitary patent system and this led to the finalisation of the UPP through enhanced cooperation.[111]

The aim of the compromise reached in Regulation 1260 is to reduce the number of translations that are necessary by means of a uniform and simple translation regime for EPUEs. However, as mentioned previously, an action was brought against the Council for authorising enhanced cooperation in this area. The translation scheme was the main reason for Spain rejecting the UPP as a whole and it was a key concern in both sets of cases brought to the CJEU.

It was argued that the true object of the Council's decision to use enhanced cooperation was not to achieve integration, but instead to exclude Spain and Italy from the negotiations and to deprive them of the right to oppose the language arrangements.[112] Spain and Italy also argued that a distortion of competition and discrimination between participating and non-participating Member States in terms of trade and language would result from the enhanced cooperation procedure.

Enhanced cooperation does generate an allowable differentiation in pursuing EU integration. Certain policies can advance without the active participation of all Member States. Enhanced cooperation is a method by which those Member States that are ready and willing to implement deeper integration between them can move forward on the basis that those unable or unwilling at that time can do so in future; however, these policies cannot be used to exclude those who are not participating.[113] This was argued to be the case in the situation at hand.

Under Article 118(2) TFEU, unanimity is required when deciding on a language arrangement for the creation of European intellectual property rights. Spain and Italy argued that the use of enhanced cooperation was to circumvent this requirement of unanimity, to their exclusion. Furthermore, the only way for non-participating Member States to join in future is to comply with the acts already adopted in that framework.[114] Spain and Italy were willing to implement a unitary patent; however, neither was (at the time) willing to sacrifice its language. Article 328 TFEU mandates that the enhanced cooperation be open to all Member States, subject to compliance with the decisions that have been made.[115] It had been argued that this is not possible because Spain will not currently accept the language regime and is therefore permanently excluded.[116]

[111] Article 20 TEU.

[112] *Spain and Italy v Council* [2013], para 27.

[113] For a more detailed examination of the use of enhanced cooperation in this area, see M Lamping, 'Enhanced Cooperation – A Proper Approach to Market Integration in the Field of Unitary Patent Protection?' (2011) 42(8) *IIC* 879; F Fabbrini, 'Enhanced Cooperation under Scrutiny: Revisiting the Law and Practice of Multi-Speed Integration in Light of the First Involvement of the EU Judiciary' (2013) 40(3) *Legal Issues of Economic Integration* 197. This is also discussed in Chapter 3.

[114] Article 328(1) TFEU.

[115] Lamping, 'Enhanced Cooperation' 897.

[116] Jaeger, 'Back to Square One' 290.

It was also argued that negotiations had by no means been exhausted and therefore the implementation of enhanced cooperation was not a last resort, as necessitated by Article 20 TEU.[117] A question is raised here regarding the interpretation of 'last resort'. Thomas Jaeger asks whether it is based on an ability or a willingness to integrate,[118] the answer being determinative as to whether enhanced cooperation in this area was a last resort.

There are a few matters to consider in this context. The lack of unanimity on a language regime has persisted across decades. It has been argued that

> the 'last resort' condition is not satisfied only where Member States disagree with the very idea of proposed legislation; it should also be considered satisfied whenever agreement among all Member States seems impossible to reach in the foreseeable future, regardless of the reasons why

and so could be acceptable in this situation.[119] According to Ullrich, demonstrating lengthy discussions and a long-lasting division of opinion may not be enough – 'there must be sufficient evidence of the seriousness of a search for a compromise'.[120]

The CJEU ruled that the Council was best placed to determine whether the Member States had demonstrated any willingness to compromise.[121] It was found that a considerable number of language arrangements for the EPUE were discussed and that 'none of those arrangements, with or without the addition of elements of compromise, found support capable of leading to the adoption of a full "legislative package"' for the EU.[122] It was accepted that all means had been exhausted.

There is an overall interest in achieving a unitary system but there is a refusal to do so based on deeply rooted, fundamentally legitimate, national interests.[123] Alternative language regimes were put forward that could have been given more consideration but were rejected.[124] The differentiation resulting from enhanced cooperation in this case is seen by some, therefore, as Matthias Lamping puts it, as neither an opt-out nor a failure to meet admissibility requirements; it is arguably exclusion.[125] Nevertheless, the CJEU ruled that it was 'permissible for those taking part in this cooperation to prescribe rules with which those non-participating

[117] *Spain and Italy v Council* [2013], para 42.
[118] Jaeger, 'Back to Square One' 290.
[119] Peers, 'Constitutional Implications' 250.
[120] H Ullrich, 'Enhanced Cooperation in the Area of Unitary Patent Protection and European Integration' (2013) 13 *ERA Forum* 589, 595.
[121] *Spain and Italy v Council* [2013], para 53.
[122] ibid paras 54–56.
[123] Lamping, 'Enhanced Cooperation' 909.
[124] Interestingly, Spain suggested that English be the only language used for the UPP, however this was strongly rejected by France. See Council Document (EU) 13031/10 of 31 August 2010 on Reflection from the Spanish delegation on a possible model for the Regulation on translations [2010] LIMITE PI 94.
[125] Lamping, 'Enhanced Cooperation' 910; and Ullrich, 'The Untamable Union Patent' 22.

states would not agree if they did take part' and so it was decided that the Council was competent to adopt its decision.[126]

Additionally, Regulation 1260 was criticised as being an infringement of the principle of non-discrimination by introducing a scheme that would be to the detriment of persons whose first language is not English, French or German and that the scheme was disproportionate to the objective pursued.[127]

This aspect is highly relevant when considering justifications for the patent system based on providing new and innovative information to society through disclosure. If a patent is only available in certain languages, this raises barriers for inventors without the language in question and without the financial means to translate the necessary documentation. There is a possibility that inventors will not be aware of the latest developments and could spend time and money developing an invention that has already been protected but the information about it is not available in their language. It is also possible that a similar invention could be developed and sold, potentially infringing a previously patented invention. Article 4(4) Regulation 1260 provides some consideration of this in the case of damages:

> In the event of a dispute concerning a claim for damages, the court hearing the dispute shall assess and take into consideration, in particular where the alleged infringer is a SME, a natural person or a non-profit organisation, a university or a public research organisation, whether the alleged infringer acted without knowing or without reasonable grounds for knowing, that [they were] infringing the European patent with unitary effect before having been provided with the translation referred to in paragraph 1.

However, this does not align with the justification of divulging innovative information to society in return for patent protection. Commentators have argued that the language regime has been too narrowly considered:

> [T]he problem is that the language issue has been approached from too narrow a perspective with a view only to maintain[ing] existing structures and to benefit[ing] from them rather than to also review[ing] them in the interest of all market actors and all Member States.[128]

The provisions included in the Regulations to solve issues in relation to the lack of translations being available in the transitional period, particularly for individual inventors and SMEs, are inadequate.

Spain also argued that the rules were disproportionate and would lead to a distortion of competition in the internal market – market access would be more difficult for some, and this could not be justified.[129] Advocate General Bot acknowledged that there would be discrimination but that the EU legislature

[126] *Spain and Italy v Council* [2013], para 82.
[127] *Spain v Council* [2015], para 22.
[128] Ullrich, 'The Untamable Union Patent' 16.
[129] *Spain v Council* [2015], para 24.

was pursuing the legitimate objective of reducing translation costs,[130] those in the field were previously acquainted with the languages of the EPO,[131] and most patent applications are from states with these languages.[132] He believed these claims were unfounded and the rules implemented were proportionate.

In deciding on this matter, the CJEU noted that a difference in treatment on the grounds of language must indeed observe the principle of proportionality. It was held that the aim of creating a uniform, simple and cost-effective regime for the EPUE to ensure legal certainty, stimulate innovation and benefit SMEs was legitimate.[133] Moreover, the language regime was found to be appropriate, maintaining the necessary balance between various interests without going beyond that which was deemed necessary to achieve the legitimate objective pursued.[134]

It is important to remember that the language regime is the same as it is for the EPO, and it is expected that machine translations will become increasingly prevalent as quality improves. However, it is also important to remember that the EU Trade Mark operates in English, French, German, Spanish and Italian. Implementing a similar scheme for the EPUE may have been a more proportionate response as it may have resulted in all EU Member States agreeing to the Regulations at the time.[135] This is especially pertinent given the expected reliance on machine translations in the future.

This integration effort is still technically open to Spain, though this would require a significant shift in principles and values. A change of government in Italy resulted in acceptance of the Regulations, and opposition parties in Spain appear to be in favour of joining the system.[136] However, whether Spain will decide to join is questionable and unlikely due to the language regime but also because of the predicted overall impact of the system on SMEs. The latter is a concern shared by other Member States and is expanded on further below.

Although concerns related to the use of enhanced cooperation and the language regime were dismissed by the CJEU, an underlying sense of exclusion remains among commentators. The overall impact is that the system will become more fragmented because some EU Member States will not be participating in the EU system for some time, but more importantly, some may *never* participate. Different laws will be applicable in the Member States participating in the

[130] *Spain v Council* [2015], Opinion of AG Bot, para 50.

[131] ibid para 57.

[132] ibid para 58.

[133] *Spain v Council* [2015], para 34.

[134] ibid para 47.

[135] As mentioned, Croatia joined the EU shortly after but has since indicated that it is not interested in acceding to the unitary patent package.

[136] As reported by G Barrett and M Rey-Alvite Villar, 'Spanish government provides further reasons for not joining unitary patent and UPC system' (*Bristows*, 24 May 2018) available at www.bristowsupc.com/latest-news/spanish-government-provides-further-reasons-for-not-joining-unitary-patent-and-upc-system/.

procedure compared to those that oppose it. This limits participation in the EPUE and increases fragmentation by introducing a new system that fails to cover not only all EU Member States, but also countries outside the EU and therefore the European patent system more broadly. With or without the introduction of this system, fragmentation will remain.

iii. Users of the UPP

A separate but related consideration for participation is the likely users of the system.

Cost will be a major consideration for users because this is one of the most controversial and significant issues of the current European patent system.

In relation to the grant of patents, the main cost is the requirement of translations being filed at the national level. As previously mentioned, in 2017, the approximate cost of a European patent with designations in 25 Member States was €32,119; broken down, the cost of translations was €20,145.[137] In relation to enforcement, the cost of patent litigation in Europe is extortionate in certain Member States. For example, according to a study undertaken by Christian Helmers and Luke McDonagh, the costs involved in litigating in the UK are between £1 million and £6 million.[138]

A central aim of the UPP is to reduce these costs by granting patents that do not need to be translated for all participating Member States and by introducing the UPC to reduce duplicated litigation. There is no concrete provision in either Regulation 1257, Regulation 1260 or the UPCA that provides clarity on costs. For the best part of the duration of the negotiations, deliberations and even acceptance of the UPP, the specific costs of the UPP were never disclosed or decided.

On the cost of grant, application fees will be the same as the European (EPC) patent because the application process for an EPUE will also be the same. The Preamble of Regulation 1260 suggests that translations will no longer be required owing to machine translations and this will eventually reduce costs. The remaining question is over renewal fees. From an initial examination, a patentee would be better off with national patents if patent protection were only necessary in a small number of countries. If protection is deemed necessary in all Member States, the unitary patent renewal fees are likely to be significantly cheaper. However, the cost of the unitary patent must also cover its expenses, and so the unitary patent still runs the risk of being too expensive, in the initial period of operation at least.

The UPC aims to tackle costs in relation to enforcement. However, the Court is to be self-financing and therefore high initial costs are expected.[139] Concerns

[137] As seen from the figures compiled by the European Commission, available at www.bristowsupc.com/assets/files/UPC%20Comm%20Slides2.pdf.

[138] C Helmers and L McDonagh, 'Patent Litigation in the UK' [2012] *LSE Legal Studies Working Papers* 12/2012 available at https://papers.ssrn.com/sol3/papers.cfm?abstract_id=2154939.

[139] Article 36 UPCA.

have been raised that the UPC will be 'prohibitively expensive', not only in terms of Court fees, but also because its structure involves various divisions as well as training, mediation and arbitration facilities, all of which will increase the cost for the user.[140]

Additionally, for both the EPUE and the UPC, any fees that have been determined and any analysis therefrom should be reconsidered taking the UK's decision not to participate in the UPP into account. This is especially important for the UPC given the costs of enforcement in the UK outlined above, which will no longer be included. Fees should be significantly reduced.

The costs involved will have a significant impact on who will use the system. If it is too expensive, it will only be firms that require expansive, EU-wide protection regardless, such as those in the pharmaceutical sector, that will use the system.

Indeed, the UPP can be strongly criticised as being inadequate for SMEs. There are a few provisions included with the aim of considering the position of SMEs. For example, Regulation 1260 includes a compensation scheme for translations to be filed during the transitional period for SMEs, natural persons, non-profit organisations, universities, and public research organisations, whose residence or principal place of business is within a participating Member State. Since an application can be submitted in any language under Article 14(2) EPC, for patent applicants filing applications at the EPO in an official language of the EU that is not an official language of the EPO, reimbursement of translation costs where an EPUE is registered will be available. However, this reimbursement is capped at a lump sum of €500, which may be insufficient.[141]

In relation to the UPCA, Mediation and Arbitration Centres are to be set up in Ljubljana and Lisbon to deal with patent disputes out of court, which could have the effect of a reduction in costs.[142] However, the patent cannot be revoked or limited in the process. It has been said that the new centres will be advantageous to the European patent field and particularly to SMEs. However, the threat and fear of litigation are often enough to stop SMEs from entering a field or from continuing to develop and sell their products. The issue runs deeper than the availability of mediation and arbitration.

Provisions have also been included for SMEs in relation to the language of proceedings of the UPCA. The language of proceedings at a local or regional division will be one of the official languages of the Member State hosting the division.[143] Alternatively, participating Member States can designate one or more of the official languages of the EPO.[144] Parties can also agree to use the

[140] D Xenos, 'The European Unified Patent Court: Assessment and Implications of the Federalisation of the Patent System in Europe' (2013) 10(2) *SCRIPTed* 245, 265.

[141] Article 5(2) Regulation 1260.

[142] Article 35 UPCA. For a detailed analysis on this Centre, see S Granata, 'The Patent Mediation and Arbitration Centre: a centre of opportunities' in C Geiger, CA Nard and X Seuba (eds), *Intellectual Property and the Judiciary* (Edward Elgar 2018).

[143] Article 49(1) UPCA.

[144] Article 49(2) UPCA.

language in which the patent was granted, subject to approval by the judicial panel.[145] At the central division, the language of proceedings will be that in which the patent was granted.[146] The language used before the Court of First Instance will be used before the Court of Appeal.[147] The complicated nature and impact of this regime is significant. Clement Salung Petersen and Jens Schovsbo give the following example:

> The proposal would allow a case brought in Denmark to be handled in Danish. This, however, would presuppose that the Danish judge could be joined by two Danish speaking judges from the pool. In the event of an appeal the Court of Appeal would hear the case in Danish. If, however, the case involves the issue of invalidity and that issue is brought before the central division it is the 'language of the patent', which decides the language of the proceedings.[148]

Although reducing language choice is necessary for a centralised, specialised court containing a multinational composition of judges, it may have an undesirable effect on users, especially SMEs. For some, the language of proceedings may not be one with which parties to the proceedings are familiar. Translation of documents is available in certain circumstances;[149] however, the language of proceedings will remain the same.

On an inspection of the Rules of Procedure, the situation increases in complexity. Although a clause has been inserted so that small local operations are only sued in their own language,[150] an 'English limited' clause has also been inserted.[151] This allows for the language of proceedings to be changed to English in reasonable circumstances. In such cases, the judge can change the language of proceedings, but the written decision could remain in the original language. The difference in languages throughout proceedings has been criticised as having the potential to cause problems.[152] If decisions are being translated, technical terms could be construed differently, which could result in a lack of clarity and quality. The quality of decisions is of the utmost importance and the risk of alternating languages within the same case puts that quality at risk.

Concerning damages, as mentioned, if the alleged infringer is one of the previously mentioned groups/persons, the Court shall take into account whether they 'acted without knowing or without reasonable grounds for knowing, that they were infringing the EPUE before having been provided with a translation'.[153] However, this places the burden on the individual inventor/SME.

[145] Article 49(3) UPCA.
[146] Article 49(6) UPCA.
[147] Article 50 UPCA.
[148] CS Petersen and J Schovsbo, 'On Law and Policy in a European and European Union Patent Court (EEUPC) – What Will It Do to Patent Law and What Will Patent Law Do to It?' in H Koch, K Hagel-Sørensen and JHH Weiler (eds), *Europe: The New Legal Realism* (Djøf Forlag 2010) 630.
[149] Article 51(3) UPCA.
[150] Rules of Procedure, Rule 14.
[151] ibid.
[152] Petersen and Schovsbo, 'On Law and Policy' 21.
[153] Article 4(4) Regulation 1260.

These provisions for SMEs are inadequate and could lead to their exclusion.[154] This may lead to an increase in fragmentation by limiting the integrative effects of the UPP to certain patentees only and thus encouraging the persistence of numerous titles of (domestic, EPC and unitary) patents in Europe and the different systems that exist to support them.

This is even more likely given the possibility for those with European (EPC) patents to opt out of the UPC during the transitional period.[155] To do so, the patentee must notify the Registry. The request will be registered and the European (EPC) patent will progress as if the UPC does not exist.

Whether to opt out is of particular concern before the introduction of the UPP as European patents will otherwise be automatically opted in to the new system.[156] The opportunity is given to opt out; however, once the transitional period comes to an end, the UPC will have exclusive jurisdiction in the participating Member States of the UPCA concerning patent disputes relating to all European (EPC) patents.

If proceedings have been brought to the UPC prior to an opt-out registration, there will be no choice; the case must come before the court in question.[157] A patent can also be opted back in and so the reverse situation is also true. Unless an action has been brought before a national court, the patentee can withdraw their opt-out from the register.[158] Of relevance here are the Rules of Procedure of the UPC. Stipulated therein is a provision which states that if an action is taken at either level, there is from that point an absolute bar on an opt-out or withdrawal of an opt-out, which makes the decision of patentees extremely important.[159]

The main legislative concern with the opt-out was whether it could in fact be registered before action was taken at the UPC since the Registry is to come into existence on the same day as the Court.[160] The other issues raised regarding the opt-out were in respect of the lack of clarity as to when the opt-out would take effect and whether it would have retrospective effect.[161] This was resolved with the introduction of a 'sunrise period'. This allows the patentee to opt out before the UPCA is functional.[162] As a result, whether to opt out will now depend on the

[154] Additional disadvantages for SMEs have been raised in D Xenos, 'The Impact of the European Patent System on SMEs and National States and the Advent of Unitary Patent' (2020) 36(1) *Prometheus – Critical Studies in Innovation* 51.

[155] Article 83 UPCA. For more on the transitional period and the opt-out, see W Tilmann, 'The Transitional Period of the Agreement on a Unified Patent Court' (2014) 9(7) *JIPLP* 575, 581–84.

[156] For more, see P England, 'In? Out? What's It All About? Patent Opt-out and Withdrawal in the UPC' (2014) 9(11) *JIPLP* 915, 915.

[157] Article 83(3) UPCA.

[158] Article 83(4) UPCA.

[159] Rules of Procedure, Rule 5.7 and Rule 5.9.

[160] England, 'Patent opt-out' 919.

[161] These concerns were expressed at the Oral Hearing of the Preliminary set of provisions for the Rules of Procedure ('Rules') of the Unified Patent Court, 17th draft of 31 October 2014.

[162] England, 'Patent opt-out' 919.

preference of the individual patentee. Although originally set at €80 per patent family, it has since been decided that there will be no opt-out fee, which has come as a relief for firms with heavy patent portfolios and for SMEs.[163]

The decision to remain within the competence of the UPC or to opt out must involve a balance between the positive effects of having a court implementing cross-border judgments and the negative effects resulting from the institutional confusion that may arise on its implementation, as well as the possibility for central revocation. The effect of numerous opt-outs may cause significant initial cost to those remaining within the competence of the UPC and may also cause confusion and higher search costs if different patents are opted in and opted out of the system. This could be highly detrimental to the initial functioning and legitimacy of the UPC.

C. Institutional Fragmentation

The potential for institutional fragmentation already exists in the European patent system. There are numerous domestic and supranational decision-making bodies (including the Boards of Appeal of the EPO and the CJEU) interpreting principles of European patent law and enforcing patents, which can lead to divergence in decision-making.

The UPCA is the latest attempt to address this issue by creating a single European patent court with exclusive jurisdiction for European patents (EPC and EPUE) – the UPC. However, the UPCA will add another institution to the European patent system, which is only open to EU Member States, thus automatically increasing the potential for institutional fragmentation and risking further possible divergence.

Although the UPC is a new institution, the current decision-making bodies of the European patent system remain. It is therefore essential that the UPC has respect for the pre-existing institutions, namely the national courts, the CJEU and the Boards of Appeal of the EPO.[164] Without this respect, institutional division may arise more often. This aspect will be discussed in detail in Chapters 5 and 6.

Additionally, the structure of the UPC and some transitional period provisions in relation to jurisdiction and competence raise some concerning aspects that also have the potential to increase the level of fragmentation within the UPC and in the European patent system. These will now be discussed in turn.

[163] As reported on here: D Smyth, 'Preparatory Committee launches consultation on the UPC Fees' (*IPKat*, 8 May 2015) available at http://ipkitten.blogspot.co.uk/2015/05/preparatory-committee-launches.html.

[164] This has also been discussed in F Baldan and E van Zimmeren, 'The Future Role of the Unified Patent Court in Safeguarding Coherence in the European Patent System' (2015) 52 *Common Market Law Review* 1529.

i. Internal Structure of the UPC

As well as adding an institution to the European patent system, the UPC will also have numerous internal divisions which introduces the possibility of fragmentation *within* the UPC.

The UPCA provides that the UPC will comprise a Court of First Instance and a Court of Appeal.[165] However, this 'unified' Court can be criticised for not having many qualities associated with uniformity. It is suggested that the structure and quantity of divisions may cause confusion rather than predictability.

First, the Court of First Instance will have a central division, as well as local and regional divisions.[166] Local divisions can be established in any participating Member State upon request. Panels of local divisions will sit in a composition of one legally qualified judge who is a national of the participating Member State hosting the division, and two legally qualified judges who are not nationals of the participating Member State concerned.[167] If a local division hears more than 50 cases per year, the panel will consist of two legally qualified judges who are nationals of the Member State, and one legally qualified judge who is not.[168] This would be the case in, for example, Germany, France and Italy. The composition of the panels maintains the diversity of a multi-Member State court and is one of the most beneficial aspects of the UPC.

Regional divisions shall be set up for two or more participating Member States, designating the seat of the division concerned. The composition of the panel will include two legally qualified judges chosen from a list of regional judges, who shall be nationals of the participating Member States concerned, and one legally qualified judge who is not a national of the participating Member States concerned.[169] All local and regional panels have the option to request a technically qualified judge with qualifications and experience in the field of technology concerned, allocated from the Pool of Judges.[170] Sweden, Lithuania, Latvia and Estonia have already formed an agreement on a regional division of the UPC.[171] Actions relating to infringement, counterclaims for revocation, provisional and protective measures, injunctions, and damages or compensation derived from provisional protection and/or prior use, will come before local or regional divisions.[172]

[165] Article 6 UPCA.
[166] Article 7 UPCA.
[167] Article 8(2) UPCA.
[168] Article 8(3) UPCA.
[169] Article 8(4) UPCA.
[170] Article 8(5) UPCA.
[171] European Commission Statement, 'Commissioner Barnier welcomes the conclusion of the first agreement on a regional division of the Unified Patent Court by Sweden, Lithuania, Latvia and Estonia' (4 March 2014) available at http://europa.eu/rapid/press-release_STATEMENT-14-46_en.htm.
[172] Article 32 UPCA.

The central division will be in Paris, with branches in Munich and another participating Member State.[173] It shall sit in a composition of two legally qualified judges who are nationals of different participating Member States and one technically qualified judge allocated from the Pool of Judges.[174] It was originally intended that the central division would consist of a single seat; however, a political dispute ensued. Certain participating Member States gave ultimatums, and controversy surrounded the debate until the 'Brussels Compromise' was reached.[175] This compromise resulted in the central division being split between Paris, Munich and London. As mentioned, following Brexit, the London branch must be relocated.

Each seat of the central division will hear cases depending on the technology in the case at hand. London had been appointed human necessities, chemistry and metallurgy; Munich will be responsible for mechanical engineering, lighting, heating, weapons and blasting; and Paris, taking the main seat, will be accountable for the remainder, including electronics and computer sciences.[176] The central division will deal with revocation or non-infringement actions unless this matter has previously been raised at a local or regional division.

Although fault has been found with the structure of the UPC for being highly complex, by having a single Court of Appeal the risks of divergent decisions for insignificant reasons are reduced.[177] The Court of Appeal will be situated in Luxembourg and shall sit in a multinational composition of five judges – three legally qualified judges who are nationals of different participating Member States, and two technically qualified judges.[178] This Court will hear every case on appeal from all the central, local and regional divisions. Therefore, the Court of Appeal has the opportunity and responsibility to ensure that the body of case law arising from the new UPC is clear, coherent and consistent; however, criticisms remain.[179]

The UPCA will add a significant number of divisions of the Court of First Instance into the European patent system. Determining which division takes a case may lead to uncertainty in the system. For example, it has been suggested that there is substantial scope for patentees to decide in which division they take their case.[180] It has been argued that, on the one hand, due to the unification of

[173] Previously, the second branch was to be in London but following Brexit and the UK decision to withdraw ratification of the UPCA, the seat will be relocated.

[174] Article 8(6) UPCA.

[175] European Commission Memo, 'Commissioner Barnier welcomes the European Council's agreement on the seat of the Unified Patent Court – the final element in the patent package' (29 June 2012) available at http://europa.eu/rapid/press-release_MEMO-12-509_en.htm.

[176] Article 7 UPCA and Annex II UPCA.

[177] Baldan and van Zimmeren identify some further mechanisms that could assist in judicial coherence such as dissenting opinions and amicus curiae briefs. See Baldan and van Zimmeren, 'The Future Role of the Unified Patent Court'. This will be further discussed in Chapters 5 and 6.

[178] Article 9 UPCA.

[179] Ullrich, 'The European Patent and Its Courts' 3.

[180] A Johnson, 'Looking Forward: A User Perspective' in J Pila and C Wadlow (eds), *The Unitary EU Patent System* (Hart Publishing 2015) 184.

the litigation system, competition among courts/divisions will be removed.[181] However, from a user perspective, it has been suggested that in most cases an action could be taken in any division using trap purchases and other strategic tactics.[182]

This new structure may therefore allow for extensive forum shopping, or more accurately, 'division shopping'.[183] This observation is interesting because a truly unified court system would not have such a problem. However, it has been predicted by Jan Smits and William Bull that 'even if a unified patent court is created, the experience in the United States of America (US) suggests that forum shopping would not be eliminated'.[184] The US patent court system is federal in nature, with 94 district courts (comparable to the UPC local, regional and central divisions) and a Court of Appeals for the Federal Circuit.[185] Smits and Bull highlight that forum shopping still occurs in this system because of some differences between the districts.[186] Considering that a similar structure will be introduced by the EU unitary patent system, it can be questioned whether the same difficulty will persist in Europe.

The structure of the UPC may also make it more feasible for patent assertion entities to enter the European patent system.[187] Patent assertion entities, or non-practising entities, are a type of company that does not contribute to society by conducting research, but instead buys patents and uses them to sue others. They have also been described as 'patent owners who obtain broad patents … to ensnare real innovators who might inadvertently cross the boundaries' and infringe the patent.[188] Evidence from the US experience shows a significant issue with patent assertion entities, and because of the previously described similar court/division structures, the same problem could arise in the UPC. However, this may not be the case entirely. According to Alan Johnson, the prevalence of patent assertion entities in the US stems from some features that are not present in the EU unitary

[181] J Brinkhof and A Ohly, 'Towards a Unified Patent Court in Europe' in A Ohly and J Pila (eds), *The Europeanization of Intellectual Property Law: Towards a European Legal Methodology* (Oxford University Press 2013) 214.

[182] Johnson, 'Looking Forward' 184.

[183] For more on forum shopping, see S Luginbuehl, *European Patent Law: Towards a Uniform Interpretation* (Edward Elgar 2011) chapter 2; A Johnson, 'Unitary Patents and the Unified Patent Court – Part 3: Forum Shopping and Jurisdictional Battles' [2013] *Chartered Institute of Patent Attorneys* available at www.bristowsupc.com/assets/files/cipa-journal-114-upc3.pdf; Brinkhof and Ohly, 'Towards a Unified Patent Court'.

[184] J Smits and W Bull, 'The Europeanization of Patent Law: Towards a Competitive Model' in A Ohly and J Pila (eds), *The Europeanization of Intellectual Property Law: Towards a European Legal Methodology* (Oxford University Press 2013) 48.

[185] ibid 48.

[186] ibid.

[187] For more on the risks of patent assertion entities, see ES-K Ng, 'Patent Trolling: Innovation at Risk' (2009) 31(12) *EIPR* 593; RC Dreyfuss, 'An International Perspective I: A View from the United States' in J Pila and C Wadlow (eds), *The Unitary EU Patent System* (Hart Publishing 2015); McDonagh, 'Exploring Perspectives of the Unified Patent Court'; and Kaisi, 'Finally a Single European Right'.

[188] Ng, 'Patent Trolling' 596.

patent system, such as the cost of litigation and the inability to recover costs.[189] The risk of this occurring in the UPC is therefore lower, but not negligible.

The structure of the UPC raises multiple instances of legal uncertainty and could allow for forum/division shopping to thrive. This may lead to some divisions being used more often than others and the decisions of that division becoming the main voice of the UPC. This is clearly not an ideal situation and could lead to institutional divergence and fragmentation within the UPC.

ii. Jurisdiction and Competence of the UPC and the Transitional Period

Jurisdiction provisions related to the transitional period of the UPCA may also increase fragmentation. Jurisdiction can be established in accordance with, for example, Regulation 1215/2012 (Brussels I Regulation)[190] and the Lugano Convention.[191]

The UPC has exclusive jurisdiction for the participating Member States of the UPCA. Therefore, if an EPUE or a European (EPC) patent is subject to an action outlined in Article 32 UPCA, the case will be taken before the UPC.[192] The UPC has competence in respect of actions in relation to patents, including actual or threatened infringements, declarations of non-infringement, provisional and protective measures, revocation of patents and declarations of invalidity, as well as decisions of the EPO in carrying out the tasks assigned to it by Article 9 Regulation 1257.[193]

However, over a seven-year period, both the UPC and national courts will have jurisdiction. As a result, actions for infringement or revocation of a European (EPC) patent may still be brought before national courts or other competent national authorities. Paul LC Torremans has outlined examples where the same case could be brought before the national courts and the UPC and discusses the potential impact.[194] If this happens and proceedings at one court are not stayed, it could lead to a situation where a national court declares a European (EPC) patent valid and awards damages, and at the same time, the UPC declares all

[189] Johnson, 'Looking Forward' 179.

[190] Council Regulation (EU) 1215/2012 of 12 December 2012 on jurisdiction and the recognition and enforcement of judgments in civil and commercial matters [2012] OJ L 351/1 (Brussels I Regulation).

[191] Convention on jurisdiction and the recognition and enforcement of judgments in civil and commercial matters [2007] OJ L 339/3 (Lugano Convention). For a detailed analysis of the jurisdictional rules relevant to the UPP, see PLC Torremans, 'An International Perspective II: A View from Private International Law' in J Pila and C Wadlow (eds), *The Unitary EU Patent System* (Hart Publishing 2015); and TB Larsen, 'A "Bundle" of National Patents v a European Patent with Unitary Effect: A Jurisdictional Comparison' in GB Dinwoodie (ed), *Intellectual Property and General Legal Principles: Is IP a Lex Specialis?* (Edward Elgar 2015).

[192] That is unless the European (EPC) patent has been opted out.

[193] Articles 31 and 32 UPCA.

[194] Torremans, 'An International Perspective II' 175.

designations of that patent void.[195] Avoiding this situation would depend on the judges involved, who may stay proceedings because *lis pendens* would possibly not operate if the courts had different actions albeit with similar issues (infringement with counterclaim of invalidity versus revocation).[196] Otherwise, the situation would depend on the likelihood of the defendant dropping the case at the national court. Torremans accurately maintains that this situation is not ideal and could cause further confusion.[197]

iii. Bifurcation

Article 33(3) UPCA allows for the possibility of bifurcation in the new system. This could potentially raise significant issues.[198] If a counterclaim for revocation is brought before a local or regional division, that division has a choice on how to proceed: first, both the action for infringement and the counterclaim can be judged simultaneously; second, the counterclaim can be referred to the central division and proceedings on infringement can be stayed at the local or regional division first seized; and finally, the entire action can be referred to the central division.

Bifurcation is the second option and has been described as a 'dysfunction' in the design of the UPC.[199] Only courts in certain participating Member States, such as Austria, Poland and Germany, are familiar with this process.[200] Therefore, having this procedure available, with which many of the prospective participants are unfamiliar, could be problematic, hindering predictability and causing unnecessary confusion.

Regardless of arguments against its inclusion,[201] it has been accepted that bifurcation will be an option for the new system; however, it was suggested that in a bifurcated case, invalidity should be expedited and further matters

[195] ibid.

[196] ibid 177.

[197] ibid 175. Jurisdictional issues could also arise in relation to the UPC exercising what has been called 'long arm jurisdiction' to make decisions on damages incurred by infringement in countries outside the UPC, and the use of 'torpedoes' to block/force UPC/national court actions.

[198] R Vary, 'Bifurcation: bad for business' (*Presentation to UKIPO*, 2012) available at www.unitary-patent.eu/sites/www.unitary-patent.eu/files/nokia_vary_bifufcation.pdf.

[199] Jaeger, 'Unitary Patent Package' 23; R Hilty, T Jaeger, M Lamping and H Ullrich, 'The Unitary Patent Package: Twelve Reasons for Concern' [2012] *Max Planck Institute for Intellectual Property & Competition Law Research Paper* No 12-12 available at http://papers.ssrn.com/sol3/papers.cfm?abstract_id=2169254, 3.

[200] For more detail on the bifurcation process in Germany, see M Haedicke and H Timmann, *Patent Law: A Handbook* (CH Beck 2013) 835–47.

[201] As stated in *European Central Bank v Document Security Systems Incorporated* [2007] EWHC 600 (Pat) [88]: 'This case therefore seems to me to be a very powerful illustration of why it is desirable to try infringement and validity issues together, where at all possible. If they are tried separately it is all too easy for the patentee to argue for a narrow interpretation of his claim when defending but an expansive interpretation when asserting infringement'.

should be stayed until there has been a decision on validity.[202] This would remedy the fear of an injunction gap – the situation in which a case is bifurcated, validity is delayed, and an injunction is granted on what turns out to be an invalid patent. Therefore, a rule has been reintroduced into the Rules of Procedure requiring the central division to set a date for validity proceedings prior to the infringement action.[203]

Still, the introduction of bifurcation into the UPP means that different divisions will be responsible for the outcome of the same case. The effect of splitting a case is to add another division into the process, which could lead to additional forum/division shopping and uncertainty for the patentee. Parties can agree to bring most actions before the division of their choice, including the central division,[204] and as mentioned, during the transitional period of the UPCA, actions for infringement or revocation may still be brought before national courts or other competent authorities.[205]

Concerns relating to the introduction of bifurcation to the EU unitary patent system relate to an increase in fragmentation. If used, different court divisions will be responsible for the outcome of the same case increasing the potential for institutional fragmentation within the UPC.

IV. Further Fragmentation

The aim of the UPP, as with all unitary systems, is to unify the European patent system for its contracting parties and reduce cost and instances of fragmentation associated with the current regime. However, many commentators identify the complete opposite, that the UPP will also increase fragmentation in the European patent system.

Overall, it can be concluded that the most important criticisms and issues related to the UPP reflect a concern that rather than unifying the European patent system, the package will serve to further fragment it in many ways. The EU unitary patent system builds upon rather than replaces the current domestic and supranational patent systems in Europe. It will only apply in a subset of EU Member States, with the identity of those states potentially changing frequently. The UPCA will add another specialist patent institution into the European patent system. Depending on the ratification process, not only will the system add another legislative and institutional layer, further layers may be added following subsequent

[202] Oral Hearing of the Preliminary set of provisions for the Rules of Procedure ('Rules') of the Unified Patent Court, 17th draft of 31 October 2014.

[203] Rules of Procedure, Rule 40(b).

[204] Article 33(7) UPCA.

[205] Article 83 UPCA.

ratifications. Finally, the jurisdiction and competence issues surrounding the transitional period may allow for duplicated cases with potentially divergent results.

These issues and others impact the perceived legitimacy and functioning of the UPP. Many will result in increasing legal uncertainty for users of the system. An increase in fragmentation will also undoubtedly follow the introduction of the UPP, or any other attempted unitary patent system that does not replace previously existing systems. Some of the issues raised can and should be addressed. However, as fragmentation will remain a part of the European patent system, focus must turn towards developing additional and alternative responses to it.

PART II

Alternative Perceptions of Fragmentation

Part I has shown that the European patent system is fragmented and that overall, the forthcoming system will increase fragmentation. This is an overarching concern reflected in many of the criticisms which have been discussed. To respond to fragmentation, there have been numerous attempts, and an almost constant motivation, to introduce a unitary patent system. Most of these attempts have failed, and despite some benefits, the forthcoming system has many concerning features. One of the main criticisms against it is that instead of unifying the European patent system, as intended, the unitary patent package will serve to further fragment it.

Despite significant concerns with fragmentation, we have not paused to comprehensively consider the concept itself and whether we are responding to it in an effective manner. Part II thus presents alternative perceptions of and responses to fragmentation outside the patent system. The chapters in this part will consider fragmentation in both European law-making and the international legal system. It will be shown that fragmentation is an expected and inherent part of supranational legal systems. It need not be feared if responded to appropriately, and furthermore, it can be a means to make progress towards convergence, while also recognising value pluralism.

3

Fragmentation in European Law-Making

Developments in the European patent system have been heavily influenced by the historical development of Europe and the EU. Numerous attempts have been made to connect the patent policies and practices of countries in Europe by the EU and more broadly. However, both the current and forthcoming patent systems have been criticised for the fragmentation they cause and will likely cause.[1] The forthcoming EU unitary patent system has been especially criticised because although it is an EU system, not all EU Member States will be participating. It is argued, correctly, that this will increase fragmentation in the European patent system.

The concept of fragmentation may appear, at first glance, to run entirely contrary to EU objectives of an integrated community. However, this chapter argues that over time, as the EU has developed and expanded, so too have its objectives, ideals and methods of integration. From peace, prosperity and supranationalism, focus has shifted to a recognition of values and value pluralism. The introduction of methods of differentiated integration, such as enhanced cooperation, allows for a recognition of value pluralism and provides a space for fragmentation in areas where unanimity cannot be achieved, or where it is not desirable.

This chapter examines the development of Europe and the EU, the European patent system, and the evolution of differentiation and fragmentation in EU law-making. A distinction is made between European union, meaning the convergence of European principles more broadly, and the European Union, relating specifically to the EU. It is split into two main sections. First, it examines the original aims and motivations for uniting Europe and initial proposals for a European patent system. Second, it investigates the impact of EU enlargement on the EU integration project, the introduction of mechanisms of differentiated integration (which allow a level of fragmentation in EU laws), and developments in the patent system both inside and outside the EU. It concludes with the situation today, where the EU Treaties place a significant focus on values and harmonisation, and, moreover, methods of differentiated integration have been used in the European patent system.

[1] See Chapters 1 and 2.

Even within the EU framework, where harmonisation among all Member States is a key priority, allowing for fragmentation in specific circumstances is seen as a way to make progress towards integration. Differentiated integration may involve a level of difference, causing fragmentation; however, it also specifically allows for it. This could be seen as a positive aspect of a legal system, one that takes national diversity and value pluralism into account. It is concluded that so long as it does not exclude Member States, fragmentation resulting from differentiated integration does not go against the vision of European unity – its inevitability was predicted. Perceiving fragmentation as such allows for more flexibility and an appreciation of the reality of law-making in a supranational system. In specific circumstances, allowing a level of fragmentation may be necessary on the path to convergence.

I. Constructing Europe and the European Patent System

The initial construction of Europe and the European patent system is mainly linked to two institutions – the Council of Europe and the EU.[2] Both had a huge influence on foundational developments in this area.

A. Council of Europe – Longchambon Proposal

Following the devastation of World War II, attempts to unite Europe began. Plans for a peaceful and unified Europe materialised with the 1948 Hague Congress for economic and political union. The Hague Congress subsequently led to the establishment of the Council of Europe through the Treaty of London in 1949. The aim of the Council of Europe was and is 'to achieve a greater unity between its members for the purpose of safeguarding and realising the ideals and principles which are their common heritage and facilitating their economic and social progress'.[3] Following the establishment of the Council of Europe, work began on the creation of a European patent as one means of pursuing the Council's aim of promoting unity between its members.[4]

The first proposal for a European patent system was from a French Senator, Henri Longchambon, in 1949.[5] Longchambon submitted his proposal for the

[2] Note that the Council of Europe and the EU are completely separate entities. Today, the Council of Europe has 47 member states, including all EU Member States.

[3] Article 1(a) Statute of the Council of Europe.

[4] F Froschmaier, 'Patents, Trade Marks and Licences within the Community' in The British Institute of International and Comparative Law, *Legal Problems of the European Economic Community and the European Free Trade Association* (Stevens & Sons Limited 1961) 59.

[5] C Wadlow, 'Strasbourg, the Forgotten Patent Convention, and the Origins of the European Patents Jurisdiction' (2010) 41(2) *IIC* 123, 125.

creation of a European Patent Office to the Consultative Assembly of the Council of Europe.[6] Though national patent offices were to retain a key role, the proposed European Patent Office would have been involved in search and examination and would have provided a conclusive decision on certain aspects of patentability.[7] Encouraging the aims of European union, a meeting of the Committee on Economic Questions took place to discuss the possibility of integrating the search and examination procedure of European patent law. The Committee concluded that Longchambon's plan was too ambitious, given the differences in national patent laws at the time, but that the idea was at least worth pursuing.[8] The proposal was used as inspiration for future plans and a committee of governmental experts, the Committee of Experts on Patents, was established to continue work on the matter.[9]

B. European Coal and Steel Community

Fears of another war prompted the Schuman Declaration of 1950, initiating the launch of another bid to create a united Europe.[10]

Robert Schuman, French Finance Minister at the time, in a speech to a meeting of ministers, stated that creative efforts were required to protect world peace.[11] What followed, the Schuman Declaration, was a proposal to unite the coal and steel industries of France, Germany and any other nations; however, its subsequent impact ensures its place in European history. The rationale behind this proposal was to bind France and Germany, both economically and politically, to secure peace in Europe. The Declaration proclaimed that 'the solidarity in [coal and steel] production thus established will make it plain that any war between France and Germany becomes not merely unthinkable, but materially impossible'.[12] This was the foundation of the Treaty of Paris 1951, which in turn established the European Coal and Steel Community (ECSC).[13] The ECSC formed the foundations of what has become the EU.

Belgium, France, Italy, Luxembourg, the Netherlands and Germany (the 'Inner Six') demonstrated their support for the Schuman Plan. However, the UK

[6] D Stauder, 'The History of Art. 69(1) EPC and Art. 8(3) Strasbourg Convention on the Extent of Patent Protection' [1992] *IIC* 311, 313. For more detail on the Longchambon plan see Wadlow, 'Strasbourg' and A Plomer, 'A Unitary Patent for a (Dis)United Europe: The Long Shadow of History' (2015) 46(5) *IIC* 508.

[7] Wadlow, 'Strasbourg' 126.

[8] ibid 127.

[9] ibid 126.

[10] D Chalmers, G Davies and G Monti, *European Union Law* (4th edn, Cambridge University Press 2019) 11. This was the beginning of what would eventually become the EU. It began with the ECSC, later adding the EEC, which was succeeded by the EC, all of which were eventually succeeded by the EU.

[11] The Schuman Declaration 1950. This speech was inspired by J Monnet. The full text is available at https://europa.eu/european-union/about-eu/symbols/europe-day/schuman-declaration_en.

[12] ibid.

[13] Chalmers and others, *European Union Law* 12; Treaty establishing the European Economic Coal and Steel Community 1951 (Treaty of Paris).

refused to accept the supranational governing authority (High Authority) that was stipulated in the plan as it believed this would weaken national sovereignty.[14] Integration was being pursued; however, diversity and national sovereignty remained of paramount importance.

The aims of the ECSC were to create 'the basis for a broader and deeper community' and 'to lay foundations for institutions which [would] give direction to a destiny henceforward shared' (similar to those of the Council of Europe).[15] In other words, the goal of the ECSC was to 'reconstruct the economies of the European continent … and ensure a lasting peace' in Europe.[16] It can therefore be concluded that the original objective of what would become the EU was to promote peace, which was pursued through the establishment of the coal and steel community. These aims focused on the internal issues of the newly formed Community and repairing relations between participatory nations to create a common market.

Peace was arguably not the only motivation for the beginning of European union. Joseph HH Weiler has identified what he believes to be two other ideals – prosperity and supranationalism – first witnessed by this unification of the coal and steel community.[17]

The creation of a common market for coal and steel had the effect of securing peace. However, it also had the effect of encouraging trade between nations, which in turn increased prosperity. Still, the countries of Europe would only commit to a treaty of this kind if it were to be of benefit to them individually. Although the ECSC came with the price tag of vesting power in the High Authority, some countries were willing to accept this to boost their own economy: 'peace was to breed prosperity and prosperity was to consolidate peace'.[18]

Over time, the ECSC had proved worthy of compromising some national sovereignty to encourage peace in Europe and in turn increase prosperity. Further integration was attempted in particular areas, such as defence and politics, but these were not successful.[19] Nationalistic attitudes of European states were preventing progress; however, the construction of a common economic market had been proposed in earlier discussions and was seen as an area where progress could be achieved.[20] This paved the way for the Inner Six to go further in their attempts at integration.

[14] A Dashwood, M Dougan, BJ Rodger, E Spaventa and D Wyatt, *Wyatt and Dashwood's European Union Law* (6th edn, Hart Publishing 2011) 4; Chalmers and others, *European Union Law* 12.

[15] ECSC Preamble.

[16] A Kur, T Dreier and S Luginbuehl, *European Intellectual Property Law* (2nd edn, Edward Elgar 2019) 39.

[17] JHH Weiler, 'Europe After Maastricht – Do the New Clothes Have an Emperor?' [1995] *Jean Monnet Working Papers* No 12 available at www.jeanmonnetprogram.org/1995-jean-monnet-working-papers/.

[18] JHH Weiler, '60 Years Since the first European Community – Reflections on Political Messianism' (2011) 22(2) *European Journal of International Law* 303, 303.

[19] Paul Craig and Gráinne de Búrca, *EU Law: Text, Cases and Materials* (7th edn, Oxford University Press 2020) 4.

[20] ibid.

The objectives of European union had subsequently developed from the unification of the coal and steel community into something much more. In 1955, ministers from ECSC states agreed that it was necessary to make 'a fresh advance towards the building of Europe', particularly in the economic area.[21] It was decided that atomic energy and the creation of a common market were to be considered, and so an intergovernmental committee was formed to discuss these objectives, with Belgian Foreign Minister Paul-Henri Spaak as chair.[22] The aims of European union were developing.

The Spaak Report of 1956 promoted the establishment of an economic community within Europe.[23] Significantly, it distinguished matters that would require a supranational decision and those that could be left to Member States.[24] It was not an entirely unified, but rather an integrated community. This report was the basis of negotiations for new legislation, which culminated in the signing of the Treaty establishing the European Economic Community 1957 (EEC Treaty) and the Treaty establishing the European Atomic Energy Community 1957 (EURATOM).[25]

The common market that was established (the EEC) was said to 'represent the fusion of two movements towards unity, the one economic and the other political … strengthening cooperation between European States and … reducing commercial fragmentation'.[26] The ECSC initiated this objective, which was then advanced through subsequent discussions, negotiations and ultimately the EEC Treaty. Under Article 2, the aims of the EEC are 'to promote throughout the Community a harmonious development of economic activities, a continuous and balanced expansion, an increase in stability, an accelerated raising of the standard of living and closer relations between the States belonging to it'. A reflection of the original objectives and ideals of an integrated Europe can be seen in these aims – an increase in stability (peace), an accelerated standard of living (prosperity), and closer relations between the states belonging to it (supranationalism). However, the EEC also went further towards integration. Its additional aims were to cover all areas of the economy, not just coal and steel; to introduce provisions abolishing customs duties; to implement the free movement of goods, persons, services, and capital; and to introduce procedures for the harmonisation of national laws.[27]

With the achievements of the ECSC, Community perspectives and objectives had stared to expand. This formed the basis of the establishment of a common

[21] Dashwood and others, *European Union Law* 7.

[22] ibid.

[23] Chalmers and others, *European Union Law* 12.

[24] ibid 12 and 13.

[25] As discussed in ibid. Also known as the Treaties of Rome.

[26] J Deniau, 'The Objectives and Constitutional Structure of the European Economic Community' in The British Institute of International and Comparative Law, *Legal Problems of the European Economic Community and the European Free Trade Association* (Stevens & Sons Limited 1961) 1.

[27] Article 3 Treaty establishing the European Economic Community (EEC) 1957.

market among the Inner Six through the EEC Treaty, developing and transforming the six individual markets into a single market, eliminating all obstacles to intra-state trade.[28] A fresh and sustained focus on economic integration via the single market was initiated.

The expansion of European objectives was also reflected in the European patent debates of the time. The creation of the EEC had a major impact on the creation of a European patent system. In 1959, only two years later, patent law became a focus of internal market policy when Hans von der Groeben made a speech promoting the harmonisation of national laws and a patent that would cover the entire Community.[29] As discussed by Bob van Bentham, the 'EEC phase', so named by the chair of a committee established to consider this, Kurt Haertel, culminated in a Draft Agreement on a European Patent, which was to centralise the grant of patents in Europe.[30] However, due to 'political reasons' and disagreements on content and differing patent philosophies, work on the EEC patent was put to one side.[31]

C. Council of Europe – Strasbourg Patent Convention

Meanwhile, by 1953 the Council of Europe, through the Committee of Experts on Patents, concluded that the complete unification of patent law in Europe was far too ambitious.[32] There were far too many differences in the laws between countries in Europe.[33] Furthermore, as seen in negotiations for the ECSC, nation states placed a high value on diversity and sovereignty, which had to be acknowledged. The Committee of Experts on Patents had been given a choice between two proposals: one from Eduard Reimer and another from Cornelis Johannes de Haan.[34]

As elaborated by Christopher Wadlow, the Reimer proposal would have established a European patent and a European Court of Justice – the patent would have been granted by national offices and the Court would have dealt with revocation and some cases of infringement, alongside national courts.[35] Wadlow goes on to discuss that de Haan, on the other hand, had taken Reimer's proposal and had pointed out the apparent inefficiencies of this plan, including the reality of divergent patent examination standards existing across Europe, and that a dualist court system would impact legal certainty.[36] He had proposed that an administrative

[28] Deniau, 'Objectives and Constitutional Structure' 3.

[29] O Bossung, 'The Return of European Patent Law to the European Union' (1996) 27(3) *IIC* 287, 288.

[30] JB van Bentham, 'The European Patent System and European Integration' (1993) 24(4) *IIC* 435, 437; Bossung 'The Return of European Patent Law' 288; and J Schade, 'Is the Community (EU) Patent Behind the Times? – Globalisation Urges Multilateral Cooperation' (2010) 41(7) *IIC* 806, 807.

[31] Van Bentham, 'The European Patent System' 437; and J Pila, 'The European Patent: An Old and Vexing Problem' (2013) 62(4) *ICLQ* 917, 924.

[32] Wadlow, 'Strasbourg' 129.

[33] ibid.

[34] ibid.

[35] ibid. For more detailed information on the Reimer plan see, for example, ibid 129–35.

[36] ibid 134. For more detailed information on the De Haan plan see, for example, ibid 134–38.

European Patents Council be set up to deal with the grant of independent European patents; that national patents remain, with the option of either European or national protection; and that European and national patents be treated the same if before a judge in a national court.[37] De Haan stated:

> The system proposed here affords the possibility of coming gradually to European unity in the matter of patents without imposing for this as a prime necessity important changes in the law of the contracting countries or any measures leading to the abandonment of national sovereignty.[38]

This plan seemed to underline the importance of national diversity, yet remain true to the objectives of European integration. However, despite many considerations, neither proposal was successful. Projects Reimer and de Haan were 'practically abandoned'.[39] According to Wadlow, 'the Committee had decided that the partial unification of substantive patent law had to precede the creation of a European patent' and that more research was necessary to achieve that end.[40]

Discussions concerning a European patent recommenced at the Council of Europe in the early 1960s, culminating in the entry into force of the Convention on the Unification of Certain Points of Substantive Law on Patents for Invention 1963 (Strasbourg Patent Convention).[41] The Strasbourg Patent Convention was responsible for the harmonisation of substantive patent law. Having achieved this significant development, the Council of Europe withdrew and patent policy was left to the EEC.

D. European Economic Community, the EPC and the CPC

In 1965, the Merger Treaty amalgamated the executives of the ECSC, the EEC and EURATOM into a single Commission and Council for the advancement of the objectives of European integration by simplifying procedural aspects.[42] In addition, Charles de Gaulle, who had twice vetoed UK entry into the EEC, resigned in 1969, opening the Community for new members.[43]

Attempts towards a European patent system for the Community also regained momentum. Van Bentham notes how, at this time, concepts of European integration, as well as economic necessity, encouraged the centralisation of the patent grant procedure.[44] A decision was made to open this procedure to countries

[37] ibid 137.

[38] ibid 139, referring to the Proposal for the granting of European patent by setting up of a European Patent Council, presented by M. de Haan. EXP/Brev B (54) 1 (Paris, March 6, 1954).

[39] Froschmaier, 'Patents, Trade Marks and Licences' 59.

[40] Wadlow, 'Strasbourg' 145.

[41] ibid.

[42] The Merger Treaty 1965 (Brussels Treaty); Chalmers and others, *European Union Law* 15.

[43] Chalmers and others, *European Union Law* 18.

[44] Van Bentham, 'The European Patent System' 437.

outside the Community to deal with backlogs and make it more attractive to business.[45] The Draft Agreement on a European Patent was thus divided into the EPC[46] and the Community Patent Convention (CPC).[47]

Discussions commenced, and from then onwards a group of five (Bob van Bentham, Kurt Haertel, Albrecht Krieger, Romuald Singer and Klaus Pfanner) worked together on the drafting of the EPC and the CPC to further the objectives of the Community in the patent area.[48]

It was intended that the EPC would create a centralised procedure for the grant of patents in Europe based on a uniform substantive patent law, strongly influenced by the Strasbourg Patent Convention.[49] In 1973, at a meeting in Munich, the EPC was signed. As laid down in its Preamble, its aim, reflecting the wider goal of European union, was 'to strengthen cooperation between the States of Europe in respect of the protection of inventions, [and ensure] that such protection may be obtained in those States by a single procedure for the grant of patents and by the establishment of certain standard rules governing patents so granted'.[50] The EPC was not an EEC instrument and is not today an EU instrument. It is an international convention with individual Contracting States. Its provisions on substantive patent law have been implemented into the national laws of all its signatories. It does not replace pre-existing national systems but has harmonised the substantive law from which each system operates. The implementation of the EPC furthered goals of European union but not purely on the level of the EEC. Today, the EPC applies to 38 European states.[51]

The EPC, through the EPO, has also set up a procedure for the grant of European (EPC) patents. This has harmonised the search and examination process, but ultimately produces a bundle of national patents rather than a unitary right.[52] Its implementation was clearly beneficial; however, it was first approached with 'understandable caution, as it was a new and untested system'.[53] Further, national laws were being replaced and countries were taking a risk in this new system.[54] National patent systems remained, although they were now based on this updated substantive patent law.

[45] ibid.

[46] Convention on the Grant of European Patents of 5 October 1973. This would include countries outside the Community.

[47] Convention for the European Patent for the Common Market (15 December 1975). This would include countries within the Community.

[48] Van Bentham, 'The European Patent System' 435.

[49] For a significantly detailed analysis of the EPC, see M Van Empel, *The Granting of European Patents* (Sijthoff 1975).

[50] Preamble, EPC.

[51] For a current list, see www.epo.org/about-us/foundation/member-states.html.

[52] For more detail, see Chapter 1.

[53] T Dickinson, 'Seven Organisations Assess the Impact of the EPC' (*Managing Intellectual Property, Europe IP Focus*, 2013) available at www.managingip.com/IssueArticle/3263177/Supplements/Seven-organisations-assess-the-impact-of-the-EPC.html?supplementListId=90047.

[54] Managing Intellectual Property, 'Analysing 40 years of the EPO: what has it done for us?' (*Managing Intellectual Property, European IP Focus*, 2013) available at www.managingip.com/

The CPC was to be implemented alongside the EPC and provide a unitary patent and court for EEC Member States.[55] However, as elaborated by Justine Pila, it was not intended as a replacement for national systems because the EEC Member States recognised the importance of national values and cultural diversities and foresaw a role for national law in areas such as entitlement and infringement.[56]

Returning to the objectives above, it can be seen here that one of the main aims of a European patent system was that of unification. By attempting to introduce a unitary patent, the original drafters were in line with the efforts of policy-makers to realise visions of unity through the Community. This is clear from the goals of the CPC, which strived, to some extent, to introduce a unified patent system for the internal market of the European Community.[57] Nevertheless, it was also clear to those involved that complete unification would not be possible, and efforts would have to take place alongside pre-existing structures.

Although the CPC was seen as 'vital' to achieving the integrationist goals of the EEC, it never entered into force.[58] The CPC was signed, however many difficulties arose with ratification due to problems including the UK government's concerns regarding dispute settlement and the validity of the Community patent, as well as the requirement of referenda in Ireland and Denmark to continue the ratification procedure.[59] The CPC was redrafted as the Community Patent Agreement some years later but, again, never entered into force.[60] Van Bentham ties the failure of the CPC to the division of the Draft Agreement on a European Patent; evidently, the European patent community were pleased with the EPC and there was then less urgency for the introduction of a unitary patent system.[61]

E. Shifting Perspectives and Objectives

The European evolution, according to Weiler, created a benchmark for post-war reconstruction and inspired reconciliation between nations.[62] Gráinne de Búrca also maintains that the 'European Union experiment' was considered a success, in that it ensured peace and prosperity by making war 'virtually impossible' and introduced a number of endeavours, including the internal market, which have

IssueArticle/3263110/Supplements/Analysing-40-years-of-the-EPC-What-has-it-done-for-us.html?supplementListId=90047, referring to P Griset, *The European Patent: A Success Story for Innovation* (Kösel Burch Altusried-Kuugzell 2013).

[55] S Luginbuehl, 'A Stone's Throw Away from a European Patent Court: The European Patent Litigation Agreement' (2003) 25(6) *EIPR* 256, 258.

[56] Pila, 'The European Patent' 923.

[57] ibid 857.

[58] A Krieger, 'When Will the European Community Patent Finally Arrive?' (1998) 29(8) *IIC* 855, 857.

[59] Van Bentham, 'The European Patent System' 438.

[60] Council Agreement 89/695/EEC of 15 December 1989 relating to Community Patents [1989] OJ L 401/1.

[61] Van Bentham, 'The European Patent System' 439.

[62] Weiler, '60 Years Since the first European Community' 303.

benefited Member States economically.[63] The internal market also brought about a form of 'transnational cooperation' without nations having to relinquish full sovereignty.[64]

At this point, it can be said that the pursuit and development of a European patent system was motivated by the same aims of prosperity and supranationalism. However, these pursuits apply beyond the EU to Europe more broadly. Through the Strasbourg Patent Convention, substantive patent laws were harmonised, and these criteria have formed the basis for all future developments in the area. The EPC has also had a huge impact on the European patent system by streamlining the application process for patents in Europe.

Importantly, for the patent system, integration had up to this point been pursued more successfully through harmonisation rather than unification. The only pursuit aimed at unifying the patent system to any degree, the CPC, was not successful. National diversity and territoriality remain key features of European patent law, features that are likely to remain.

The EEC at this point had nine Member States.[65] Perspectives and objectives were further expanding, which allowed the EEC to successfully go further in its attempts at integration. However, there was also a subsequent expansion in its scope, membership and values, which had and has an impact on the pursuit of integration and the methods used to achieve these goals. Perspectives and objectives had to shift once again to adapt to these expansions.

II. The Impact of Expansion

After a period of political stagnation or 'malaise' in the Community, the Single European Act was introduced in 1986, which has been described as a 'kick-start' to the further fulfilment of the economic goals of the Community.[66] According to Paul Craig and de Búrca, this was due to the new Article 100a EEC, which stated that 'The Council shall … adopt the measures for the approximation of the provisions laid down by law, regulation or administrative action in Member States which have as their object the establishment and functioning of the internal market'.[67] Adding to this, they note that provisions introduced on regional policy and the environment reinforced the view of a truly common market that would bring Europe closer.[68] The objectives of European integration were further

[63] G de Búrca, 'Europe's *Raison d'être*' [2013] *Public Law & Legal Theory Research Paper Series*, Working Paper No 13-09 available at http://papers.ssrn.com/sol3/papers.cfm?abstract_id=2224310, 2.

[64] ibid. Note that De Búrca goes on to discuss how, following the economic crisis, the EU's reason for being is in question.

[65] Between 1973 and 1975, the EEC expanded from six to nine, to include Denmark, Ireland and the UK.

[66] Craig and de Búrca, *EU Law* 10.

[67] ibid.

[68] ibid, citing JHH Weiler, 'The Transformation of Europe' (1991) 100(8) *The Yale Law Journal* 2403, 2458.

expanding. However, as mentioned in the EEC Treaty text, this was again to be done through the approximation rather than the unification of laws, which appreciated the diversity and value pluralism that existed between nations.

Succeeding the implementation of the Single European Act, the TEU was signed in Maastricht in 1992.[69] This created the EU, encompassing the well-known three-pillar structure, which included the European Communities (ECSC, EEC/EC,[70] and EURATOM), Common Foreign and Security Policy, and Cooperation on Justice and Home Affairs. It importantly introduced the principle of subsidiarity, which is to ensure that the EU acts only if it is not possible for the Member States to achieve the same goal.[71]

The TEU was criticised extensively for threatening the 'cohesiveness and unity of the Community order'.[72] This was because it also introduced mechanisms of differentiated integration such as closer/enhanced cooperation.[73] While enhanced cooperation can permit derogations to Member States from EU law and result in fragmentation, it also enables integration where this is the only way forward, no longer optional but a 'necessary condition of progress' and a 'last resort'.[74] Craig and de Búrca note that while lack of unity and increased fragmentation may emerge, this was compensated for by allowing the Community to progress in areas that might otherwise have stagnated the process of integration entirely.[75]

The introduction of these provisions reflects a change in attitude regarding European integration, moving towards differentiated integration and value pluralism. This risked and risks increasing fragmentation but was and is necessary to protect diversity among nation states, which will be discussed in more detail below.

In 1997, the TEU was amended by the Treaty of Amsterdam to enhance the democratic legitimacy of the EU by increasing the powers of the European Parliament. It also arguably legitimised differentiated integration in the form of closer/enhanced cooperation by somewhat simplifying that process.[76]

In addition to European objectives developing and expanding, focus was turning to the promotion of the values of the EU.[77] In 2001, the TEU was

[69] Treaty on European Union 1992.

[70] The EEC Treaty was succeeded by the Treaty establishing the European Community 1993 (EC Treaty). As a result, the EEC developed into the EC.

[71] Article 5 TEU; Craig and de Búrca, *EU Law* 11.

[72] D Curtin, 'The Constitutional Structure of the Union: A Europe of Bits and Pieces' (1993) 30 *Common Market Law Review* 17, 67, cited in Craig and de Búrca, *EU Law* 13.

[73] Craig and de Búrca, *EU Law* 13.

[74] G Majone, 'Unity in Diversity: European Integration and the Enlargement Process' (2008) 33(4) *European Law Review* 457; Article 20 TEU. Note that the CJEU has ruled in the *Omega* case that further derogations from EU law can be justified by an overriding reason of public interest: Case C-36/02 *Omega Spielhallen- und Automatenaufstellungs-GmbH v Oberbürgermeisterin der Bundesstadt Bonn* ECLI:EU:C:2004:614. For more, see R Bellamy and S Kröger, 'Differentiated Integration as a Fair Scheme of Cooperation' [2021] *Review of Social Economy* 1.

[75] Craig and de Búrca, *EU Law* 13.

[76] ibid 15 and 16.

[77] J Larik, 'From Speciality to a Constitutional Sense of Purpose: On the Changing Role of the Objectives of the European Union' (2014) 63(4) *ICLQ* 935.

amended by the Treaty of Nice, which reformed the institutional structure of the Community to sustain membership expansion and enlargement in general.[78] Further provisions were also introduced on enhanced cooperation, including a statement that it would be 'aimed at safeguarding the values' of the EU.[79]

The Lisbon Treaty 2009 was introduced in response to the failure of the Constitutional Treaty and made significant changes to the TEU. It removed the three-pillar structure, which created a more solid basis for the EU to adopt autonomous acts on trade in services and commercial aspects of intellectual property law.[80] The EC Treaty was succeeded by the Treaty on the Functioning of the European Union, and the EU was and is now based on it and the TEU.

Important changes were also made to the introduction of the TEU. A new Recital was inserted into the Preamble, which now states that the EU is

> RESOLVED to mark a new stage in the process of European integration undertaken with the establishment of the European Communities,
>
> DRAWING INSPIRATION from the cultural, religious and humanist inheritance of Europe, from which have developed the universal values of the inviolable and inalienable rights of the human person, freedom, democracy, equality and the rule of law

Article 2 TEU was inserted and declared that the Union is 'founded on the values of respect for human dignity, freedom, democracy, equality, the rule of law and respect for human rights ....'[81] Article 3 TEU was replaced and in subsection (3) it now states:

> The Union shall establish an internal market. It shall work for the sustainable development of Europe based on balanced economic growth and price stability, a highly competitive social market economy, aiming at full employment and social progress, and a high level of protection and improvement of the quality of the environment.
>
> It shall promote scientific and technological advance. It shall combat social exclusion and discrimination, and shall promote social justice and protection, equality between women and men, solidarity between generations and protection of the rights of the child.
>
> It shall promote economic, social and territorial cohesion, and solidarity among Member States.
>
> It shall respect its rich cultural and linguistic diversity, and shall ensure that Europe's cultural heritage is safeguarded and enhanced.[82]

As observed by Joris Larik, for the first time, the values of the EU (Article 2 TEU) appear before its objectives (Article 3 TEU) and although the order of the Treaty

[78] Craig and de Búrca, *EU Law* 16.
[79] Text of the Treaty of Nice, Article 27a TEU, renumbered as Article 20 TEU.
[80] Chalmers and others, *European Union Law* 31–38.
[81] Inserted as Article 1a TEU and renumbered as Article 2 TEU.
[82] Originally an amendment to what was Article 2 TEU and renumbered as Article 3 TEU.

provisions does not equate to their importance, this represents a 'paradigm shift from a legal entity that, in the first place, exists to strive for certain goals to one which, above all, expounds what it stands for'.[83]

EU interests have clearly progressed far beyond mere trade initiatives and have unquestionably entered the social policy realm. This is indicative not only of the success of the EU, but also of its far-reaching power and motivation to take account of the interests of Member States, public policy, and fundamental rights, such as human dignity.[84] The objectives of the EU expanded exponentially and so a focus on its values gave the EU a solid foundation that would speak more personally to its Member States. A commitment to the idea of an integrated Europe remains; however, a recognition of value pluralism is becoming more apparent.

It can be argued that one of the reasons for this evolution of EU interests is that it was seen as necessary to expand the scope of the internal market because there were far more Member States than originally envisaged. The increase in membership of the EU through this time period was unprecedented.[85] With the continued expansion of both the legal and geographical scope of the EU, methods of achieving European integration have had to adapt. For example, the Lisbon Treaty also revised provisions on enhanced cooperation to make them easier to enforce. The harmonisation of laws, with options for differentiation, was pursued to encourage integration in Europe, while also considering increasing membership, national diversity, and value pluralism.

A. Impact on the Patent System

EU expansion and related developments have also had an impact on law-making in the European patent system. In general, the EU shares competence with Member States in relation to the internal market.[86] Intellectual property is not included in the exclusive competences of the EU and so the principles of proportionality and subsidiarity must be considered.[87]

Following the implementation of the Lisbon Treaty, the EU was given express competence to establish unitary intellectual property rights in the TFEU. When implementing EU legislation in the field of intellectual property law, the legal basis relied on is either Article 114 TFEU (in the case of harmonising directives) or Article 118 TFEU (in the case of regulations establishing unitary intellectual

[83] Larik, 'From Speciality' 951.

[84] This can be seen clearly in the patent field in the area of biotechnological inventions, which will be discussed in Chapter 6.

[85] Between 1973 and 1975, Denmark, Ireland and the UK joined the Community. It then saw a large expansion and grew quite quickly in the 2000s.

[86] Article 3 TFEU.

[87] Article 5 TEU and Protocol (No 2) on the Application of the Principles of Subsidiarity and Proportionality [2008] OJ C 115/1, annexed to the TEU and TFEU by the Treaty of Lisbon 2007.

property rights).[88] Either way, the overarching reason behind the introduction of EU legislation in intellectual property law is to promote the functioning of the internal market, to reduce barriers to trade, and to reduce fragmentation within the EU. For example, Article 118 TFEU states:

> In the context of the establishment and functioning of the internal market, the European Parliament and the Council, acting in accordance with the ordinary legislative procedure, shall establish measures for the creation of European intellectual property rights to provide uniform protection of intellectual property rights throughout the Union and for the setting up of centralised Union-wide authorisation, coordination and supervision arrangements.

Furthermore, the Charter of Fundamental Rights for the EU (Charter),[89] which received the political approval of Member States in December 2000, was elevated to the status of the Treaties.[90] Contained in this Charter is Article 17(2), which states that 'Intellectual property shall be protected'.

From a reading of Article 118 TFEU it can be seen that the creation of unitary intellectual property rights, including, by implication, patent rights, is important in order to advance European integration through the implementation and development of the internal market. From a reading of its Preamble, the Charter is also seen to promote value pluralism. It states, in very similar terms to Article 2 TEU as quoted above, that 'the Union is founded on the indivisible universal values of human dignity, freedom, equality and solidarity … while respecting the diversity of the cultures and traditions of the peoples of Europe'.[91]

Although steps have been taken at an EU level to create European intellectual property rights that provide uniform protection throughout the EU, previous developments outside the EU have arguably delayed advancements.[92] The EPC has succeeded in harmonising further the requirements of patentability and the application process for patents in Europe.[93] Due to its success, further integration of patent law by the EU became more of a challenge.[94] It has been said that this success has 'overshadowed' the efforts of the EU to introduce a unitary patent.[95] Some EU attempts towards unifying and harmonising the European patent system have been successful, though this has been predominantly for specific subject matter.[96]

[88] Article 118 TFEU.

[89] Charter of Fundamental Rights of the European Union (2000) OJ C 364/01.

[90] Article 6 TEU.

[91] Preamble, Charter of Fundamental Rights of the European Union 2000.

[92] Plomer, 'A Unitary Patent for a (Dis)United Europe' 532; C Seville, *EU Intellectual Property Law and Policy* (Edward Elgar 2009) 70.

[93] See Chapter 1. For a critical assessment of the EPC's success, see J Willems, 'The EPC: The Emperor's Phantom Clothes? A Blueprint Instead of a Green Paper' [1998] 1 *IPQ* 1.

[94] Plomer, 'A Unitary Patent for a (Dis)United Europe' 524.

[95] H Ullrich, 'Patent Protection in Europe: Integrating Europe into the Community or the Community into Europe?' (2002) 8(4) *European Law Journal* 433; H Ullrich, 'Harmony and Unity of European Intellectual Property Protection' in D Vaver and L Bently (eds), *Intellectual Property in the New Millennium* (Cambridge University Press 2004).

[96] Council Regulation (EC) 469/2009 of 6 May 2009 concerning the supplementary protection certificate for medicinal products (codified version) [2009] OJ L 152/1; Council Regulation (EC) 1610/96

However, the introduction of alternative methods of integration has clearly been useful for the forthcoming EU unitary patent system. The use of the enhanced cooperation procedure was authorised for the UPP.

As mentioned, enhanced cooperation allows a group of Member States to implement new EU laws without the participation of all Member States. The result is differentiation. It must only be used as a 'last resort'.[97] The reason for using the enhanced cooperation procedure is to make progress towards integration among this group of Member States, when it is not possible to do so as a bloc. Although fragmentation may result, these differences are seen as permissible. However, it cannot be used to permanently exclude those who are not participating, because the integration effort must always be open to non-participating Member States.[98] Careful consideration is required to ensure that the line between acceptable differentiation and exclusion is drawn appropriately. Therefore, it is important to pay close attention to the reasons why Member States will not join the integration effort.

Examples are scarce and so reflecting on the reason behind its inclusion in the EU Treaties is useful. With an expanding membership, it was predicted that reaching unanimous agreement would become more difficult, in part due to the existence of an increasing variety of legal, moral and social values. Therefore, it is likely that reasons for disagreement will be based on value pluralism. The use of enhanced cooperation requires a consideration of these values because, if fundamentally important and legitimate concerns are raised, which could result in permanent exclusion, the process becomes problematic. Subsequent progress towards integration would be stifled.

When the enhanced cooperation process was authorised for the UPP Regulations, its use was extensively criticised. It was arguably used to exclude Spain and Italy rather than as a last resort, when both states refused to agree to the proposed language regime.[99] The CJEU dismissed objections relating to the authorisation of enhanced cooperation, a decision that has also been criticised.[100]

It is unclear whether a consideration of value pluralism was undertaken to the extent necessary in this case; whether the motivation for using this procedure

of 23 July 1996 concerning the creation of a supplementary protection certificate for plant protection products [1996] OJ L 198/30; Council Directive 98/44/EC of the European Parliament and of the Council of 6 July 1998 on the legal protection of biotechnological inventions [1998] OJ L 213/13 (Biotech Directive); Directive 2004/48/EC of the European Parliament and of the Council of 29 April 2004 on the enforcement of intellectual property rights [2004] OJ L 195/16 (Enforcement Directive). For a discussion on the specialisation of patent law, see DL Burk and MA Lemley, 'Policy Levers in Patent Law' (2003) 89(7) *Virginia Law Review* 1575.

[97] Article 20 TEU.

[98] Article 20 TEU in accordance with Article 328 TFEU.

[99] See Chapter 2.

[100] Joined Cases C-274 and 295/11 *Kingdom of Spain and Italian Republic v Council of the European Union* ECLI:EU:C:2013:240; Case C-146/13 *Kingdom of Spain v European Parliament and the Council of the European Union* ECLI:EU:C:2015:298; Case C-147/13 *Kingdom of Spain v Council of the European Union* ECLI:EU:C:2015:299. For criticisms, see Chapter 2.

was based on recognising a plurality of values or being used to push through the unitary patent system by any means necessary. There was enormous political momentum and pressure to implement the UPP at the time.[101] However, a complicating factor is that a change of government in Italy resulted in a change of opinion on the language regime, and so Italy has now accepted the terms of the adopted framework. Opposition parties in Spain also appear to be in favour of signing up to the UPP.[102] Therefore, it is possible to say that Spain may join in future, though it is currently highly unlikely. It is also therefore not possible to say with confidence that the process permanently excludes Spain, raising a separate question as to what circumstances would be considered a permanent exclusion.

Whether these values were considered to the extent necessary can no longer change the outcome. Progress towards integration is being made and the process is still officially open to Spain. However, this is relevant when considering current perceptions of fragmentation in the European patent system. The use of the enhanced cooperation procedure should indicate the beginning of a change in attitude towards fragmentation. However, it seems more likely that the process was used to push the system through, rather than as a result of any change in perception.

Drawing a distinction between the purpose of the enhanced cooperation procedure and how it was used for the creation of an EU unitary patent system, fragmentation resulting from enhanced cooperation is part of the process. As long as it does not exclude Member States, additional progress can be made towards integration, and this may eventually result in all Member States joining the integration effort. To make use of this procedure in the most appropriate manner will require a high significance to be placed on considerations of value pluralism. It can be deduced that in a supranational system there may be a place for fragmentation in law-making while a plurality of values remains.

III. Fragmentation as a Means of Integration

In terms of original objectives, European union has been successful. France and Germany did not go to war and nations prospered and rebuilt functioning economies. As the historical analysis of the EU and European legal systems presented above highlights, European objectives have evolved over time. At first, objectives and ideals of peace, prosperity and supranationalism were of the utmost importance; subsequently, focus turned towards the importance of values and value pluralism.

[101] See Chapter 2.

[102] As reported by G Barrett and M Rey-Alvite Villar, 'Spanish government provides further reasons for not joining unitary patent and UPC system' (*Bristows*, 24 May 2018) available at www.bristowsupc.com/latest-news/spanish-government-provides-further-reasons-for-not-joining-unitary-patent-and-upc-system/.

As the scope, membership and values of the EU have expanded, new law-making methods have been introduced, such as enhanced cooperation. These methods can be used to promote European integration in an alternative manner, when all other avenues have failed. Although laws will not always be uniform, enhanced cooperation, which inherently causes fragmentation, also allows progress towards integration in a way that recognises value pluralism. Based on these amendments to the EU Treaties, in specific circumstances, there is a place for fragmentation in EU law-making.

Many of these historic developments are reflected in the attempts that have been made towards a European unitary patent system. Its creation has been a major focus of internal market policy for decades. In the most recent attempts towards an EU unitary patent system, these new methods are being used to make progress towards integration, though not without criticism, or an obvious change in perception towards fragmentation.

Overall, the introduction of enhanced cooperation in EU law-making suggests that fragmentation as a concept is more nuanced than 'good' or 'bad'. Allowing a level of difference to persist while a plurality of values exists reflects the reality of law-making in a supranational system. Importantly, as the process cannot be used to exclude, consensus can be built, and more Member States may join the integration effort. Allowing a level of fragmentation in these specific circumstances can therefore still lead to convergence in the long term. Perceiving fragmentation as such allows for much needed flexibility in supranational efforts towards harmonisation.

4

Fragmentation in the International Legal System

Fragmentation is not a concept that is specific to the European patent system. It is a predominant feature in other legal fields, such as in international law.

International law is made up of different legal rules, norms and various institutions. There has never been a single global legislature or a global centralised court with general compulsory jurisdiction to implement a uniform body of law applicable internationally, and therefore, there is no generally agreed hierarchical order that exists to resolve disputes between differing norms and institutions.[1] The absence of such hierarchy, coupled with the expansion and proliferation of rules and legal norms, tribunals and institutions at the international level, has increased interest in the nature and effects of fragmentation in the field of international law. A vast amount of scholarship therefore exists in this area, enabling the effect of fragmentation and responses to it within the European patent system to be considered from an alternative perspective.

Indeed, for those who see fragmentation as an inherent part of a system, it can be 'a fruitful perspective by which to study almost any legal system or subsystem'.[2] Graeme B Dinwoodie has reflected on the 'multiplication of sources and institutions playing in the [international] intellectual property space' and the commonalities shared with discussions of fragmentation in the international legal system.[3] Henning Grosse Ruse-Khan has examined this in detail in relation to the protection of intellectual property law in international law.[4]

Similar issues arise on a regional level in the European patent system, particularly in relation to the multiplicity of institutions, and so the concepts and

[1] MA Young, 'Introduction: The Productive Friction between Regimes' in MA Young (ed), *Regime Interaction in International Law: Facing Fragmentation* (Cambridge University Press 2015) 2. Some courts have attempted to instil a hierarchy, for example the CJEU has stated that it cannot review UN decisions, see Joined Cases C-584/10 P, C-593/10 P and C-595/10 P *Commission and Others v Kadi* ECLI:EU:C:2013:518.

[2] M Andenas and E Bjorge (eds), *A Farewell to Fragmentation: Reassertion and Convergence in International Law* (Cambridge University Press 2015) 1.

[3] GB Dinwoodie, 'Diversifying Perspectives of the International Intellectual Property System' in C Geiger (ed), *The Intellectual Property System in a Time of Change: European and International Perspectives* (LexisNexis 2016) 224.

[4] H Grosse Ruse-Khan, *The Protection of Intellectual Property in International Law* (Oxford University Press 2016).

arguments used to analyse and approach fragmentation in international law can be used to support an original analysis of fragmentation in the European patent system.

Specifically, when considering fragmentation in international law, one must consider law-making and decision-making. To deal with various issues, numerous treaties are drawn up with diverse membership and scope. Each will involve a forum for decision-making, increasing the number of institutions in the field. If a question arises on the interpretation of a concept that each treaty contains in any or all of these fora, each one could provide a different answer. As there is no centralised court to provide a single answer, these differences, this fragmentation, could impact legal certainty. This can also occur within a field, such as in human rights law, where multiple institutions interpret similar subject matter for similar purposes.[5]

In the European patent system, the same thing happens on a more local level, predominately in decision-making. Despite all countries basing their national laws on the same international conventions,[6] each has its own rules and institutions that operate individually, and these fora can interpret substantive patent law provisions differently, leading to institutional fragmentation. Furthermore, in the decisions being made, consideration of concepts relevant to other legal fields may be required, which, if not undertaken carefully, may lead to substantive fragmentation. An abundance of institutions are involved. As there is no centralised body or court to provide a single answer, these differences, this fragmentation, can become embedded in the system and cause conflict.

Due to these similarities, methods developed in the context of international law could prove useful in determining how to perceive and effectively approach and respond to fragmentation in the European patent system. This chapter will offer a theoretical analysis of fragmentation as a feature of supranational legal systems. Drawing on jurisprudence from international law, where fragmentation is inherent, raises a question as to whether the European patent system can learn from this response.

I. Fragmentation in the International Legal System

The International Law Commission (ILC) mentions the 'phenomenon' of fragmentation in its report and conclusions on fragmentation.[7] In terms of historical

[5] For an in-depth analysis, see M Ajevski, 'Special Issue: Fragmentation in International Human Rights Law – Beyond Conflict of Laws' (2014) 32(2) *Nordic Journal of Human Rights* 87; M Payandeh, 'Fragmentation within International Human Rights Law' in M Andenas and E Bjorge (eds), *A Farewell to Fragmentation: Reassertion and Convergence in International Law* (Cambridge University Press 2015).

[6] Particularly the Convention on the Grant of European Patents of 5 October 1973.

[7] International Law Commission, 'Fragmentation of International Law: Difficulties arising from the diversification and expansion of International Law: Report of the Study Group of the International Law Commission, finalised by Martti Koskenniemi' [2006] A/CN.4/L.682, 14 (ILC Report).

background, two reasons are given for the existence of fragmentation in international law: that the law was being made by groups separate from one another and also being developed and revised separately.[8] It explains that the current problem with the development of specialised regimes (eg trade law, human rights law, etc) is that this takes place without considering what is happening in the surrounding fields and results in 'conflicts between rules or rule-systems, deviating institutional practices and, possibly, the loss of an overall perspective on the law'.[9] From this, there are two aspects to consider when examining this phenomenon – the existence of multiple rules and the inconsistent development and interpretation of these rules.

In the relevant literature, there are numerous variations in the characteristics attributed to fragmentation in the field of international law. Nevertheless, a similar breakdown can be seen. For example, Margaret A Young views it as 'the uneven normative and institutional development and evolution in inter-state trade',[10] and as 'conflicting norms between regimes',[11] but also as 'the existence of separate norms and institutions, instigated by non-identical groupings of states, often in response to specific functional issues'.[12] Phillipa Webb mentions 'conflicts between substantive bodies of law such as trade law and environmental law' and, separately, 'two courts seized of the same issue rendering contradictory decisions' and 'a significant divergence in the reasoning on the same/similar legal issue or in relation to the same/similar factual scenario'.[13] Andrew Moravcsik looks at 'the differences in the understanding and application of international legal principles between states'.[14] Tomer Broude and Yuval Shany mention a similar point when they discuss 'normative or institutional conflicts'.[15] Michael Zürn and Benjamin Faude consider fragmentation to be a result of 'institutional variety in the absence of hierarchical coordination'.[16] Here we can see an understanding of fragmentation that not only mirrors its historical development, but also brings that understanding into current practice.

[8] ILC Report, paras 5 and 6, citing W Jenks, 'The Conflict of Law-Making Treaties' (1953) 30 *British Yearbook of International Law* 403.

[9] ILC Report, para 8.

[10] MA Young, 'Fragmentation' in T Carty (ed), *Oxford Bibliographies in International Law* (Oxford University Press 2014) 1.

[11] MA Young, 'Regime Interaction in Creating, Implementing and Enforcing International Law' in MA Young (ed), *Regime Interaction in International Law: Facing Fragmentation* (Cambridge University Press 2015) 85.

[12] Young, 'Fragmentation' 1.

[13] P Webb, *International Judicial Integration and Fragmentation* (Oxford University Press 2013) 5 and 6.

[14] A Moravcsik, *The Choice for Europe: Social Purpose and State Power from Messina to Maastricht* (Cornell University Press 1998).

[15] T Broude and Y Shany, 'The International Law and Policy of Multi-Sourced Equivalent Norms' in T Broude and Y Shany (eds), *Multi-Sourced Equivalent Norms in International Law* (Hart Publishing 2011) 12.

[16] M Zürn and B Faude, 'On Fragmentation, Differentiation, and Coordination' (2013) 13(3) *Global Environmental Politics* 119, 119.

Different norms and institutions have developed independently from one another, often originating within 'semi-isolated "regimes", with conflicts resolved by specialised courts and tribunals'.[17] A regime has been described as a 'union of rules laying down particular rights, duties and powers and rules having to do with the administration of such rules, including in particular rules for reacting to breaches'.[18] Young has found that the scholarly literature on regimes focuses 'on disparate sets of norms, decision-making procedures, and organisations that have developed to address functional issue areas' and that this scholarship seeks 'to understand how such regimes take one another into account during conflict resolution and in more general circumstances of law-making and implementation'.[19]

Eyal Benvenisti and George Downs discuss 'the increased proliferation of international regulatory institutions and ambiguous boundaries' but also consider that fragmentation could be seen as a 'harmless side effect' of international political pluralism.[20] Others, such as Andreas Fischer-Lescano and Gunther Teubner, speak of fragmentation as 'an ephemeral reflection of a more fundamental, multidimensional fragmentation of global society itself' and 'a legal reproduction of collisions between the diverse rationalities within a global society'.[21] The outlook here is that fragmentation is something that is inevitable in such a system.

Despite the variations in language used by commentators, from this overview some generalisations can be deduced. Considerations of fragmentation in international law come down to divergence, be it of rules, norms, regimes, institutions or interpretations. Various scholars have suggested that this is the result of a multiplicity of international regulations,[22] the specialisation of international regulations,[23] and the proliferation of courts and tribunals.[24] In the eyes of international legal scholars and international relations scholars, fragmentation is the result of an 'absence of hierarchical coordination'.[25] For most, the resulting divergence is an inherent aspect of the international legal system, given its nature.

[17] Young, 'Fragmentation' 1.

[18] A Fischer-Lescano and G Teubner, 'Regime-Collisions: The Vain Search for Legal Unity in the Fragmentation of Global Law' (2004) 25 *Michigan Journal of International Law* 999, 1013.

[19] Young, 'Fragmentation' 2.

[20] E Benvenisti and GW Downs, 'The Empire's New Clothes: Political Economy and the Fragmentation of International Law' (2007) 60(2) *Stanford Law Review* 595, 596, citing M Koskenniemi and P Leino, 'Fragmentation of International Law? Postmodern Anxieties' [2002] 15 *Leiden Journal of International Law* 553, 553.

[21] Fischer-Lescano and Teubner, 'Regime-Collisions' 1004 and 1017.

[22] G Hafner, 'Pros and Cons Ensuing from Fragmentation of International Law' (2004) 25 *Michigan Journal of International Law* 849, 849.

[23] ibid 850.

[24] Young, 'Fragmentation' 1.

[25] Zürn and Faude, 'On Fragmentation' 119. For an excellent account of the varying responses of international legal scholars and international relations scholars to fragmentation, including how it should be responded to, see C Kreuder-Sonnen and M Zürn, 'After Fragmentation: Norm Collisions, Interface Conflicts, and Conflict Management' (2020) 9(2) *Global Constitutionalism* 241, 245–49.

These factors that are seen as being responsible for fragmentation – some of which are also apparent in the context of the European patent system – are often seen as risks for the development of regimes involving international law. One of the many questions therefore posed by fragmentation in general, and considered by this book in the context of the European patent system, is whether the law can develop consistently with the existence of so many laws and courts.[26] A possible answer to this question lies in the ways in which the international community has viewed fragmentation and its growth in the area.

A. Analysis of Fragmentation

Fragmentation has been, is and always will be a characteristic of the international legal system. However, how it has been perceived varies according to the priorities of commentators and according to how fragmentation has an impact in practice. It has therefore been viewed positively, negatively and neutrally.

For example, Gerhard Hafner theorises that fragmentation can have both positive and negative effects on the rule of law in international law.[27] He argues that on the positive side, it can induce stricter compliance with international law, as nations may be 'more inclined to comply with norms of a regional nature that better reflect the particular political situation of the [nations] in that region'; and on the negative side, it can expose the 'frictions and contradictions between the various legal regulations' that exist.[28]

One of the main arguments that has been made regarding the issue is that since fragmentation is an inherent aspect of international legal orders, it can be expected to remain. Rather than focusing on whether it ought to exist, therefore, attention should turn to how it can be harnessed.[29] In essence, this recognises that while some of the effects of fragmentation can be negative, those negative effects can also be minimised by means of certain mechanisms, including but not limited to *lex specialis*, *lex posterior* and systemic integration, elaborated on below.[30]

More generally, classifying a certain level of fragmentation as 'good' or 'bad' is not accepted by certain authors, who believe that this classification would require an 'intuitive comparative threshold that can effectively substitute for [an] apparently missing theoretically derived benchmark'.[31] Using differentiation

[26] This question was raised in the international law context by Webb, *International Judicial Integration and Fragmentation* 1.

[27] Hafner, 'Pros and Cons'.

[28] ibid 850 and 851.

[29] C Greenwood, 'Unity and Diversity in International Law' in M Andenas and E Bjorge (eds), *A Farewell to Fragmentation: Reassertion and Convergence in International Law* (Cambridge University Press 2015) 39.

[30] Zürn and Faude, 'On Fragmentation' 127.

[31] ibid 126.

theory to conceptualise fragmentation, some of those authors, including Zürn and Faude, argue that functional differentiation,[32] which can lead to fragmentation, is a 'rational response to an increasingly complex society' – it is argued that a 'high degree of institutional differentiation … is an important characteristic of modernity'.[33] They come to the conclusion that the mere existence of institutional fragmentation is not undesirable, but rather creates a need for coordination.[34] Andreas Paulus argues along similar lines and believes that 'issue areas are held together by … common values'.[35] Furthermore, he believes that a 'case can be made for an international order based on the rule of law' which goes so far as to 'celebrate functional fragmentation, but does not lose sight of the necessity of a substantive coherence of laws and institutions'.[36] From this, it can be seen that fragmentation is expected and inherent.

Focus is on the coordination of laws rather than their unification, promoting a joint understanding of the rule of law. It is believed that if sufficient coordination is achieved, conflicts between institutions will be minimised and laws will remain diverse enough to respect the profound differences in society.[37] Fragmentation is seen as providing an 'open-endedness that makes for the flexibility and contextual responsiveness of the international legal system'.[38] However, if coordination is the method by which fragmentation is to be managed, a question arises as to how this is best achieved.

B. Responses to Fragmentation

The ILC identified a number of different methods by which fragmentation ought to be (and is being) treated, including the use of the Vienna Convention provisions on the interpretation of treaties,[39] various maxims for conflict resolution, and the principle of systemic integration.[40] These will be explored in sequence immediately below. The general overview is that it is important to consider the relationship

[32] Described by Zürn and Faude, ibid 122, as 'wherein the subsystems [of a whole] are defined by the coherence of particular types of activity and their distinction from other types of activity, and difference does not stem merely from rank'.

[33] ibid 120.

[34] ibid.

[35] AL Paulus, 'Commentary to Andreas Fischer-Lescano and Gunther Teubner: The Legitimacy of International Law and the Role of the State' (2004) 25 *Michigan Journal of International Law* 1047, 1050.

[36] ibid 1057 and 1058.

[37] Zürn and Faude, 'On Fragmentation' 128.

[38] A Lindroos, 'Addressing Norm Conflicts in a Fragmented Legal System: The Doctrine of *Lex Specialis*' (2005) 74(1) *Nordic Journal of International Law* 27, 29.

[39] Vienna Convention on the Law of Treaties (Vienna, 23 May 1969, 1155 UNTS 331).

[40] ILC Report and International Law Commission, 'Conclusions of the work of the Study Group on the Fragmentation of International Law: Difficulties arising from the Diversification and Expansion of International Law' (2006) 2(2) *Yearbook of the International Law Commission* 1.

between competing norms and that these norms should be interpreted as much as possible in a harmonised manner.

The main sources of interpretation for international law are those enshrined in the Vienna Convention, specifically Articles 31–33 on the interpretation of treaties. The main provision, Article 31, requires that a treaty be interpreted 'in good faith in accordance with the ordinary meaning to be given to the terms of the treaty in their context and in the light of its object and purpose'. Articles 32 and 33 provide that the preparatory materials for the convention in question can be used as a supplementary means of interpretation and give guidance on when a treaty has been officially published in more than one language.

In areas of conflict, certain rules and principles can be applied such as *lex specialis*, *lex posterior*, *jus cogens*, *obligations erga omnes* and the principle of systemic integration.[41] Numerous rules, whether general or specific, can apply to the same factual issue, creating friction that may lead to divergent interpretations of substantive law depending on which rule is used in which circumstance.[42] International law has seen an increase in institutional fragmentation, which has served to strengthen the role of specialist regimes; this, in turn, has subsequently given rise to concerns over regime conflicts.[43]

Lex specialis is the principle prescribing that a legal norm in force that is more specific will be applied instead of the general norm of the area. *Lex posterior* is the principle that gives primacy to more recent rules over former rules on the same issue. When generalist legal regimes compete with more specialised regimes, this has required the use of such interpretative principles.[44]

Other interpretative methods used to deal with conflict include *jus cogens* and *obligations erga omnes*. Peremptory norms, or *jus cogens*, are the fundamental principles of international law from which no derogations are permitted. If these principles are in question, they must always come first. *Obligations erga omnes* refer to the predetermined obligations that states have towards the international community. These obligations are used to designate the scope of application of the relevant rule and procedural consequences.

Systemic integration can also be used in conflicts, which involves attempting to apply all rules that exist regarding the case at hand in a harmonious fashion, to integrate those rules and fulfil the intention of the legislator. Once a matter comes before a tribunal and this interpretative approach is being applied, all relevant rules must be taken into account and considered against one another. The most effective use of this approach would be one that leads to a harmonious response to the area or legal concept, with all variations considered.

[41] Young, 'Fragmentation' 2.

[42] For example, there may be a conflict between two regimes, such as between international trade law and environmental law.

[43] Lindroos, 'Addressing Norm Conflicts' 32 and 33.

[44] Hafner, 'Pros and Cons' 856.

Young has also identified certain mechanisms for countering the negative effects of fragmentation.[45] These include regime interaction, as well as principles of pluralism and constitutionalism. Young considers regimes and regime interaction to be a 'central concept' in the analysis and understanding of fragmentation.[46] Certain regimes are seen to build up around specific subject matter. To 'face' the fragmentation that is introduced by the existence of numerous regimes, one option to ensure the proper functioning of the international legal system is for regimes to interact with one another, creating a dialogue between them.[47] It has been argued that regime interaction and the resulting 'productive friction' will 'lead to a more responsive and effective international legal system', which takes into account numerous opinions and interpretations of substantive law, rather than a system which focuses purely on a single rule.[48] However, it has also been argued that rather than regime interaction being of benefit, the result will be cooption,[49] or regime collision,[50] and due to political, ideological and other differences, a harmonised interpretation is often not possible.[51] These concerns must be taken into account and addressed.

There are also those who are in favour of recognising pluralism as offering a framework for conceiving and responding to fragmentation. Pluralism, the existence of multiple and overlapping legal rules, allows for diversity and flexibility within a legal system. Legal pluralism can be described as 'the presence in a social field of more than one legal order in which law and legal institutions are not subsumable within one system but have various sources';[52] or, as a system that 'contains inconsistent rules of recognition that cannot be legally resolved from within the system'.[53] Pluralist legal systems survive without hierarchy and, according to Nicholas Barber, create a situation in which the risk of divergence is known and an effort made to avoid it by harmonious interpretation of the law.[54] According to this argument, acknowledging the existence of inconsistencies allows

[45] Young, 'Fragmentation'.

[46] ibid 26. Other authors have taken the concept of regimes further. For example, Laurence Helfer discusses how international relations scholars have developed the concept of international regimes to be broader than a particular organisation or treaty in LR Helfer, 'Regime Shifting: The TRIPs Agreement and New Dynamics of International Intellectual Property Law Making' (2004) 29 *The Yale Journal of International Law* 1, 10.

[47] One of the seminal texts in this regard is MA Young (ed), *Regime Interaction in International Law: Facing Fragmentation* (Cambridge University Press 2015).

[48] Young, 'Introduction' 11.

[49] M Koskenniemi, 'Hegemonic Regimes' in MA Young (ed), *Regime Interaction in International Law: Facing Fragmentation* (Cambridge University Press 2012) 319.

[50] In general, see Fischer-Lescano and Teubner, 'Regime-Collisions'.

[51] S Humphreys, 'Structural Ambiguity: Technology Transfer in Three Regimes' in MA Young (ed), *Regime Interaction in International Law: Facing Fragmentation* (Cambridge University Press 2012).

[52] J Griffiths, 'What Is Legal Pluralism?' (1986) 24(1) *Journal of Legal Pluralism* 55, 1.

[53] N Barber, 'Legal Pluralism and the European Union' (2006) 12(3) *European Law Journal* 306, 306. On legal pluralism, see also BZ Tamanaha, 'Understanding Legal Pluralism: Past to Present, Local to Global' (2008) 30 *Sydney Law Review* 375.

[54] Barber, 'Legal Pluralism' 327 and 328.

for political compromise and allows parties who disagree regarding the specific interpretation of a rule to all emerge victorious.[55] Adopting a pluralist response to fragmentation, it can be argued that, on balance, it is positive because it allows for the divergences that give different states their cultural, moral, economic and political identities. However, there remains the possibility that unnecessary divergence and inconsistency could occur and consequently a pluralist approach has been questioned.[56]

Principles of constitutionalism have also been used to respond to and gain a deeper understanding of fragmentation in international law.[57] It has been noted that the lack of a global constitutional system is the reason for fragmentation, however constitutional practices can be used and developed in order to respond to existing fragmentation.[58]

Also arising in the literature on responses to fragmentation in international law are discussions of what have been named 'multi-sourced equivalent norms'.[59] Multi-sourced equivalent norms are described as the 'multiplication of similar rules arising from different legal sources',[60] or as

> [t]wo or more norms which are (1) binding upon the same international legal subjects; (2) similar or identical in their normative content; and (3) have been established through different international instruments or 'legislative' procedures or are applicable in different substantive areas of the law.[61]

In these discussions, focus is on the risks arising due to fragmentation from the perspective of normative parallelism – parallels between similar rules, rather than conflicts between different norms. For example, from the perspective of normative parallelism the discussion would focus on the risks arising from a divergence in human rights law and humanitarian law, whereas the focus of general discussions of fragmentation in international law is on the conflict between, for example, international trade law and environmental law. It has also been suggested that multi-sourced equivalent norms are 'comprised of equivalences as well as differences that create legal and political alternatives … [that] can be seen as enhancing flexibility and enabling regime shifts'.[62] This is said to either strengthen international normativity or, alternatively, promote and facilitate forum shopping and manipulative behaviour.[63]

[55] ibid 328.
[56] For an overview, see Young, 'Fragmentation' 38.
[57] ibid 35.
[58] See ibid 35–38.
[59] Broude and Shany, *Multi-Sourced Equivalent Norms in International Law*.
[60] M Poiares Maduro, 'Foreword' in T Broude and Y Shany (eds), *Multi-Sourced Equivalent Norms in International Law* (Hart Publishing 2011) vii.
[61] Broude and Shany, 'International Law and Policy' 5.
[62] ibid 12.
[63] ibid.

This discussion has also examined the potential responses to these associated risks and commentators are quite optimistic that they can be interpreted in a consistent manner if certain precautions are taken and if certain mechanisms are put into place. Suggestions include the use of secondary rules,[64] and judicial borrowing and dialogue.[65]

Webb, in her seminal text *International Judicial Integration and Fragmentation*, distinguishes between the fragmentation that results from conflicts between distinct areas and fragmentation that results from conflicting decisions relating to the same legal or factual scenario.[66] The latter, she explains, could be two courts coming to a different decision on the same issue or a court diverging from a previous decision without explanation.[67] She expands on the importance of treating similar cases in a consistent manner in such scenarios, with room to determine the best way forward in the short term, leading towards reconciliation in the long term.[68] Judicial integration could be a way to achieve this, though it is recognised that this will never lead to uniformity – on this, Webb states that

> judicial integration requires that similar factual scenarios and similar legal issues are treated in a consistent manner, and that any disparity in treatment is explained and justified. The desired outcome is harmony and compatibility, which allow for the co-existence of minor variations and for tailoring of solutions for particular cases.[69]

C. Judicial Dialogue and Cooperation

It appears from this overview of responses that a widely supported technique to promote coordination in multiple areas of fragmentation is interaction. Particularly key to such interaction is judicial dialogue and cooperation. In the long term the hope is that judicial dialogue and cooperation will lead to a general joint understanding and harmonisation of substantive law. This technique offers particular hope due to the proliferation of international courts and tribunals in the international legal system – which is itself a contributing factor to the fragmentation of

[64] A Nollkaemper, 'The Power of Secondary Rules to Connect the International and National Legal Orders' in T Broude and Y Shany (eds), *Multi-Sourced Equivalent Norms in International Law* (Hart Publishing 2011).

[65] B Pirker, 'Interpreting Multi-Sourced Equivalent Norms: Judicial Borrowing in International Courts' in T Broude and Y Shany (eds), *Multi-Sourced Equivalent Norms in International Law* (Hart Publishing 2011). For more on the judicial perspective in international law, see T Treves, 'Fragmentation of International Law: The Judicial Perspective' (2009) 16(27) *Agenda Internacional* 213. For more on judicial dialogue in European patent law, see discussion in subsequent chapters of this book and J Brinkhof, 'The Desirability, Necessity and Feasibility of Co-operation Between Courts in the Field of European Patent Law' (1997) 19(5) *EIPR* 226.

[66] Webb, *International Judicial Integration and Fragmentation* 6.

[67] ibid.

[68] ibid.

[69] ibid 5.

international law – and is for similar reasons of interest for the European patent system.[70]

Even the use of 'proliferation' as a description has negative connotations, which some commentators see as misleading; the increase of courts and tribunals is arguably a natural response to the increase of legal norms in an area.[71] However, the mere fact that a number of courts or tribunals exist in a specific area, or in conflicting areas, creates the risk that differing interpretations of law will arise, which may in turn lead to negative results, such as forum shopping. Therefore, following a detailed analysis of the potential ways forward, a model has been proposed by Webb, based on judicial dialogue and cooperation, with a prominent (yet not hierarchical) role for international courts, such as the International Court of Justice (ICJ), and a shared responsibility for integration among all key actors.[72]

Judicial dialogue can take multiple forms, including reciprocity, interaction and informal communications.[73] Thomas Buergenthal maintains that courts and tribunals need to 'recognise that they are all part of the same legal system' and should respect each other's decisions – if so, the legitimacy and efficacy of international law should, in theory, prevail.[74]

Certain risks need to be considered, and the risk of judicial law-making taken into account. However, as long as the dialogue is not taken so far as to introduce new rules, or unfounded interpretations of rules, the judicial dialogue model can be of benefit.[75] Courts and tribunals must also be wary of judicial deference, ensuring that scope for change remains, in case a rule ought to be changed or updated.[76] In addition, it has been argued that despite its apparent positive results, integration and regime interaction can lead to the 'co-opting' of a weaker regime, resulting in a coordination that is not necessarily desirable.[77] However, if the judiciary take these risks into account and remain aware of the negative consequences of certain actions or decisions, this method can be successful.

It is true that multiple courts and tribunals can have negative consequences, such as differing jurisprudence that 'can erode the unity of international law' and promote conflicting legal doctrine that can 'threaten the universality of international law'.[78] However, it has been persuasively argued that so long as these

[70] For more, see A-M Slaughter, 'Judicial Globalization' (2000) 40 *Virginia Journal of International Law* 1103.

[71] G Abi-Saab, 'Fragmentation or Unification: Some Concluding Remarks' (1999) 31 *NYU Journal of International Law and Politics* 919, 925; and Treves, 'Fragmentation of International Law'.

[72] Webb, *International Judicial Integration and Fragmentation* 208–28. For more on judicial integration and the tendency of courts to integrate, see, for example, Abi-Saab, 'Fragmentation or Unification'.

[73] G Cornelisse and M Moraru, 'Introduction: Judicial Dialogue on the Return Directive – Catalyst for Changing Migration Governance?' in G Cornelisse, M Moraru and P De Bruycker (eds), *Law and Judicial Dialogue on the Return of Irregular Migrants from the European Union* (Hart Publishing 2020).

[74] T Buergenthal, 'Proliferation of International Courts and Tribunals: Is It Good or Bad?' (2001) 14(2) *Leiden Journal of International Law* 267, 274.

[75] ibid 273.

[76] ibid.

[77] Koskenniemi, 'Hegemonic Regimes' 322.

[78] Buergenthal, 'Proliferation of International Courts' 272.

potential consequences are taken into account, and decisions from other courts and tribunals are considered, a joint understanding could emerge.[79] Overall, a coordinated approach would have the benefit of ensuring that all voices and implemented policies are taken into account.

Concerns remain, however, and some commentators contend that the fragmentation of international law is more concerning than generally acknowledged.[80] Instead of focusing on fragmentation, discussion is now focused on diversity, and it has been claimed that this takes away the negative connotations of fragmentation, but not its negative consequences.[81]

Benvenisti and Downs argue that fragmentation is the result of a 'calculated strategy by powerful states' who can lead the direction of development in their favour.[82] However, as outlined above, the fragmentation of international law has just as much to do with the increase in functional differentiation and specialised regimes being introduced to more fully understand the law and apply it in the correct manner. If states do use this strategy to increase fragmentation for their benefit, the expected results are left in the hands of the judiciary, who are encouraged to interpret the law in a consistent and coherent manner.

D. From Fear to Acceptance

Considering the responses to fragmentation above, it can be suggested that, for the most part, the international community accepts the existence of fragmentation as a reality of the international legal system. While there is also extensive awareness and discussion of its possible risks, responses to fragmentation in the field of international law have developed and have certainly been constructive.[83]

Scholarly discussion regarding the fear of fragmentation in international law, including the proliferation of courts and tribunals, mostly took place in first decade of the 2000s. Since then, the field of international law has continued to grow and develop without too much controversy surrounding the dangers of fragmentation. Initial fears have diminished.[84] As Webb puts it, 'the fragmentation of international law has become a phenomenon to be monitored rather than feared'.[85]

[79] ibid 273.

[80] Benvenisti and Downs, 'The Empire's New Clothes' 597.

[81] B Simma, 'Fragmentation in a Positive Light' (2004) 25 *Michigan Journal of International Law* 845, 847.

[82] Benvenisti and Downs, 'The Empire's New Clothes' 597.

[83] Telling evidence of this is the revision of the section of the ILC Report referring to the 'risks ensuing from fragmentation' to refer instead to the 'difficulties arising from the diversification and expansion of international law' – as discussed in Simma, 'Fragmentation' 846–47. Further evidence points to scholarship in the area, including chapters in Andenas and Bjorge, *A Farewell to Fragmentation* and papers in 'Special Issue: After Fragmentation' (2020) 9(2) *Global Constitutionalism*.

[84] For a detailed study arguing how convergence has taken over from fragmentation, see Andenas and Bjorge, *A Farewell to Fragmentation*.

[85] Webb, *International Judicial Integration and Fragmentation* xiii.

As explored above, the discussion on fragmentation in international law has somewhat shifted towards diversity and particularly coordinated fragmentation. This reflects a belief that so long as coordination and dialogue between institutions continues, numerous rules and legal norms, courts and tribunals can exist without unification or hierarchy.

II. Application to the European Patent System

Many of the causes, nature and effects of fragmentation in the international legal system can also be seen in the sub-system of European patent law. However, despite the change in attitude towards fragmentation in the international legal system, discussion in the European patent system remains focused on its removal, with little attention on how to do so outside introducing a unitary patent system.

Fragmentation in the international system has been attributed to the abundance of not only courts and tribunals, but also legal norms – be they concerned with different aspects of a multifaceted issue or multi-sourced equivalent norms. Additionally, institutional hierarchy does not exist in the international legal system. A court that has the power to preside over all legal systems and render decisions that are applicable in all countries does not exist.

Prior to the initiation of international agreements, a country would only comply with, and have its citizens abide by, its own laws and customs – its national legal system. Presently, each country's national laws remain in place; however, most territories also participate in international treaties and special regimes, often distinguished by function. Therefore, these countries must not only consider their own national legal system, but also the international conventions of which they are members. By embracing an international legal system, the situation often arises where a decision must be made regarding which law is to be applied in certain situations and which court has jurisdiction in the matter.

As discussed extensively above, conflict of laws rules assist with this, as well as regime interaction and judicial dialogue and cooperation. These mechanisms have been seen to reduce the risk of the negative consequences associated with fragmentation in the international legal system and have encouraged a shift in attitude towards fragmentation in that sphere. As a result of that shift, fragmentation has come to be seen not only as less of a threat to the goals of international integration than previously, but also as helping to realise those goals through a flexible and contextual response.

Different norms, laws and institutions have also developed independently from one another in the European patent system. Prior to the enactment of the Paris Convention,[86] countries in Europe were solely dependent on national laws for

[86] Convention for the Protection of Industrial Property 1883.

the protection of industrial property. Even today, each state has an office to deal with the granting of patents in that territory, as well as a court system to decide on matters regarding infringement, validity, revocation and other post-grant matters. Following the implementation of the Paris Convention, and thereafter the Strasbourg Patent Convention,[87] the EU Treaties and the EPC, the patent law landscape in Europe changed drastically.

Today, each European country retains its national patent laws. However, as party to the above-mentioned international agreements, each country must also consider the rules therein. For example, patent law in the UK is subject to the Patents Act 1977. However, the UK is also a signatory to the Paris Convention and the Strasbourg Patent Convention, a former Member State of the EU, and a Contracting State to the EPC. Therefore, in deciding on matters relating to patents in the UK, rulings must be made that reflect and are consistent with the provisions of the above numerous legal instruments.

The Paris Convention and the Strasbourg Patent Convention have been incorporated into patent laws throughout Europe through the EPC. These legal provisions have also been incorporated into the national laws of the Contracting States to the EPC.[88] Many national laws were also brought into line with the Community Patent Convention, although it never entered into force.[89] Furthermore, substantive patent law at EU level has also been implemented (to varying degrees) into the legal systems of Member States. Additionally, the main EU Directive in patent law, the Biotech Directive, has been incorporated into the Implementing Regulations to the EPC as a supplementary means of interpretation.[90] It therefore appears that the harmonisation of substantive legal norms in the patent field has essentially been achieved.

Although legal rules and norms have been implemented domestically in a harmonised fashion, since patent law remains territorial post-grant, national offices and courts must still make the final decisions on matters of infringement, validity and revocation. Therefore, the interpretation of substantive patent law provisions has been left largely to each individual country. Consequently, one of the main causes of the fear of fragmentation in the European patent system is the number of domestic courts and tribunals, responsible for interpreting and applying the same or very similar substantive legal principles, alongside the CJEU (as guardian of the intellectual property law provisions of the EU Treaties and the patent provisions of the Biotech Directive) and the EPO (as guardian of the EPC), with minimal institutional hierarchy between them.

[87] Convention on the Unification of Certain Points of Substantive Law on Patents for Invention 1963.
[88] See Chapter 1.
[89] Convention for the European Patent for the Common Market (15 December 1975).
[90] Implementing Regulations to the EPC 2000.

Focusing on the European tribunals specifically, the CJEU is the 'Supreme Court' of the EU; however, with regard to European patent law, the CJEU does not have jurisdiction to interpret the provisions of the EPC, and its decisions are binding on EU Member States only.[91] The Boards of Appeal of the EPO are specialised 'European' patent law tribunals (not EU, but applicable in all EU Member States and beyond); however, they do not have jurisdiction over the interpretation of domestic provisions by national courts, and their decisions are only of persuasive authority to both national courts and the CJEU. In this context of different national and European courts being required to interpret and apply the same principles of substantive patent law, it is inevitable that conflicts will arise – between different national regimes, between national regimes and the Boards of Appeal of the EPO, between national regimes and the CJEU, and between the Boards of Appeal of the EPO and the CJEU.

Additionally, patent law does not exist in a vacuum and so concepts from other areas of law, including competition law, human rights, contract law and more, can be heard in patent law cases. Therefore, conflicts can also arise on the interpretation of particular concepts, leading to substantive fragmentation.

Furthermore, when the EU unitary patent system enters into force, there will be an additional source of patent law principles that will require interpretation and application, and another specialist patent tribunal in Europe with yet another different sphere of competence and jurisdiction. This potential effect of the EU unitary patent system in contributing further to the abundance of laws and courts in Europe, and thereby compounding further the degree of fragmentation in the field, is seen as one of the main criticisms of the system.[92]

Institutional and substantive fragmentation are a concern in the European patent system that can be responded to in additional ways. Given the context, the analysis around institutional/regime interactions and judicial integration/fragmentation are the most relevant to the European patent system. Both are seen to encourage a response with a strong focus on judicial dialogue and cooperation. As mentioned, Webb particularly endorses an approach that combines structured judicial dialogue, a prominent (yet not hierarchical) role for the ICJ, and a shared responsibility for integration among all stakeholders, not only the judiciary.[93] An important question emerges at this point – whether the mechanisms used, and suggestions made to respond to fragmentation in the international legal system, can be used to strengthen responses to fragmentation in the European patent system.

[91] However, its interpretation of the provisions of the Biotech Directive are highly persuasive to the Boards of Appeal of the EPO since its provisions have been incorporated into the Implementing Regulations to the EPC 2000 as a supplementary means of interpretation.

[92] See Chapter 2.

[93] Webb, *International Judicial Integration and Fragmentation* 208–28.

III. Fragmentation as an Inherent Aspect of a Legal System

From the perspective of international legal scholars, fragmentation is perceived as an inherent aspect of the international legal system, and effective mechanisms have been put in place or developed to reduce the risks associated with it and harness its effects. The question that then arises is what implications this might have for the European patent system. Specifically, is it useful or even possible to see the fragmentation that currently exists within the European patent system as an inherent and/or constructive element? Moreover, is it possible to use similar mechanisms to assist in responding to it? The purpose of the following chapters is to consider these questions.

PART III

Fragmentation and Substantive Patent Law

Part II has shown that fragmentation as a concept can be perceived and responded to in multiple ways. In European law-making, methods of differentiated integration have been introduced to allow progress towards integration for an expanding supranational system. In the international legal system, fragmentation was at first feared. However, as mechanisms were used to respond to it, perceptions changed. It is now also perceived in neutral and positive terms.

Fragmentation is likely to remain a feature of the European patent system and so perceptions of and responses to it should alter similarly. Part III investigates how substantive patent law is being interpreted and how institutions are currently responding to fragmentation. It will be argued that fragmentation can and should be seen as an inherent aspect of the European patent system. In certain circumstances, responding to it could also mean allowing it to persist while consensus is built appropriately, if possible and desirable. Our focus should therefore be on developing additional mechanisms to respond to fragmentation, which can also recognise value pluralism and the wider impact of patent law on society.

5

Responding to Fragmentation as an Inherent Aspect of the European Patent System

Fragmentation is and likely always will be part of the European patent system. Without complete unification, territorial and procedural fragmentation will remain and so, too, the potential for institutional fragmentation. Substantive fragmentation will also remain a factor for consideration, though this arises less regularly. Since national patent systems will remain operational to the benefit of a variety of stakeholders, unitary rights will be for participating EU Member States only,[1] and further legislative reform is highly improbable, responding to the risks of institutional fragmentation will become even more important.

One of the standout features of the European patent system is the multiplicity of institutions that deal with patent law, be it grant or enforcement. This includes every national patent office, the EPO, every national court tasked with deciding issues of patent law, the Boards of Appeal, the Enlarged Board of Appeal, the Opposition Divisions of the EPO, and the CJEU. The UPC will soon be added to that list.

As previously discussed, all Contracting States have amended national laws to implement the EPC,[2] some have also implemented provisions related to enforcement from the CPC,[3] and EU Member States have implemented relevant EU laws.[4] The institutions involved all interpret substantive patent law based on these provisions, take various approaches towards the criteria for patentability, and make decisions on the validity and enforcement of patents. Divergence can arise and has arisen in the interpretation of substantive patent law. As expected, patent offices and courts interpreting the same laws can do so differently and can make diverse decisions in relation to the same patent, all resulting in institutional fragmentation.

[1] With the exception of Switzerland and Liechtenstein, where there is also a unitary patent.

[2] Convention on the Grant of European Patents of 5 October 1973, it being based on the Convention on the Unification of Certain Points of Substantive Law on Patents for Invention 1963.

[3] Convention for the European Patent for the Common Market (15 December 1975).

[4] For example, Directive 98/44EC of the European Parliament and of the Council of 6 July 1998 on the legal protection of biotechnological inventions.

This chapter will investigate areas where divergent approaches persist and the attempts that have been made to respond to fragmentation and reduce divergence in decision-making.[5] It will focus on three key areas: inventive step, patentable subject matter, and claim construction. It does so with a focus on national courts (particularly the UK) and the EPO, with a brief mention of the CJEU. EU involvement in the interpretation of substantive patent law and the response to fragmentation in relation to the exceptions to patentability will be discussed in the next chapter.

In the previous chapter it was asked if the methods used and suggestions made when responding to fragmentation in the international legal system could be applied in the European patent system. When considering fragmentation and integration within regimes, particularly the risks of institutional fragmentation, a relevant and promising suggestion was made – that the most effective way to respond to the risks of institutional fragmentation was through structured judicial dialogue, a prominent yet not hierarchical role for a central court, and a shared responsibility for integration by all stakeholders.[6] This suggestion can and should be adapted and applied in the European patent system. In fact, the process has already begun.

It will be shown that in the interpretation of substantive patent law, methods being used to respond to fragmentation in the European patent system are similar to those being used in the field of international law. There is a recognition of the potential for differences arising, alongside attempts by the institutions involved to minimise divergence through the implementation of various strategies, including judicial dialogue and cooperation. However, it is suggested that these attempts should be more formally recognised, harnessed and further developed.

I. Areas of Divergence

The EPC was created to strengthen 'co-operation between the States of Europe in respect to the protection of inventions', whereby such protection 'may be obtained by a single procedure for the grant of patents'.[7] Prior to the implementation of the EPC, numerous differences existed between the patent laws of Contracting States, including the term of patent protection, the scope of prior art for novelty purposes, the possibility of protecting chemical compounds, and standards of search and examination.[8] Significant changes were made to national patent laws; however, the impact was mixed.

[5] Substantial parts of this chapter were previously published in K Walsh, 'Promoting Harmonisation across the European Patent System through Judicial Dialogue and Cooperation' (2019) 50(4) *IIC* 408.

[6] P Webb, *International Judicial Integration and Fragmentation* (Oxford University Press 2013) 208–28.

[7] EPC, Preamble. For more on the EPC, see Chapter 1.

[8] M Jewess, *Inside Intellectual Property: Best Practice in Intellectual Property Law, Management, and Strategy* (Chartered Institute of Patent Attorneys 2013) Appendix 20.2, 430.

A. Implementation of the EPC

National patent laws were substantially harmonised, which led to more legal certainty and higher-quality patents. However, even where possible, the exact wording of the provisions of the EPC was not transposed directly into national laws, leading to some unnecessary confusion.[9] For example, English is one of the three authentic texts of the Convention, and so a change in the wording of the provisions when implemented by the UK was both unnecessary and confusing. If differences exist between the wording of the Act and the Convention, the approach in the UK is to construe the Act in the same sense as that of the Convention.[10] There is an important provision in the Patents Act 1977 (UK) that promotes the consistent interpretation of UK patent law with the EPC in relation to certain provisions. Section 130(7) Patents Act 1977 (UK) states:

> Whereas by a resolution made on the signature of the Community Patent Convention the governments of the member states of the European Economic Community resolved to adjust their laws relating to patents so as (among other things) to bring those laws into conformity with the corresponding provisions of the European Patent Convention, the Community Patent Convention and the Patent Co-operation Treaty, it is hereby declared that the following provisions of this Act, that is to say, sections 1(1) to (4), 2 to 6, 14(3), (5) and (6), 37(5), 54, 60, 69, 72(1) and (2), 74(4), 82, 83, 100 and 125, are so framed as to have, as nearly as practicable, the same effects in the United Kingdom as the corresponding provisions of the European Patent Convention, the Community Patent Convention and the Patent Co-operation Treaty have in the territories to which those Conventions apply.

The provision has, however, been described as 'preposterous' by the UK Court of Appeal as it would not be necessary if the exact wording of the Convention had been used.[11] If the wording of the provisions of the EPC had been transposed directly, there would have been less confusion and less need for section 130(7) Patents Act 1977 (UK).

B. Approaches to Patentability

Additionally, most post-grant matters are determined by national courts. The UK Patent Act provides guidance that the courts ought to take judicial notice of the EPC and interpret laws in accordance with the EPC.[12] However, the interpretation of the EPC by the EPO and Boards of Appeal is not binding on national courts,

[9] G Paterson, *The European Patent System: The Law and Practice of the European Patent Convention* (2nd edn, Sweet & Maxwell 2001) 36.

[10] *Smith Kline and French Laboratories Ltd v RD Harbottle (Mercantile) Ltd* [1980] RPC 363.

[11] *Grimme Maschinenfabrik GmbH & Co KG v Derek Scott (t/a Scotts Potato Machinery)* [2010] EWCA Civ 1110 [82].

[12] Section 91(1)(a) Patents Act 1977 (UK).

and the EPC contains minimal guidance on enforcement. Furthermore, there is no common European patent court for all 38 EPC Contracting States, which would lead to a binding uniform interpretation of the law. As a result, numerous institutions interpret the provisions of the EPC, which can lead to institutional fragmentation.

The *Improver* case is the most well-known example of divergence in parallel proceedings. Here, the same European patent, with various designations, was litigated in several Contracting States with divergent outcomes.[13] Stefan Luginbuehl has also identified additional cases with divergent outcomes: *Novartis AG and Cibavision AG v Johnson & Johnson Medical Ltd and others* 2009/2010 resulted in different decisions regarding the validity of a European patent between France and the Netherlands on the one hand, and the UK and Germany on the other; *Document Security Systems v European Central Bank* 2008, where the Dutch courts came to the opposite conclusion to that of the German and French courts, as well as the Austrian patent office; *Pozzoli v BDMO SA* 2007, where the patent was revoked in the UK and France, but held to be valid and infringed in Germany; *Angiotech Pharmaceuticals v Conor Medsystems Inc* 2007, which resulted in different outcomes in the UK and the Netherlands; and *Muller v Hilti* 1999/2000, where the decision of the German Court was at odds with the decisions of the courts of Switzerland and France.[14] Malwina Mejer and Bruno van Pottlesberghe de la Potterie consider some of these decisions and more in detailed case studies highlighting the uncertainty and complexity this creates.[15] Further empirical research in this area provides evidence that in the majority of cases litigated in multiple jurisdictions across Europe, the result is divergent outcomes and that the practices of the four countries in the study are indeed substantially different.[16]

Divergence can also arise in the interpretation of substantive patent law provisions more generally. Two important areas where divergent approaches are apparent when comparing the UK with the EPO and other countries in Europe are the substantive patent law criteria of inventive step and patentable subject matter.[17]

[13] UK: *Improver Corp v Remington Consumer Product Ltd* [1990] FSR 181; Germany: Decision of the Oberlandesgericht Düsseldorf, 21 November 1991 – 2 U 27/89 '*Improver*', translated in 'Improver Corp & Sicommerce AG v Remington Products Inc' (1993) 24 *IIC* 838; Netherlands: translated in (1993) 24 *IIC* 832.

[14] S Luginbuehl, *European Patent Law: Towards a Uniform Interpretation* (Edward Elgar 2011) 10.

[15] M Mejer and B van Pottlesberghe de la Potterie, 'Economic Incongruities in the European Patent System' [2009] *Bruegel Working Paper*.

[16] K Cremers, M Ernicke, F Gaessler, D Harhoff, C Helmers, L McDonagh, P Schliessler and N Van Zeebroeck, 'Patent Litigation in Europe' [2016] *European Journal of Law and Economics* available at http://link.springer.com/article/10.1007/s10657-016-9529-0. See also SJH Graham and N Van Zeebroeck, 'Comparing Patent Litigation Across Europe: A First Look' (2014) *17 Stanford Technical Law Review* 655; P-O Bjuggren, B Domeij and A Horn, 'Swedish Patent Litigation in Comparison to European' (2015) 5 *Nordisk Immateriellt Rättsskydd* 504.

[17] Inventive step is discussed first because analysis related to the approaches to patentable subject matter relate to what is considered at the inventive step stage. Further areas of divergence can be gleaned from discussions contained in 17th European Patent Judges' Symposium, [2015] *Supplementary Publication*, OJ EPO 5.

i. Inventive Step

According to Article 56 EPC and section 3 Patents Act 1977 (UK), to be patentable an invention must involve an inventive step. This criterion will be fulfilled if, and only if, with regard to the state of the art, the invention is not obvious to the person skilled in the art. There are slight variations in the wording of these provisions; however, section 3 is included in section 130(7) Patents Act 1977 (UK), which, as previously mentioned, states that it is to have the same effect in the UK, or as nearly as practicable, as the corresponding provision in the EPC.

The approach by which the UK and the EPO, as well as the Netherlands, France and Germany, decide whether there has been an inventive step differs: in the UK the *Windsurfing/Pozzoli* approach is used, whereas the EPO and others use the problem and solution approach.[18]

The UK approach involves a four-step test, introduced by the Court of Appeal in *Windsurfing International v Tabur Marine*. In order to assess the question of obviousness without the benefit of hindsight it should be hypothesised what would have been obvious at the priority date to the person skilled in the art.[19] This test was elaborated upon and restated in *Pozzoli*[20] to be used alongside the *Windsurfing* approach.[21] Essentially, the test requires the identification of the person skilled in the art, their relevant common general knowledge, the inventive concept of the claim and what differences exist between the state of the art and the inventive concept. Once these are identified, the question asked is: 'Viewed without any knowledge of the alleged invention as claimed, do those differences constitute steps which would have been obvious to the person skilled in the art or do they require any degree of invention?'[22]

In all but exceptional cases, the EPO applies the problem and solution approach. This was first established in *Bayer/Carbonless copying paper* and confirmed in G1/19.[23] According to the EPO Guidelines for Examination and the Enlarged Board of Appeal, there are three main steps: determining the closest prior art; establishing the objective technical problem to be solved; and considering whether or not the claimed invention, starting from the closest prior art and the objective technical problem, would have been obvious to the person skilled in the art.[24] The technical problem refers to 'the aim and task of modifying or adapting the closest prior art to provide the technical effects that the invention provides over the closest prior art'.[25] If there is no technical contribution, the invention is not inventive.

[18] *Windsurfing International Inc v Tabur Marine (Great Britain) Ltd* [1985] RPC 59 (*Windsurfing*); *Pozzoli SPA v BDMO SA* [2007] EWCA Civ 588 (*Pozzoli*).

[19] *Windsurfing*, 71.

[20] *Pozzoli*, 878.

[21] Intellectual Property Office, *Manual of Patent Practice*, October 2021 (UK), Section 3.12.

[22] Step 4 of both *Windsurfing* and *Pozzoli*.

[23] T1/80 *Bayer/Carbonless copying paper* of 06.4.1981; G1/19 *Pedestrian simulation* of 10.3.21.

[24] EPO, Guidelines for Examination, March 2021, G.VII.5; G1/19.

[25] ibid G.VII.5.2.

Of relevance here are the differences between these approaches and the impact this difference has in practice. The problem and solution approach has been criticised by the UK courts.[26] It was also once criticised by the Boards of Appeal.[27] The main reasons for criticism are its reliance on hindsight, its limit to one piece of (closest) prior art, and its artificiality in cases where an invention breaks new ground.[28] The UK courts have elaborated that the approach may make sense in the context of an examining office, but when it comes to a national court making a full multi-factorial assessment of all relevant factors, it may not be as applicable.[29] However, there are similarities between the problem and solution approach and aspects related to the UK test, particularly the obvious-to-try test.[30] This alternative point of view was also expressed in *Generics (UK) Ltd v Daiichi Pharmaceutical Co Ltd*:

> Some have suggested that [*Windsurfing/Pozzoli*] is different from the EPO's problem/solution approach. It is not. The problem/solution approach only applies at stage four. The first three stages must be carried out implicitly as much for the problem/solution approach as for any other.[31]

Indeed, the main question answered by both tests is whether the invention is obvious to the person skilled in the art.

It can also be argued that the differences between these two approaches would not result in a divergent outcome when taking a holistic view of the criteria for patentability. Coupled with the tests for patentable subject matter, both the UK and EPO consider similar questions overall. This is another area where there is a divergence in approach.

ii. Patentable Subject Matter

In European patent law, a positive definition of an invention does not exist. Instead, examples of non-patentable subject matter are listed in Article 52(2) EPC and section 1(2) Patents Act 1977 (UK). This includes discoveries, scientific theories, mathematical methods, aesthetic creations, schemes, rules and methods for performing mental acts, playing games or doing business, programs for computers, and presentations of information (all not deemed to be 'inventions').[32] However, these activities are only excluded 'as such'. Once more, the wording of these

[26] *Actavis UK Ltd v Novartis AG* [2010] EWCA Civ 82.
[27] T465/92 *Alcan/Aluminium alloys* of 14.10.1994.
[28] *Actavis UK Ltd v Novartis AG* [2010] EWCA Civ 82.
[29] See, for example, ibid [25]–[50].
[30] P England and S Parker, 'Obviousness in the New European Order' (2012) 7(11) *JIPLP* 805.
[31] *Generics (UK) Ltd v Daiichi Pharmaceutical Co Ltd* [2009] EWCA Civ 646 [20].
[32] Literary, dramatic, musical or artistic works are also explicitly excluded from patentability in the Patents Act 1977 (UK). These works fall under 'aesthetic creations' in the EPC provision. For a detailed discussion on the requirement of an invention in patent law, see J Pila, *The Requirement for an Invention in Patent Law* (Oxford University Press 2010).

provisions is not identical, however section 1(2) is also subject to section 130(7) Patents Act 1977 (UK). Although the provisions should have the same effect in both the UK and at the EPO, the way they are interpreted and applied differs.

There have been attempts by various courts to clarify what is an invention. The most relevant is the *Red Dove* case, where the nature of an invention was defined for pre-EPC German law.[33] The German Supreme Court defined an invention as requiring 'technical teaching', which was subsequently characterised as 'teaching to methodically utilize controllable natural forces to achieve a causal, perceivable result'.[34] In 2010, the Enlarged Board of Appeal stated that the standard set by *Red Dove* 'still holds good today and can be said to be in conformity with the meaning of the EPC'.[35] Courts in the UK have not yet considered its applicability.

The current approach in the UK to patentable subject matter and the requirement of an invention, the technical contribution approach, originated at the EPO and was first applied in *VICOM/Computer-related invention*.[36] The decisive aspect of this approach is a consideration of what technical contribution the invention makes to the known art. The technical contribution approach was adopted by the UK in *Genentech's Patent* and confirmed in *Merrill Lynch*, *Gale's Application* and *Fujitsu*.[37] In affirming it, the UK courts aligned themselves with the approach that was then being taken by the EPO.[38]

However, the EPO subsequently abandoned the technical contribution approach and adopted a new, less demanding approach requiring technical character. This is to be assessed independently of the other requirements of patentability, such as novelty and inventive step.[39] The reason for the change in approach was because the assessment of technical character can be achieved without any recourse to the prior art, unlike the technical contribution approach.[40] When deciding on the technical character of an invention, and thus whether it fulfils the initial requirement of an invention, the EPO follows the decisions of the Enlarged Board of Appeal supporting the approach adopted in the *Red Dove* case.

There is also a short-cut approach for the patentability of programs for computers specifically, the any hardware approach. This approach was established in *PBS PARTNERSHIP/Controlling pension benefits system* and was

[33] Decision of the Bundesgerichtshof, 27 March 1969 (X ZB 15/67) – '*Rote Taube (Red Dove)*'.

[34] ibid, Reasons, 3.

[35] G2/07 *Broccoli/PLANT BIOSCIENCE* of 09.12.2010; G1/08 *Tomatoes/STATE OF ISRAEL* of 09.12.2010, Reasons, 6.4.2.

[36] T208/84 *VICOM/Computer-related invention* of 15.7.1986.

[37] *Genentech's Patent* [1989] RPC 147; *Merrill Lynch's Application* [1989] RPC 561; *Gale's Application* [1991] RPC 305; *Fujitsu's Application* [1997] RPC 608.

[38] There were variations in the way in which this test was adopted but in all cases 'technical effect' was the important factor.

[39] European Patent Office, *Case Law of the Boards of Appeal of the European Patent Office* (9th edn, Druckerei CH Beck 2019) I.A.1.2.

[40] ibid I.A.1.4.1.b.

recently summarised in G1/19.[41] Originally, it was introduced for apparatus claims as opposed to apparatus and method claims. It was held that if a computer or system had 'the character of a concrete apparatus in the sense of a physical entity, man-made for a utilitarian purpose' it would be an invention for the purpose of the EPC.[42] The distinction between method claims and apparatus claims was blurred,[43] and eventually disappeared altogether.[44] Subsequently, the any hardware approach applies to both apparatus claims and method claims, confirming that the requirement for an invention in the case of computer-related subject matter is easily satisfied. Essentially, any subject matter that is a concrete apparatus, or is involved in the use of a concrete apparatus, will avoid exclusion under Article 52 EPC.

In *Aerotel/Macrossan* the UK Court of Appeal rejected the EPO any hardware approach.[45] It considered three approaches and, instead of following the jurisprudence of the EPO, it followed common law rules of precedence and continued to use the technical contribution approach. To simplify its application, a four-step test was established. According to that test, following claim construction, the actual contribution should be identified and an assessment undertaken as to whether it falls solely within excluded subject matter. Finally, the court decides whether the contribution is technical in nature.[46]

The High Court refused to follow the jurisprudence of the EPO in *Re Symbian's Application*.[47] However, in *Symbian v Comptroller General of Patents, Designs and Trademarks*,[48] the Court of Appeal believed that both approaches could be reconciled as a matter of broad principle. It was stated that by conflating the third and fourth steps of the *Aerotel/Macrossan* approach, the test could amount to the same as that of the EPO.[49] It was further emphasised that 'there is a need for a two-way dialogue between national tribunals and the EPO, coupled with a degree of mutual compromise', and that there must be an attempt to ensure that the consequent differences in terms of the outcome in particular patent cases are minimised.[50]

Both approaches have been criticised. The EPO has criticised the technical contribution approach for introducing issues of inventive step into the question

[41] T931/95 *PBS PARTNERSHIP/Controlling pension benefits system* of 08.9.2000; G1/19 *Pedestrian simulation* of 10.03.21.

[42] T931/95 *PBS PARTNERSHIP/Controlling pension benefits system* of 08.9.2000, Reasons, 5.

[43] T258/03 *HITACHI/Auction Method* of 21.4.2004.

[44] T424/03 *MICROSOFT/Data transfer with expanded clipboard formats* of 23.2.2006.

[45] *Aerotel Ltd v Telco Holdings Ltd & Macrossan's Patent Application* [2006] EWCA Civ 1371 (*Aerotel/Macrossan*).

[46] This test was subsequently modified in *Symbian Ltd v Comptroller General of Patents, Designs and Trademarks* [2008] EWCA Civ 1066 (*Symbian*).

[47] *Re Symbian's Application* [2009] RPC 1.

[48] *Symbian* [2008] EWCA Civ 1066.

[49] ibid [11].

[50] ibid [61].

of whether there is patentable subject matter.[51] The UK has criticised the technical character approach for setting the bar for patentability too low. However, both the EPO and UK courts seem to agree that when considered alongside the other requirements of patentability, there is unlikely to be any divergence in the outcome of individual cases overall.[52] The main reason is the EPO's requirement that for an invention to be inventive, it must be inventive by reason of its technical aspects only.[53] Therefore, an application could fulfil the requirement of having technical character at the EPO and therefore be an invention; however, it may fail under the test for inventive step, which takes into account the objective technical problem to be solved by the invention. Taking a holistic view, both the UK and the EPO require that the subject matter of an invention make a technical contribution to be patentable, albeit at different stages of examination.

In summary, the formal approach of UK courts and the EPO differ in these two areas of substantive patent law. Although these differences in approach may not be an issue when taking a holistic view of patentability, risks related to fragmentation in the form of inconsistent decisions remain here and in relation to the interpretation of various concepts. Importantly however, attempts towards convergence are being encouraged.

II. Towards Convergence – Judicial Dialogue and Cooperation

Strong attempts are being made by the institutions involved to interpret the EPC in a consistent manner. Methods similar to those being used in the field of international law are being used to respond to fragmentation in the European patent system, particularly judicial dialogue and cooperation. There is evidence of a concern on the part of the judiciary to implement patent law in line with the provisions of the EPC and the jurisprudence of the Boards of Appeal, other national courts and the CJEU.[54] Judicial dialogue and cooperation is happening quite successfully and is something that should be encouraged and formalised among all the institutions of the European patent system.

[51] *PBS PARTNERSHIP/Controlling pension benefits system* admitted a low hurdle for patentability but reiterated that the requirement for technicality would be required to pass the threshold of inventive step.

[52] N Fox and W Corbett, 'UK and EPO Approaches to Excluded Subject Matter and Inventive Step: Are Aerotel and Pozzoli Heading for the Rocks?' (2014) 36(9) *EIPR* 569, 573.

[53] T641/00 *Two identities/COMVIK* of 26.9.2002.

[54] For a discussion of this issue from the perspective of former and current UK judges, see R Jacob, 'The Relationship between European and National Courts in Intellectual Property Law' in A Ohly and J Pila (eds), *The Europeanization of Intellectual Property Law: Towards a European Legal Methodology* (Oxford University Press 2013) and C Birss, 'Unitary Rights and Judicial Respect in the EU – "Bringing Cool Back"' (2013) 3(3) *Queen Mary Journal of Intellectual Property* 195. See also Luginbuehl, *European Patent Law* 128–33.

There are two ways in which this is currently being achieved. First, judges from various institutions of the European patent system are considering one another's decisions. Second, additional initiatives are underway: members of the judiciary meet to discuss developments in patent law and areas where harmonisation can be achieved; national court judges are being appointed as external members on the Enlarged Board of Appeal; and judges can undertake judicial internships at the EPO.

A. Decision-making

The consideration of judgments is taking place in multiple forms: national courts consider decisions from the Boards of Appeal, other national courts and the CJEU; the Boards of Appeal consider decisions from national courts and the CJEU; and the CJEU also considers Board of Appeal decisions and judgments from national courts.

i. National Courts Considering Board of Appeal Decisions

UK courts have been very active in this regard. The promotion of a consistent interpretation of the EPC is evident in many judicial decisions. For example, in *Merrell Dow v Norton* it was stated by the UK House of Lords (now Supreme Court):

> It is … the *duty* of the United Kingdom courts to construe Section 2 so that, as far as possible, it has the same effect as Article 54 [EPC]. For this purpose, it must have regard for the decisions of the European Patent Office (EPO) on the construction of the EPC. These decisions are not strictly binding upon courts in the United Kingdom but they are *great persuasive authority*: first, because they are decisions of expert courts (the Boards of Appeal and the Enlarged Board of Appeal of the EPO) involved daily in the administration of the EPC and secondly, because *it would be highly undesirable for the provisions of the EPC to be construed differently* in the EPO from the way they are interpreted in the national courts of a Contracting State [emphasis added].[55]

Indeed, there is a duty upon the UK to interpret EPC provisions in a way that, as far as possible, has the same effect as the EPC provisions. This duty emanates from the previously mentioned section 130(7) Patents Act 1977, which states as much. This provision has been observed in case law of the UK Court of Appeal, such as in *Genentech Inc's Patent*, where it was declared:

> If observance to this provision involves what might appear to be a heretical departure from established practice then this must be laid at the door of the legislator, and taken as disclosing the intention of Parliament to observe the European Patent Convention.[56]

[55] *Merrell Dow Pharmaceutical Inc v Norton & Co Ltd* [1996] RPC 76, 82.
[56] *Genentech Inc's Patent* [1989] RPC 147, 197.

In *Merell Dow*, the Court made clear that the decisions of the Boards of Appeal should be considered persuasive authority and considered by the UK courts. This was further emphasised in *Biogen v Medeva*, where Lord Hoffmann's judgment realigned the practice of the UK courts and the Boards of Appeal on sufficiency.[57] Although, in the end, the UK Court came to a different final conclusion to that of the Technical Board of Appeal, it was said that there was no divergence in the jurisprudence of the courts.[58] As pointed out by Ian Karet, the Court 'went out of their way' to present the decisions of the UK courts as consistent with those of the EPO, confirming the relevance of EPO decisions in the UK.[59] In its judgment, the divergent outcomes in the case were attributed to the different issues that had been argued before the House of Lords and the EPO, as well as the EPO having seemingly ignored previous jurisprudence that supported the conclusion of the UK Court.[60]

The UK Supreme Court also considered in detail a Board of Appeal decision concerning the same patent in *Human Genome Science v Eli Lilly*.[61] However, the Court also noted that although this practice of considering the decisions of the Boards of Appeal should happen, that did not mean that the UK courts had to follow the Board's reasoning.[62] It was stated that

> [w]hile consistency of approach is important, there has to be room for dialogue between a national court and the EPO (as well as between national courts themselves). Nonetheless, where the Board has adopted a consistent approach to an issue in a number of decisions, it would require very unusual facts to justify a national court not following that approach.[63]

The Supreme Court is promoting a consistent approach to interpretation; however, it is also leaving a door open in case the Boards of Appeal are taking the law 'in an inappropriate direction'.[64] By promoting this kind of practice, courts in the UK are encouraged to follow the jurisprudence of the Boards of Appeal, yet they are not forced to do so. This allows for continued conversation and dialogue.

ii. National Courts Considering Other National Court Decisions

A second aspect of domestic judicial practice that promotes cooperation is the consideration of the decisions and interpretations of other national courts.

[57] *Biogen Inc v Medeva* [1996] UKHL 18. However, this was later overturned for product patents in *Generics (UK) Ltd v Lundbeck A/S* [2009] UKHL 12.

[58] *Biogen v Medeva*, [77].

[59] I Karet, 'Analysis: English Courts and the EPO: What Next?' (1997) 2 *IPQ* 244, 246.

[60] ibid 246.

[61] *Human Genome Sciences Inc (HGS) v Eli Lilly* [2011] UKSC 51 [42]–[92], [103]–[111], [114]–[115], [117]–[118], [120]–[123], [126]–[129], [134].

[62] ibid [87].

[63] ibid.

[64] ibid.

In *Grimme v Scott*,[65] the UK Court of Appeal emphasised the importance of taking the decisions of other national courts into account, even if no such decisions are presented to the Court by counsel.

The judges in that case decided to do their own research into the question of whether a case of contributory infringement had arisen. It was stated that while conducting this research, an opportunity arose that allowed them to ask judicial colleagues in Germany and the Netherlands if they had had any similar cases on the matter; in the course of that inquiry it was found, to the judges' reported astonishment, that the Dutch courts had previously considered a case concerning Scott's machine.[66] The Court was astonished because neither party, particularly Grimme, had brought this case to their attention. They went on to say:

> Advocates should recognise that where a point of patent law of general importance, such as the construction of a provision which by Treaty (either the EPC or the Community Patent Convention) is to be implemented by states parties to those conventions, has been decided by a court, particularly a higher court, of another member state, the decision matters here. For, despite the fact that there is no common ultimate patent court for Europe, it is of obvious importance to all the countries of the European Patent Union or the parties to the Community Patent Convention, that as far as possible the same legal rules apply across all the countries where the provisions of the Conventions have been implemented. An important decision in one member state may well be of strong persuasive value in all the others, particularly where the judgment contains clear reasoning on the point.
>
> Broadly we think the principle in our courts – and indeed that in the courts of other member states – should be to try to follow the reasoning of an important decision in another country. Only if the court of one state is convinced that the reasoning of a court in another member state is erroneous should it depart from a point that has been authoritatively decided there. Increasingly that has become the practice in a number of countries, particularly in the important patent countries of France, Germany, Holland and England and Wales. Nowadays we refer to each other's decisions with a frequency which would have been hardly imaginable even twenty years ago. And we do try to be consistent where possible.
>
> The Judges of the patent courts of the various countries of Europe have thereby been able to create some degree of uniformity even though the European Commission and the politicians continue to struggle on the long, long road which one day will give Europe a common patent court.[67]

As well as advocates being encouraged to present decisions from other courts on the same issues, which reflects the suggestions made when responding to fragmentation in the context of the international legal system, the Court has also emphasised the importance of taking the decisions of other national courts into consideration. The court again left a door open for divergence in cases where

[65] *Grimme Maschinenfabrik v Derek Scott (t/a Scotts Potato Machinery)* [2010] EWCA Civ 1110.
[66] ibid [77].
[67] ibid [79]–[81].

national courts disagree on the reasoning behind a decision, but the main point was that of promoting consideration and cooperation.

This practice was encouraged more recently by the UK Supreme Court in *Schütz v Werit*[68] and *Warner-Lambert v Generics*.[69] In *Schütz*, the Court mentioned in its reasoning that it was relevant to consider four decisions of the German courts.[70] The reason for doing so was that Germany was also a Contracting State to the EPC. However, it was also said that national courts do have different approaches in relation to many issues and that 'while complete consistency of approach may be achieved one day, it is not a feasible or realistic possibility at the moment'.[71] The Court went on to say that 'given the existence of the EPC (and the CPC), it is sensible for national courts at least to learn from each other and to seek to move towards, rather than away from, each other's approaches'.[72]

In *Warner-Lambert*, the Court considered decisions in France, Germany and Sweden on the same patent, stating that 'if courts in other jurisdictions have upheld Claim 3, that may serve as a reality check against my own, less favourable conclusions'.[73] It was stated that it would be 'unfortunate' if divergent decisions arose concerning the same patent; however, after examining other decisions, it was ultimately decided that none could be followed entirely because of the different questions that were considered.[74]

These are important statements for it is with this type of interaction that harmonisation will move forward. Although it may be a slow method, given the remaining possibility of disagreement, it appears to be an effective one because instead of waiting for legislation to be debated and entered into force, progress can be made on a case-by-case basis.[75] It was noted in the statement above by the Court in *Grimme v Scott* that the judgments of other jurisdictions are now referred to frequently by courts in England & Wales, Germany, the Netherlands and France, relative to 20 years ago. This is indeed the case as this practice of taking other national court jurisprudence into account can also be seen in other jurisdictions.

In Germany, not only has the Supreme Court ruled that German national courts have to take the decisions of the Boards of Appeal into account, it went further and stated that they must also consider the decisions of other national courts relating to similar subject matter.

The former requirement was first introduced by the German Supreme Court in the *Zahnkranzfräser* case.[76] This decision was subsequently confirmed and

[68] *Schütz v Werit* [2013] UKSC 16 (*Schütz*).

[69] *Warner-Lambert Company LLC v Generics (UK) Ltd t/a Mylan and another* [2018] UKSC 56 (*Warner-Lambert*).

[70] *Schütz*, [39].

[71] ibid [40].

[72] ibid.

[73] *Warner-Lambert*, [55].

[74] ibid [55]–[60].

[75] As will be seen below with regard to *Actavis v Eli Lilly* [2017] UKSC 48.

[76] Decision of the Bundesgerichtshof, 5 May 1998 – X ZR 57/96 '*Zahnkranzfräser (Gear rim mill)*'.

expanded in the *Walzenformgebungsmaschine* case.[77] In the latter case, the German Supreme Court also stated that the national courts, if diverging from another decision regarding similar issues, must, where appropriate, give reasons as to why this divergence is occurring.[78] However, a caveat was given. The German Supreme Court expressed that the German courts were not bound by these decisions, that any case deviating from similar judgments was not automatically defective, and this would not necessarily be an appropriate reason for an appeal to the German Supreme Court.[79]

From this judgment, it is evident that similar guidance to that of the UK national courts is being given to German national courts. The door is left open for possible divergence; however, this should only be in cases where there is an appropriate reason. The requirement that these reasons be explained will assist in discovering where the lines of divergence emerge, and how or whether those lines can be drawn closer together in order to achieve further harmonisation.

In France, proceedings from other courts are also increasingly considered.[80] Searches are conducted as to proceedings taking place in other jurisdictions, and their relevance to the case at hand is examined. Examples include *Mylan v AstraZeneca*, *Warner-Lambert v Sandoz*, *MVF 3 APS v S.A.R.L Intelligent Insect Control*, *Lilly France v Sanofi-Aventis Deutschland*, and *Akzo Nobel v Teva Sante*.[81] However, due to the brevity of French court judgments, it is not always known how relevant other decisions have been in these decisions and others. The relevant cases are cited and often analysed to a certain extent, but the importance of these decisions is not clear.

It can be argued, however, that the relevance of other decisions will depend on the similarity of the issues and the facts of the cases, some being more relevant than others. That other proceedings are even mentioned in these decisions implies that they are at least discussed and considered, even if the same conclusion is not reached.

Although some higher-level courts have been encouraging courts at different levels and in different countries to take other patent law decisions into account, it has been on the basis of this being a persuasive authority. Taking the argument one step further, judges of the European patent system may have a positive duty

[77] Decision of the Bundesgerichtshof, 15 April 2010 – Xa ZB 10/09 '*Walzenformgebungsmaschine (Roller-forming-machine)*'.

[78] Luginbuehl, *European Patent Law* 11.

[79] An English summary of the *Walzenformgebungsmaschine* case was provided by Bardehle Pagenberg, IP Report III [2011] available at http://eplaw.org/de-walzenformgebungsmaschine-2/.

[80] Including the decisions of the Boards of Appeal.

[81] Tribunal de Grande Instance de Paris, 3rd chamber 3rd section, 1 July 2016 (15/05880), *AstraZeneca v Mylan*; Tribunal de Grande Instance de Paris, 13 October 2015 (15/58725), *Warner-Lambert v Sandoz*; Cour d'Appel de Montpellier, Civil division section 2, 17 September 2015 (13/05047), *MVF 3 APS v Intelligent Insect Control*; Tribunal de Grande Instance de Paris, 23 September 2014 (14/58023), *Lilly France v Sanofi*; Tribunal de Grande Instance de Paris, 3rd chamber 3rd section, 27 September 2012 (12/13507), *Akzo Nobel v Teva Sante*.

to cooperate with one another, their respective countries having freely signed up to the EPC.

iii. EPO Interpretation and Consideration of National Court Decisions

The Boards of Appeal also contribute to the informal harmonisation of the European patent system in manners similar to those used in the international legal system. They do so when considering national court decisions and through methods of interpretation contained in the Vienna Convention.[82]

The Boards of Appeal use various methods when interpreting the provisions of the EPC. One method of interpretation used is that conveyed in Articles 31 and 32 of the Vienna Convention, which provide guidance on the interpretation of treaties. While the Vienna Convention entered into force in 1980 and only applies to treaties concluded after the entry into force of the Convention, the Boards of Appeal have nonetheless applied its rules in numerous decisions. In G5/83, the Enlarged Board of Appeal stated that

> there are convincing precedent for applying the rules for interpretation of treaties incorporated in the Vienna Convention to a treaty to which in terms they do not apply … After a careful study of the whole subject, the Enlarged Board of Appeal concludes that the European Patent Office should do the same.[83]

The result is a commitment by the EPO to interpreting the provisions of the EPC in good faith and according to their ordinary meaning, in their context, including in light of the object and purpose of the EPC, unless they can be shown to have been intended by the Contracting States to have a special meaning.[84]

In addition, the Enlarged Board of Appeal went on to say that 'in the interpretation of international treaties which provide a legal basis for the rights and duties of individuals and corporate bodies', which is the case with the EPC, it is 'necessary to pay attention to questions of harmonisation of national and international rules of law'.[85] It was expressed that this aspect of interpretation is not dealt with by the provisions of the Vienna Convention but 'is particularly important where the provisions of an international treaty', such as the EPC, 'have been taken over into national legislation'.[86] Most significantly, the Enlarged Board of Appeal stated: '[I]t is incumbent upon the European Patent Office, and particularly its Boards of Appeal, to take into consideration the decisions and expressions of opinion of courts and industrial property offices in Contracting States'.[87] Therefore,

[82] Vienna Convention on the Law of Treaties (Vienna, 23 May 1969, 1155 UNTS 331).
[83] G5/83 *Second medical indication* of 05.12.1984, Reasons, 4.
[84] G2/08 *Dosage regime/ABBOTT RESPITORY* of 19.2.2010.
[85] G5/83, Reasons, 6.
[86] ibid.
[87] ibid.

it can be seen that the Boards of Appeal also promote the informal harmonisation of European patent law, and as G5/83 displays, they are willing to consider the reasoning and interpretation of European patent laws from Contracting State courts.

Although this practice appears to be unequivocal, there have been subsequent cases where the Enlarged Board of Appeal has introduced some reservations to this statement, for example, when the national law approach contravenes the intentions of the EPC. In G1/13, the Enlarged Board of Appeal stated:

> There are of course limits on the extent to which the EPO should follow national law. For example, a provision of national law which purported to confer on a company procedural rights which were contrary to the EPC could not be acknowledged by the EPO.[88]

The Boards of Appeal have also discussed this issue and have concluded that considerations of harmonisation do not exonerate a Board from its duty to act as an independent judicial body with the function of interpreting the EPC and deciding in the last instance matters relating to patent grant.[89]

Furthermore, the emphasis placed on interpreting the EPC with a view to promoting harmonisation was criticised because not all national laws are harmonised and therefore it would be impossible to decide which interpretation from which national court the Boards of Appeal ought to follow.[90] However, through more dialogue, a Board could look at the different interpretations of national courts and decide on a 'best practice' approach.

Additionally, national decisions have no binding effect on the Boards of Appeal. The EPC is the only source of law that is binding on the EPO. Therefore, proceedings before the EPO are decided in accordance with the EPC and even if the reasoning of a national court would lead the EPO to the same conclusion, the Board must first apply the provisions of the EPC and assess the jurisprudence of the Boards of Appeal in order to make a final decision.[91] This may explain why, in practice, national decisions are still rarely explicitly taken into consideration and why, for the Boards of Appeal, the EPO has the final say in matters relating to the interpretation of the EPC.

iv. Boards of Appeal Considering CJEU Decisions and the CJEU Considering Board of Appeal Decisions

Albeit less often, the Boards of Appeal have also considered the jurisprudence of the CJEU, especially when deciding on matters to do with biotechnological inventions and vice versa. This is because the EU Directive on the protection

[88] G1/13 *Admissibility of referral* of 25.11.2014, Reasons, 8.

[89] T154/04 *Estimating sales activity/DUNS LICENSING ASSOCIATES* of 15.11.2006, Reasons, 3.

[90] T452/91 of 5.07.1995, Reasons, 5.4.1.

[91] ibid.

of biotechnological inventions has been incorporated into the Implementing Regulations of the EPC as a supplementary means of interpretation.[92] These decisions will be discussed in detail in the next chapter.

v. *Referrals by National Courts*

Judicial dialogue already exists formally within the EU between the Member States and the CJEU in matters concerning the protection of biotechnological inventions. Member States are under an obligation to refer questions on the interpretation of this Directive to the CJEU.[93] This has occurred in a number of cases and although the resulting decisions have caused quite a controversy,[94] the referral is a useful mechanism that could be introduced more broadly across the European patent system.

In fact, this was previously attempted. In *Aerotel/Macrossan*, the UK Court of Appeal attempted to make a 'reference' to the Enlarged Board of Appeal via the President of the EPO. A Board of Appeal can decide to refer questions to the Enlarged Board of Appeal or following a request from a party if it is required to ensure uniform application of the law, or if a point of fundamental importance arises.[95] The President of the EPO may also refer a point of law but only where two Boards of Appeal have given different decisions.[96] In *Aerotel/Macrossan*, the Court of Appeal proposed some questions regarding the patentability of programs for computers:

> It is formally no business of ours to define questions to be asked of an Enlarged Board of Appeal. What we say now is only put forward in case the President of the EPO finds it helpful. If he thinks it pointless or arrogant of us to go this far, he is of course entirely free to ignore all we say. Nonetheless in hope that there is a spirit of co-operation between national courts and the EPO we ventured to ask the parties what questions might be posed by the President of an Enlarged Board pursuant to Art. 112.[97]

Then President of the EPO, Alain Pompidou, replied and made no reference to the Enlarged Board of Appeal; however, the next President, Alison Brimelow, did in G3/08.[98] The questions were found to be inadmissible.[99]

The reference has been described as disappointing because the questions referred to the Board were not seen as reflecting those that had originally been

[92] Biotech Directive; Chapter V, Rule 26(1) Implementing Regulations to the EPC 2000.

[93] As a result of Article 267 TFEU.

[94] Case C-34/10 *Oliver Brüstle v Greenpeace eV* ECLI:EU:C:2011:669; Case C-364/13 *International Stem Cell Corporation v Comptroller General of Patents, Designs and Trade Marks* ECLI:EU:C:2014:2451 (*ISCC*).

[95] Article 112(1)(a) EPC.

[96] Article 112(1)(b) EPC.

[97] *Aerotel/Macrossan*, [75].

[98] Jacob, 'The Relationship between European and National Courts' 196–98.

[99] G3/08 *Programs for computers* of 12.5.2010.

proposed and the attempted experiment was ineffective.[100] Despite the inadmissibility, if an official line of communication were opened between Contracting States and the Boards of Appeal, akin to the CJEU referral mechanism, further dialogue could follow. According to Stefan Luginbuehl, however, this would require an amendment of the EPC to put a greater distance between the EPO (as an examining authority) and the Enlarged Board of Appeal (as a decision-making body), the Boards currently being part of, rather than independent of, the EPO.[101]

B. Case Study in Cooperation – Claim Construction

As shown, there have been many statements in judgments that the practice of various institutions in the European patent system should be considered and a consistent approach towards interpretation adopted where possible. Although these efforts will not always lead to convergence,[102] in some instances, they can. The most recent and potentially most impactful example of judicial cooperation as a response to fragmentation came in a decision of the UK Supreme Court and shows how this practice can promote harmonisation in the European patent system and the impact that this can have.

i. Background

Prior to the implementation of the EPC, countries in Europe also had different methods of claim construction. There were two ends of the interpretative spectrum – a strict literal approach and a sign post approach.

Originally in the UK, a strict literal interpretation of the text of the claims was used. This involved viewing the claims of the patent application as the definition of the invention: whatever was claimed was within the scope of protection of the patent and whatever was not claimed was outside it. This was the case even if the difference between the claimed invention and the alleged infringing product was insignificant to the functioning of the invention. The issue was that minor changes could be made to a protected invention and that competing products could be placed on the market without amounting to an infringement. Therefore, the UK courts began to implement a new method of interpretation – the 'pith and marrow' approach.

Here, the courts would determine the 'essential feature' of the claimed invention. If the alleged invention took the essential feature or 'pith and marrow' of the patented invention, that would constitute an infringement. However, it was

[100] Jacob, 'The Relationship between European and National Courts' 196.

[101] Luginbuehl, *European Patent Law* 144.

[102] E Lageza, 'Mapping Judicial Dialogue across National Borders: An Exploratory Network Study of Learning from Lobbying among European Intellectual Property Judges' (2012) 8(2) *Utrecht Law Review* 115, 125.

questioned from whose perspective the essential features of the invention should be determined. That problem came into focus in *Catnic v Hill & Smith*, which was decided before the EPC became law in the UK.[103]

The invention concerned steel lintels, whose rear member, in the Catnic patent application, was 'extending vertically'.[104] The Hill & Smith invention concerned a very similar product, however, the rear member 'inclined 6° or 8° from the vertical'.[105] At first instance, Whitford J held that although there had been no 'textual infringement' of the claims, Hill & Smith 'had taken all the essential features of a number of claims' and that was held to be an infringement.[106]

The case went to the Court of Appeal, where it was held that the essential feature of the invention was that the rear member extended vertically and thus, there was no infringement.[107] The issue of patent infringement reached the House of Lords, where it was stated by Lord Diplock that 'a patent specification should be given a purposive construction rather than a purely literal one'.[108]

The House of Lords decided that patent claims ought to be viewed from the perspective of the person skilled in the art, who should examine the claims from the perspective of the patentee and consider their intention. The scope of protection was therefore dependent on the intention of the patentee, striking what was seen as a fairer balance between the interests of the parties involved.

Germany was at the other end of the interpretative spectrum. Originally a signpost approach was used, the claims only serving as a guideline to the scope of protection. More important in German claim construction was the 'direct subject matter' and 'technical teaching' of the invention, and the 'general inventive idea'.[109] The actual wording of the claims was far less important, which was strikingly different to the literal approach, and a lot more flexible.[110] In comparison to the purposive approach (the early stages of which were seen in *Catnic*), the sign post approach was still significantly different, owing to its lack of focus on the wording of the claims.

The differences in these interpretative approaches were an issue because, by having such differences, contrasting decisions were more likely to emerge on cases to do with the same patented invention. That issue became even more significant on the entry into force of the EPC.

[103] *Catnic v Hill & Smith Limited* [1982] RPC 183.
[104] ibid 185.
[105] In fact, in a previous design, Hill & Smith had taken all the features of the Catnic invention. They had intended to manufacture this product until they received a writ for infringement from Catnic.
[106] *Catnic v Hill & Smith Limited* [1978] FSR 405.
[107] *Catnic v Hill & Smith Limited* [1979] FSR 619 (CA).
[108] *Catnic* [1982] RPC 183, 243.
[109] M Fisher, 'New Protocol, Same Old Story? Patent Claim Construction in 2007; Looking Back with a View to the Future' (2008) 2 *IPQ* 133, 148. For a detailed examination of claim construction in the UK up to 2007, with a focus on Germany in chapter 7, see M Fisher, *Fundamentals of Patent Law: Interpretation and Scope of Protection* (Hart Publishing 2007). For a more recent discussion, see D Booton, 'The Construction of Patent Claims' (2020) 40 *Legal Studies* 651.
[110] Fisher, 'New Protocol' 148.

ii. Impact of the EPC

Following the entry into force of the EPC, Contracting States had to comply with Article 69 EPC, which states: 'The extent of the protection conferred by a European patent or a European patent application shall be determined by the claims. Nevertheless, the description and drawings shall be used to interpret the claims.'

The Protocol on the Interpretation of Article 69 EPC was also introduced in an attempt to bring Contracting States closer together in how patent claims were interpreted. It therefore requires Contracting States to use similar methods of interpretation:

> Article 69 should not be interpreted in the sense that the extent of the protection conferred by a European patent is to be understood as that defined by the strict, literal meaning of the wording used in the claims, the description and drawings being employed only for the purpose of resolving an ambiguity found in the claims. Neither should it be interpreted in the sense that the claims serve only as a guideline and that the actual protection conferred may extend to what, from a consideration of the description and the drawings by a person skilled in the art, the patentee has contemplated. On the contrary, it is to be interpreted as defining a position between these extremes which combines a fair protection for the patentee with a reasonable degree of certainty for third parties.[111]

In 2000, in a further attempt to harmonise patent claim interpretation, the wording of the Protocol on the Interpretation of Article 69 EPC was amended slightly, and a second article was added.[112] The original article remains essentially the same, and the new Article 2 states: 'For the purpose of determining the extent of protection conferred by a European patent, due account shall be taken of any element which is equivalent to an element specified in the claims.'

The Protocol was and remains extremely vague, however, its inclusion is important. This is especially so because the EPC is a convention that is primarily for the grant of patents, not their enforcement. These legislative provisions were the EPC's attempt to harmonise a quite divergent area and the results were variable.

The Patents Act 1977 (UK) implemented the provisions of the EPC into national law in the UK. Therefore, the judiciary became obligated to take the provisions of the EPC into account. As mentioned, *Catnic* was decided before the EPC was implemented into national law in the UK. The next important case regarding patent claim interpretation was *Improver v Remington.*[113] Here, the Patents Court took the opportunity to decide on patent claim construction under the new law. In doing so, it was stated that a purposive approach towards claim construction ought to be taken and three questions were formulated that courts could ask when dealing with patent infringement and variants.

[111] Wording of the 1973 Convention.

[112] Protocol on the Interpretation of Article 69 EPC of 5 October 1973 as revised by the Act revising the EPC of 29 November 2000.

[113] *Improver Corp v Remington Consumer Product Ltd* [1990] FSR 181.

First, it is asked whether the change makes a difference to the functioning of the invention.[114] Then, it is asked whether that would have been obvious to the person skilled in the art at the date of publication.[115] Finally, the perspective of the patentee is taken into account, where it is asked whether the person skilled in the art would have thought that the patentee intended that a strict reading was an essential requirement of the invention.[116] These questions maintain the approach that had been taken in *Catnic* regarding claim construction.

The *Improver* questions became the go-to questions for any case to do with variants and infringement over the next 15 years in the UK. In subsequent cases, they became known as the 'Protocol Questions'.[117] However, how they were being used was a cause for concern to Lord Hoffmann, who took the opportunity to clarify matters in *Kirin-Amgen v Hoechst Marion*.[118]

In *Kirin-Amgen*, Lord Hoffmann explained that the Protocol Questions were to be used as guidelines because in certain instances it would be very difficult to apply the questions to the facts of the case.[119] Following that judgment, the courts in the UK showed reluctance in applying the Protocol Questions and instead followed the guidance of Lord Hoffmann in *Kirin-Amgen*. For 15 further years this practice progressed, with courts and practitioners becoming familiar with the approach taken.

This was not the only issue that caused controversy regarding claim construction. As mentioned, in 2000, an amendment was made to the EPC that had a follow-on impact in the UK. Article 2 of the Protocol on the Interpretation of Article 69 EPC was introduced, which required that due account be taken of equivalents.

The issue of equivalents was discussed in the *Improver* case since there was an equivalents clause in the description of the patent application in suit. However, the point was given more extensive consideration in *Kirin-Amgen*. Lord Hoffmann discussed the doctrine of equivalents as it exists in other countries and made it very clear that the UK had no such doctrine. He was of the opinion that a doctrine of equivalents allows the patentee to unjustifiably extend their protection beyond the claims to something that 'performs substantially the same function in substantially the same way to obtain the same result' as the invention.[120]

Lord Hoffmann said that the problem was that once the protection expanded outside the claims, a question arises as to where the line is to be drawn with variants.[121] To avoid the issue of non-infringing immaterial variations, he favoured an approach that abandoned literalism in construction, rather than the

[114] ibid 189.
[115] ibid.
[116] ibid.
[117] *Wheatly v Drillsafe* [2001] RPC 133, 142.
[118] *Kirin-Amgen Inc & Ors v Hoechst Marion Roussel Ltd & Ors* [2004] UKHL 46 (*Kirin-Amgen*).
[119] ibid 66.
[120] ibid 37 and 38.
[121] ibid 39.

introduction of a doctrine of equivalents.[122] His view was that by introducing the purposive approach to claim construction, this would take any immaterial variation into account. It was seen as an element of construction and therefore within the scope of the claims, rather than outside.

The implementation of the provisions of the EPC and the guidance on claim interpretation had little to no effect in the UK. The Protocol was and is so vague that it can accommodate several approaches to patent claim construction. It has been described as 'a masterpiece of ambiguity' and criticised for having allowed Contracting States to continue using their own differing methods of claim construction, while holding true to the provisions of the EPC.[123] This is not to say that the Protocol has been ineffective. It is difficult to ensure that all EPC Contracting States interpret patent applications in the same manner, especially given the differences that exist in national economies and procedures.

Courts in the UK had already moved away from a literal approach to claim construction, as seen in *Catnic*. Further, Lord Hoffmann made it very clear that the practice in the UK regarding equivalents at that time was in line with the EPC and with the Protocol and therefore no changes were necessary.

This was not the case in Germany. To implement the provisions of the EPC, a new Patents Act was introduced in 1981.[124] The new legislation was interpreted by the German Supreme Court in the landmark *Formstein* decision.[125] The Supreme Court stated:

> The question was not whether the 'principle' of the solution to the technical problem by the alleged infringement coincided with that of the patented invention, but whether the average person skilled in the art on the basis of his specialist knowledge could discover from the patent claims, taking the specification and drawings into account, whatever solution was used in the alleged infringement to achieve the same effect.[126]

This is a significant departure from previous practice in Germany. Following *Formstein*, a quintet of cases was heard by the German Supreme Court, where it was reiterated, again and again, that the claims were now to be 'not only a point of departure but the decisive basis for the determination of the scope of protection'.[127]

One of the most relevant of these cases was the *Schneidmesser* decision, wherein the Court took the guidance from *Formstein* and rearticulated that guidance into a

[122] ibid 42.

[123] IC Baillie, 'Where Goes Europe? The European Patent' (1976) 58 *Journal of the Patent and Trademark Office Society* 153, 167.

[124] Patentgesetz in der Fassung der Bekanntmachung vom 16. Dezember 1980 (BGBI. 1981 I S. 1), das zuletzt durch Artikel 1 des Gesetzes vom 30. August 2021 (BGBI. I S. 4074) geändert worden ist.

[125] Decision of the Bundesgerichtshof, 29 April 1986 – X ZR 28/85, translated in *Formstein (Moulded Curbstone)* [1991] RPC 597 (in the Federal Supreme Court of Germany).

[126] ibid 50.

[127] Fisher, 'New Protocol' 149.

series of questions which could be used in future cases. The questions, as expressed in English by Peter Meier-Beck, German Supreme Court Judge, are as follows:

> Does the modified embodiment solve the problem underlying the invention with means that have objectively the same technical effect? … If the first question … has to be answered in the negative, the contested embodiment is outside the scope of protection. Otherwise we have to ask the second question: Was the person skilled in the art, using his specialist knowledge, able to find the modified means at the priority date as having the same effect? … If the second question … has to be answered in the negative, the contested embodiment is outside of the scope of protection. Otherwise we have to ask the third question … Are the considerations that the person skilled in the art had to apply oriented to the technical teaching of the patent claim in such a way that the person skilled in the art took the modified embodiment into account as being an equivalent solution?[128]

As expected, these questions have been compared to the *Improver* questions on numerous occasions,[129] and are certainly similar in some respects; however, there are several differences. As elaborated on by Meier-Beck, the first *Schneidmesser* question is only interested in the result of the variant rather than the function, way and result, as in the first *Improver* question.[130] The second questions are both similar, so long as obviousness is interpreted in the same way and according to the EPC.[131] The third *Schneidmesser* question asks 'whether the considerations of the person skilled in the art are so close to the technical teaching of the patent claim that the variant appears to be an equivalent alternative to an embodiment that realises the wording of the patent claim', thus returning to the elements of the first *Improver* question relating to function.[132] Therefore, although different in certain respects, both the *Schneidmesser* and the *Improver* questions involve a value judgement.[133]

This departure from previous practice shows the impact of the legislative provisions in the EPC on the law in Germany. Courts now look at the claims of a patent as a decisive factor in determining the scope of protection. Further, the implementation of questions somewhat similar to those in *Improver* encourages harmonisation. However, it has been argued that divergences remain in decisions due to the philosophical foundations of the patent systems in Germany and the UK – the former being focused on rewarding the inventor and the latter focusing on boosting innovation.[134]

[128] P Meier-Beck, 'The Scope of Patent Protection – The Test for Determining Equivalence' (2005) 36(3) *IIC* 339.

[129] For example ibid and Lord Hoffmann's judgment in *Kirin-Amgen*.

[130] Meier-Beck, 'The Scope of Patent Protection' 343.

[131] ibid.

[132] ibid.

[133] ibid 344.

[134] Fisher, 'New Protocol' 161. See also W Aoun, '"Pith and Marrow is Dead … Long Live Pith and Marrow": The Doctrine of Equivalents after *Actavis*' (2022) 44(4) *EIPR Special Issue: Patents in a Changing Europe* 231.

iii. Divergence

Although Article 69 EPC and the Protocol did change legal practice in certain EPC Contracting States regarding the determination of the scope of protection of a patent, problems remained. National courts were reaching different outcomes in infringement actions relating to the same patented invention, despite interpreting national laws that all implemented the provisions of the EPC.

The most famous example of this is the *Improver* case. It was argued by the claimant that their European patent, designated in numerous Contracting States, was infringed by the defendant in the UK, Germany and the Netherlands. Actions were brought in each of the relevant national courts. In the UK, it was decided that there had been no infringement, whereas courts in Germany and the Netherlands decided that there had been an infringement.[135]

Despite the courts all referring to the EPC and the Protocol on Interpretation of Article 69 EPC, divergent results emerged.[136] *Improver* was not a stand-alone case. Divergent decisions in cases relating to the same patented invention happened again and again.[137]

The issue of equivalents was seen as the point where the UK courts differed from other European courts.[138] In Germany and France, for example, a doctrine of equivalents can be used. Yet how it is implemented differs from country to country.

In Germany, the *Schneidmesser* questions are used to determine if a variant is an equivalent. In France, two means can be considered equivalent if they realise the same function or result, and so the effect or purpose of the variant is the central aspect to be considered when using the French doctrine of equivalents. Furthermore, the French courts do not look at obviousness nor the intent of the patentee. However, the relevant function must be new, otherwise there will never be infringement by equivalents.

As mentioned, the courts in the UK went to extreme lengths to say that there is no doctrine of equivalents in the UK.[139] The Supreme Court was of the view that a purposive approach to claim construction included taking approximations into account, and therefore, the UK was interpreting claims in line with the EPC advice.[140] The Supreme Court also stressed that there was no longer a difference

[135] UK: *Improver Corp v Remington Consumer Product Ltd* [1990] FSR 181; Germany: Decision of the Oberlandesgericht Düsseldorf, 21 November 1991 – 2 U 27/89 '*Improver*', translated in (1993) 24 *IIC* 838; Netherlands: translated in [1993] 24 *IIC* 832.

[136] B Sherman, 'Patent Claim Interpretation: The Impact of the Protocol on Interpretation' (1991) 54(4) *MLR* 499.

[137] Luginbuehl, *European Patent Law* 10; Cremers and others, 'Patent Litigation in Europe'; Mejer and van Pottlesberghe de la Potterie, 'Economic Incongruities'.

[138] For a detailed investigation into the interpretation of patents in Austria, Switzerland, Germany, France, Italy, the Netherlands, Sweden and the UK see J Pagenberg and W Cornish (eds) *Interpretation of Patents in Europe: Application of Article 69 EPC* (Heymanns 2007).

[139] That is, until July 2017, as will be discussed below.

[140] *Kirin-Amgen*, 48.

in approach to the construction of claims in the UK and Germany.[141] However, the prevailing view at the time in Germany was that a harmonised position had not yet been reached, owing to the fact that the possibility of a formal doctrine of equivalence was rejected by Lord Hoffmann, whereas it played a significant role in the interpretation of patent claims in Germany.[142]

In 2007, following a detailed investigation by a number of authors (including academics, judges and litigators) into the practice of eight countries in Europe with regard to the interpretation of patents, Jochen Pagenberg concluded that among all questions discussed, 'one problem appears as the most difficult to solve, namely how equivalents will be treated in the various jurisdictions all over Europe'.[143] At the time, as mentioned, the UK practice towards (or in this case, against) equivalence stood out from the approaches of other European jurisdictions, and the rejection of the doctrine of equivalence was seen as disregarding the balance required by the Protocol on the Interpretation of Article 69 EPC.[144] However, developments in the UK have gone a long way in providing a solution to this most difficult problem and provide an excellent example of how judicial dialogue and cooperation can lead to greater harmonisation in practice.

iv. Convergence

In July 2017, the interpretation of patent claims was 'clarified' once again, changing legal practice in the UK significantly by aligning with its continental neighbours and also arguably with the EPC. *Actavis v Eli Lilly* has had and will continue to have a huge impact on patent law practice.[145]

The question before the Court was whether Eli Lilly's patent, on the use of pemetrexed disodium in the manufacture of a medicine for use in combination with vitamin B12 for the treatment of cancer, was infringed (directly and/or indirectly) by Actavis's proposed products that did not use pemetrexed disodium, but pemetrexed diacid, pemetrexed ditromethamine or pemetrexed dipotassium;[146] essentially, whether Eli Lilly's patent covered compounds other than pemetrexed disodium.

At first instance, Arnold J followed the well-established guidance of the UK courts on claim construction, emphasising that equivalents could not be used

[141] ibid 72–73.

[142] Fisher, 'New Protocol' 146.

[143] J Pagenberg, 'C – Conclusion and Proposals for Greater Harmonization' in J Pagenberg and W Cornish (eds), *Interpretation of Patents in Europe: Application of Article 69 EPC* (Heymanns 2007) 281.

[144] ibid.

[145] *Actavis v Eli Lilly* [2017] UKSC 48. Besides the point on infringement, whether or not equivalents should apply when it comes to the requirement of novelty has been questioned. This was discussed in *Generics (UK) Ltd and others v Yeda Research and Development Company and others* [2017] EWHC 2629 (Pat) and it was decided that it should not.

[146] *Actavis v Eli Lilly* [2017] UKSC 48, [4] and [8].

to extend the scope of protection of a patent in one instance and not the other (infringement and novelty).[147] He went on to assess whether or not an infringement had occurred by using the *Improver*/Protocol Questions and decided that Eli Lilly had intended to limit the claims to pemetrexed disodium only, and thus there was no direct infringement.[148]

On appeal, Floyd LJ restated the UK approach to the construction of claims and equivalents:

> The fact that English courts do not apply a general doctrine of equivalents to the construction of patent claims does not mean that the existence of equivalents which have no material effect on the way the invention works has no bearing on the proper, purposive interpretation of a patent claim. To the contrary, it has long been the law that such equivalents form part of the background of facts known to the skilled reader which would affect what he understands the claim to mean[149]

He said that in interpreting claims like this, English law complies with the Protocol on the Interpretation of Article 69 EPC, including Article 2. Floyd LJ followed the same line of reasoning as Arnold J at first instance and decided that there had been no direct infringement.[150]

The case was further appealed to the Supreme Court. In one of his final cases as President of the Supreme Court, Lord Neuberger took the opportunity to clarify how claims ought to be interpreted in the UK, in order to be in line with the requirements of the EPC and the Protocol on the Interpretation of Article 69 EPC. In doing so, and despite precedent from the Supreme Court in *Kirin-Amgen* pointing in the opposite direction, he introduced a doctrine of equivalents in the UK.

The reasoning behind this ground-breaking decision was to ensure that the UK complied with the Protocol on the Interpretation of Article 69 EPC. Lord Neuberger stated:

> In my view, notwithstanding what Lord Diplock said in *Catnic* [1982] RPC 183, 242, a problem of infringement is best approached by addressing two issues, each of which is to be considered through the eyes of the notional addressee of the patent in suit, ie the person skilled in the relevant art. Those issues are: (i) does the variant infringe any of the claims as a matter of normal interpretation; and, if not, (ii) does the variant nonetheless infringe because it varies from the invention in a way or ways which is or are immaterial? If the answer to either issue is 'yes', there is an infringement; otherwise, there is not. Such an approach complies with article 2 of the Protocol, as issue (ii) squarely raises the principle of equivalents, but limits its ambit to those variants which contain immaterial variations from the invention.[151]

In expressing infringement as two separate issues, Lord Neuberger asserted that the previous method of claim construction 'may have been wrong' because it conflated

[147] *Actavis v Eli Lilly* [2014] EWHC 1511 (Pat), [103].
[148] ibid [149].
[149] *Actavis v Eli Lilly* [2015] EWCA Civ 555, [45].
[150] ibid [80].
[151] *Actavis v Eli Lilly* [2017] UKSC 48, [54].

the issue of interpretation and scope of protection.[152] The reasoning behind this new approach relied on the first issue being a question of interpretation, and the second relating to facts and expert evidence.[153]

By changing the law on claim construction and allowing for a doctrine of equivalents, courts can now consider to what extent the scope of protection of a patent can extend beyond the meaning of the claims in context.[154] This is completely against the reasoning of the Supreme Court in *Kirin-Amgen* and thus changes legal practice in this area significantly. In his decision, Lord Neuberger also revived and reformulated the *Improver*/Protocol Questions.[155] Courts can now ask the following questions, which are to be used as a guideline rather than strictly:

> (i) Notwithstanding that it is not within the literal meaning of the relevant claim(s) of the patent, does the variant achieve substantially the same result in substantially the same way as the invention, ie the inventive concept revealed by the patent?
> (ii) Would it be obvious to the person skilled in the art, reading the patent at the priority date, but knowing that the variant achieves substantially the same result as the invention, that it does so in substantially the same way as the invention?
> (iii) Would such a reader of the patent have concluded that the patentee nonetheless intended that strict compliance with the literal meaning of the relevant claim(s) of the patent was an essential requirement of the invention?
>
> In order to establish infringement in a case where there is no literal infringement, a patentee would have to establish that the answer to the first two questions was 'yes' and that the answer to the third question was 'no'.[156]

Applying these questions to the case at hand, it was decided that the Actavis products directly infringed the Eli Lilly patent because all the Actavis products involved ultimately achieved substantially the same result in substantially the same way as the patented invention;[157] that the person skilled in the art would have appreciated that the products would work in the same way;[158] and that the person skilled in the art would conclude that the patentee did not intend strict compliance with the wording of the claims and would have intended that other pemetrexed salts be included in the scope of protection.[159]

[152] ibid [65].
[153] ibid [54].
[154] ibid [56].
[155] Interestingly, Neuberger J (as he then was) made the same argument (relating to the questions) in *Kirin-Amgen* in the Court of First Instance. Lord Hoffmann did not agree in the Supreme Court decision. We now have a situation where Lord Neuberger has changed the test of Lord Hoffmann in favour of his own. This is most apparent in the treatment of the second question, where in *Kirin-Amgen*, Neuberger J said that it should be assumed that the person skilled in the art is told that the variant works, which now features in the modified *Improver* questions from *Actavis v Eli Lilly: Kirin-Amgen v Transkaryotic Therapies* [2002] RPC 2, [26].
[156] *Actavis v Eli Lilly* [2017] UKSC 48, [66].
[157] ibid [68].
[158] ibid [69].
[159] ibid [74].

v. Impact

The change to the legal practice in this area has had and will have a number of significant consequences.[160]

First, as mentioned, this is a significant change to legal precedent in the UK. Owing to this decision, practice around drafting patent applications has changed, and arguments before courts in matters of infringement are being carefully considered. Attorneys have to decide whether to raise an argument of infringement by equivalents, which could imply that their case of literal infringement is weaker (literal in the patent context, not in the textual context).

Second, this judgment brings the UK more into line with other countries in Europe. The Supreme Court investigated how the doctrine of equivalents was used in other countries in its reasoning.[161] Although in this case the Court was under an obligation to consider the law from other jurisdictions because the UK Court was deciding on patent designations in a number of other countries, it can still be applauded from a dialogue perspective. By looking at the law from these jurisdictions, parallels and distinctions can be drawn, which can lead to either a more harmonised approach, or a realisation as to why divergence occurs.

Finally, the change to this area of UK law shows how judicial cooperation works at its best. The Supreme Court considered the practice in other jurisdictions as well as the previous practice and precedents in the UK.[162] In particular, the Supreme Court examined the approach of the German, French, Italian, Spanish and Dutch courts towards equivalents, discussed the divergent decisions in *Improver*, and concluded that there was a difference in approach.[163] It was ultimately decided that a harmonised approach to equivalents was the way forward. Departing from a previous interpretation of the Supreme Court is unusual, but in this case it was clearly driven by a desire for harmonisation and to ensure that the UK complies with its commitments to the EPC.[164]

As considered by Pagenberg, 'greater harmony can only be achieved, if the rules are not only consistent with the Protocol, but also correspond to those of other member countries of the EPC'.[165] *Actavis v Eli Lilly* displays how, in practice, this greater harmony can be achieved.

[160] For further discussions on *Actavis v Eli Lilly*, see J Strath and R Jacob, '*Actavis v Lilly*: The Madness Begins' (2018) 13(3) *JIPLP* 169; N Jadeja, H Smith-Willis and H Hurdle, 'Cast Back into the Sea of Uncertainty – A Doctrine of Equivalents in UK Law? The Supreme Court Ruling in *Actavis v Eli Lilly*' (2018) 13(7) *JIPLP* 564; P Johnson, 'The (re-)emergence of the doctrine of equivalents' (2017) 12(10) *JIPLP* 817; P Widera, 'Has *Pemetrexed* Revived the Doctrine of Equivalence?' (2018) 13(3) *JIPLP* 238; Aoun 'Pith and Marrow is Dead'.

[161] *Actavis v Eli Lilly* [2017] UKSC 48, [44]–[52].

[162] ibid [44]–[53].

[163] ibid [52].

[164] ibid [53]–[54].

[165] Pagenberg, 'Conclusion' 283.

vi. Post-*Actavis v Eli Lilly*

Following this decision, courts have applied the modified *Improver* questions from *Actavis v Eli Lilly* in cases of infringement by equivalents.[166] In a Court of Appeal decision, Lord Kitchin (having been recently elevated to the Supreme Court) reflected on the changes, stating that 'it is, in my view, clear that this approach is markedly different from that which the courts in this country have adopted since *Catnic*'.[167] The *Actavis v Eli Lilly* decision has been criticised for creating uncertainty around where to draw the line when it comes to equivalent inventions and whether they infringe, but from a harmonisation perspective, the approach in the UK is now more similar to the approach taken across Europe.

Indeed, the pemetrexed invention was litigated in several jurisdictions across Europe, including Austria, Finland, Germany, Italy, Sweden and Switzerland, involving multiple alleged infringers, with most courts coming to the same conclusion.[168] There have been a few exceptions, such as in the Netherlands, where a very similar case was decided differently, though in that case previous jurisprudence was still considered.[169]

Nevertheless, what can be seen is an effort to bring the European patent system closer together by judicial cooperation and explanations as to why one court may not agree with another.

C. Judicial Meetings and Appointments

Judicial cooperation is not only seen in the decisions of courts. Additional attempts are being made to bring judges together with a view to promoting a consistent approach towards the interpretation of substantive patent law.

Attempts are being made to respond to the risks of fragmentation through regular meetings of judges in the field. The EPO Academy is playing a key role in promoting this type of informal harmonisation by organising meetings where judges dealing with patent law across Europe come together to discuss recent developments.[170]

[166] The doctrine of equivalents has since been discussed in the UK by the High Court (Patents Court) in cases such as *Illumina v Premaitha* [2017] EWHC 2930 (Pat); *Fisher & Paykel v Resmed* [2017] EWHC 2748 (Pat); *L'Oréal Société Anonyme v RN Ventures* [2018] EWHC 173 (Pat); *Bose Corporation v Freebit* [2018] EWHC 889 (Pat); and *Liqwd Inc and Olaplex LLC v L'Oréal SA* [2018] EWHC 1394 (Pat); and by the Court of Appeal in *Actavis v ICOS* [2017] EWCA Civ 1671; and *Icescape Limited v Ice-World International BV & Ors* [2018] EWCA Civ 2219.

[167] *Icescape Limited v Ice-World International BV & Ors* [2018] EWCA Civ 2219, [59].

[168] R Lambers, 'The Pemetrexed Pendulum Swings Back' (*Kluwer Patent Blog*, 21 June 2019).

[169] Case C/09/541424/ HA ZA 17-1097 *Eli Lilly v Fresenius Kabi Nederland BV* ECLI:NL:RBDHA:2019:6107.

[170] They also produce a number of publications that highlight the differences in national courts, such as European Patent Academy, *Patent Litigation in Europe: An Overview of National Law and Practice in the EPC Contracting States* (5th edn, European Patent Office 2019). Efforts are also being made on the international level. WIPO held its first ever Annual IP Judges Forum in 2018 and has introduced an online tool (WIPO LEX) to assist with this.

The European Patent Judges' Symposium was one of the most well-known events in the field. In 2014, the Symposium met for the 17th time since its inauguration in 1982.[171] The reasoning behind the Symposium was put forward as a question by Friedrich-Karl Beier in the first of these meetings:

> [T]he question necessarily follows, how this harmony of law, which is intended by the legislatures and which has already been achieved at the level of enacted legislation, can now be achieved and safeguarded in judicial practice as well. And does the idea of judicial cooperation within Europe not necessarily follow, of looking more often beyond the limits of one's own jurisdiction, of fortifying the exchange of ideas amongst all of the judges who in future will have to apply the same new European patent law, who will decide the same questions and confront the same problems?[172]

Beier went on to say that European patent law will be shaped by case law, and that 'its true contours will emerge only from a multiplicity of individual decisions'.[173] Every two years, judges involved in patent law from all avenues – national courts, the Boards of Appeal and representatives from the CJEU – came together to discuss developments in patent law in order to continually develop and build up judicial cooperation across Europe. This was an extremely important event for the harmonisation of European patent law. There were also working sessions in which potential problems were raised and discussions held on how they might be handled. Every session involved presentations from national judges, and from 1994 presentations were given on certain case studies intended to highlight some difficulties in deciding patent law cases and how these cases could be decided. For example, in 2010 the case of a patent application for a folding attic stair was discussed.[174] Unfortunately, this event has not been convened since 2014.

Every year, in the autumn, European patent law judges also meet in Venice at the EPO European Judges' Forum. Similarly, annual conferences and organised events are additional opportunities for informal discussion. Similar to the Symposium, these events give judges the opportunity to discuss the latest developments in European patent law in their countries and elsewhere. These meetings will presumably continue to take place and if they do, will continue to serve the aim of European cooperation in the patent field by promoting the harmonisation of substantive patent law and procedure by informal means.

Harmonisation is further promoted by the appointment of external members to the Enlarged Board of Appeal.[175] External members are national court judges

[171] 17th European Patent Judges' Symposium, [2015] *Supplementary Publication*, OJ EPO 5.
[172] F-K Beier, 'Judicial Cooperation in European Patent Law' (1983) 6 *IIC* 707, 711.
[173] ibid 712.
[174] 15th European Patent Judges' Symposium, [2011] *Special Edition*, OJ EPO 1, 275.
[175] Luginbuehl, *European Patent Law* 145.

who can be appointed in cases where the scope of a matter referred extends beyond the internal administration of the EPO.[176]

Along similar lines, judicial internships are also available for national judges of the EPC Contracting States at the Boards of Appeal. These internships promote access to training and provide the opportunity to undertake an intensive course on patentability and procedures at the EPO, alongside the opportunity to shadow a member of the Boards of Appeal. In doing so, they enable national judges to experience the practices of the EPO, which can then be filtered back to their own national courts, if appropriate.

D. Impact of the Unitary Patent Package

This kind of understanding and respect between judges and members of the Boards of Appeal of the EPO will be even more important when the UPC is established. When implemented, there will be another highly specialised patent law judiciary at European level. Federica Baldan and Esther van Zimmeren have explored similar interactions between institutions from the perspective of multi-level governance and judicial coherence.[177] This complementary paper notes how these practices have been essential in enhancing judicial coherence and explores this particularly in relation to the UPC. They note multiple ways in which the UPC can encourage judicial coherence.

For example, regular meetings will be organised between all judges of the UPC to discuss developments in patent law and to ensure consistency in judgments.[178] However, it is important that these discussions also consider jurisprudence and developments outside of the UPC. For the UPC to be successful, dialogue between it and the current judiciaries and Boards is essential, given that not all European countries can participate, and because of the continued existence of current systems.[179]

The importance of sharing respect for one another's decisions and methods of interpretation of the law is the resulting consistency, without which divergent interpretations of substantive patent law will be more prevalent. Of course, this

[176] Article 11(5) EPC: 'The Administrative Council, after consulting the President of the European Patent Office, may also appoint as members of the Enlarged Boards of Appeal legally qualified members of the national courts or quasi-judicial authorities of the Contracting States, who may continue their judicial activities at the national level'.

[177] F Baldan and E van Zimmeren, 'The Future Role of the Unified Patent Court in Safeguarding Coherence in the European Patent System' (2015) 52 *Common Market Law Review* 1529. See also T Khuchua, 'Different "Rules of the Game" – Impact of National Court Systems on Patent Litigation in the EU and the Need for New Perspectives' (2019) 10 *Journal of Intellectual Property, Information Technology and E-Commerce Law* 257.

[178] Article 19(3) UPCA.

[179] This point was also highlighted by M Fröhlinger during a keynote presentation at the UP & UPC Conference at the EPO in Munich on 3 July 2018.

mutual respect is not mandated. The institutions involved are independent and are not obliged to follow each other's opinions. A harmonised approach is desirable where possible and appropriate, but divergent opinions may still arise. There must be a working relationship between all patent law institutions in order to strive for consistency in judgments, as well as to make clear any differences and the reasons for them.

E. Limitations of Judicial Dialogue and Cooperation

There are, of course, certain limitations to judicial dialogue and cooperation that are important to recognise and address.

The practice of judicial dialogue in the European patent system is informal and ad hoc. Considering suggestions made in the previous chapter, a more structured approach is warranted. For example, an online framework for dialogue could be introduced to support the judiciary when making decisions on European patent law. All cases could be uploaded and machine translated to assist with access. Judges could look at the decisions of other courts or decide to stay proceedings more often to await the judgment of another court hearing the same or a similar case.[180] If the case concerned a patent that had not been litigated previously, the court could investigate its approach to, for example, deciding on the patentability of an invention or sufficiency, and compare it to other courts and the Boards of Appeal. By doing so, it could learn what other European countries consider when dealing with these issues and decide whether practice could or should be changed in that country as a result. An open dialogue system could also be introduced, whereby judges could access a confidential online tool linking them to judges in other jurisdictions. In final written decisions, if departing from the status quo, all judges could also be required to expand on why they have departed from the majority view. If this were to happen more frequently, further steps could be taken in analysing how harmonisation could occur in these areas, if it should. Empirical research is currently being conducted in this area by the author to test these suggestions and determine how a more structured approach towards judicial dialogue and cooperation can be achieved.[181]

Critical consideration will also be required when implementing such practice. When deciding whether to follow the approach of another jurisdiction, there may be a tendency towards courts that are deemed experts in patent law. The expertise of the UK and German Courts is particularly well known in the patent field,

[180] Stays of proceedings are considered in many jurisdictions across Europe in relation to concurrent proceedings, particularly when an action is pending before the EPO. However, they are often refused. See, for example, P England, 'Parallel Patent Proceedings Between the European Patent Office and UK Courts' (2015) 10(7) *JIPLP* 509.

[181] This research is supported by the British Academy, Department for Business, Energy and Industrial Strategy. Reference number: SRG1819\190316.

and it is important that those with expertise are heard and considered extensively. However, this also risks the emergence of a UK/German-centric approach to the interpretation of patent law for Europe, limiting who gets heard and whose approaches are considered. There should also be attempts towards considering alternative approaches and viewpoints through judicial dialogue and cooperation. This point raises a further concern with the significant lack of diversity in the judiciary more generally.

Procedural fragmentation (the impact of differences in court procedures within Europe) can also limit the impact of judicial dialogue and cooperation in responding to fragmentation.[182] This is particularly apparent in parallel proceedings. Differences exist between practices in civil law and common law countries, in the evidence presented to the courts and how this is considered, as well as in the use of witnesses and expert testimony.[183] These differences can lead to courts coming to divergent conclusions because the decision reached in the same case in another jurisdiction may be less applicable. Therefore, as also suggested for the international legal system, all stakeholders must be involved in this process, especially when determining the information presented to courts.[184]

One of the most cited limitations of such an approach is that without a hierarchical court to make a final determination on, say, for example, the approach towards claim construction and equivalents, divergence will continue.[185] Divergence arises *within* countries, let alone *between* countries. It can be said that on appeal these internal differences can be addressed and that a hierarchical court would have the same effect more broadly. However, unless this court includes all countries in the European patent system, the potential for institutional fragmentation remains and still needs to be considered.[186]

It has been suggested that the ICJ should play a prominent, yet not hierarchical, role in the response to institutional fragmentation in the international legal system.[187] The UPC could be such a court in the European patent system. In time, the UPC will unify decision-making for participating EU Member States, which will also likely have a highly persuasive impact on decision-making outside that system. This will play a significantly important role in the European patent system. However, whether the UPC *should* have such a role is questionable. The decisions of the UPC will be highly specialised (possibly detrimentally in some cases) and will not be binding on all courts or institutions that deal with matters relating to patent law.[188] Divergence will likely continue. Additionally, if the Boards of Appeal follow

[182] Also mentioned by Webb, *International Judicial Integration and Fragmentation* 184.

[183] This is also being considered by the author in the empirical research mentioned above.

[184] Webb, *International Judicial Integration and Fragmentation* 208–28.

[185] R Arnold, 'Harmonization of European Patent Law' (2019) 14(9) *JIPLP* 657; Luginbuehl, *European Patent Law* 128–32.

[186] This too would bring with it certain problems. For example, it would take an incredibly long time for cases to be decided and an effective means of judicial review would be required.

[187] Webb, *International Judicial Integration and Fragmentation* 208–28.

[188] This will be discussed in further detail in Chapter 6 and the Conclusion.

the UPC to align jurisprudence without question, this may even be problematic for those outside the EU unitary patent system, but inside the European (EPC) patent system. As mentioned, judicial cooperation and dialogue will become even more necessary on the introduction of such a court.

III. Fragmentation as an Inherent Aspect of the European Patent System

Substantive patent law in Europe was essentially harmonised by the EPC and its predecessors, and national laws were amended to reflect this. However, some fragmentation was and is inevitable. The validity of each patent is tested against the provisions of the EPC as implemented in national laws. Matters of infringement are tested against the provisions of national laws by domestic courts applying their own rules of procedure and influenced by their own patent traditions. In this context, because of the potential for institutional fragmentation that exists in the European patent system, divergent outcomes and interpretations were and are inevitable.

This chapter has investigated responses to fragmentation in the European patent system, including some of the most prominent areas where convergence and divergence in interpretation and decision-making have occurred. Despite areas of continued divergence, there is evidence that the institutions involved are promoting consistency in the interpretation of substantive patent law where possible. The methods described in Chapter 4 for mitigating the risks of fragmentation in the field of international law are also being used to reduce the risks of fragmentation in the European patent system, particularly judicial dialogue and cooperation. The above examples illustrate some of the efforts that have been undertaken to respond to fragmentation through judicial dialogue and cooperation, and this kind of activity has become more frequent.

Other examples include the EPO's use of the rules governing the interpretation of treaties contained in the Vienna Convention; the active dialogue that exists between national court judges, facilitated by regular meetings between them; the commitment of judges to comparative reasoning and research, even in cases where counsel does not cite authorities from other jurisdictions; and the attempt by courts to explain any divergences in their outcomes from those reached by other European courts.

While certain limitations need to be considered, these methods have gone a significant way to reducing the risks associated with fragmentation. Fragmentation is inherent in the European patent system and differences will remain between courts when it comes to interpretation, but also when it comes to procedures and the evidence brought before each court in parallel proceedings. Despite these differences, decisions of other national courts, decisions of the Boards of Appeal and CJEU, and soon the UPC, can and should still be considered. Although judicial dialogue and cooperation may not always or ever lead to complete integration, it can assist with informal harmonisation where appropriate and, importantly, leave room for considerations of alternative views. It is suggested that these attempts should be more formally recognised, harnessed and further developed in line with the suggestions made, to improve our response to fragmentation in the European patent system.

6

Accepting Fragmentation as a Necessary Aspect of the European Patent System

Fragmentation is an inherent part of the European patent system and the negative aspects associated with it can be reduced if responded to appropriately. However, distinct and additional factors arise when addressing fragmentation in the area of exceptions to patentability,[1] particularly for supranational institutions.

Responding to fragmentation in this area is even more complicated because the exceptions to patentability are grounded in public policy issues. Such issues involve a variety of viewpoints that can differ for multiple reasons. This arises especially in relation to biotechnological inventions because of sometimes polarised opinions on their patentability. Additionally, in the interpretation of these exceptions, there is often a crossover with other areas of law and policy. The risk for substantive fragmentation is therefore higher. Although these differences arise in limited and specific circumstances, it is important that they are considered.

It is suggested that in these circumstances it may be more appropriate to allow a level of fragmentation to persist and that this should be considered in decision-making. This suggestion reflects conclusions drawn in Chapter 3 in relation to law-making, where there is space for fragmentation in specific circumstances. Such an approach would enable discretion in areas where consensus cannot be realised. Importantly, this would not prevent progress towards integration where possible and appropriate. In areas where fragmentation remains, judicial dialogue and cooperation can be used to make progress towards harmonisation on a case-by-case basis. However, this will require a critical reflection and consideration of the diversity that exists in the European patent system. Only then can a decision be made on whether convergence is possible or desirable.

In testing this suggestion, this chapter will consider how the exceptions to patentability are being interpreted in the European context and how the supranational institutions involved are currently responding to fragmentation. In doing so, it is important to first evaluate the significant impact of EU law in this area through

[1] Exceptions to patentability refers to subject matter that may be considered an invention but will still be refused patent protection. Specifically, for the reasons listed in Article 53 of the Convention on the Grant of European Patents of 5 October 1973.

the Biotech Directive.[2] The Biotech Directive harmonised the criteria and exceptions to patentability for biotechnological inventions for all EU Member States. Some of its provisions were incorporated into the Implementing Regulations to the EPC and it is also used as a means of supplementary interpretation.[3] As a result, similar laws apply in all EPC Contracting States. Furthermore, with these aspects of substantive patent law now emanating from the EU, the CJEU has jurisdiction over its interpretation, thus increasing the possibility of institutional fragmentation.

This chapter will examine the impact of this additional law and additional institution on the interpretation of substantive patent law in Europe. Then, informed by practices in the field, it will examine how the exceptions to patentability have been interpreted by the institutions involved, particularly in relation to the exception to patentability for the use of human embryos for industrial or commercial purposes and the patentability of products resulting from essentially biological processes.

In both areas, convergence has been a clear motivating factor in decision-making by the CJEU and the Enlarged Board of Appeal of the EPO. Crucially, these institutions make decisions that are of binding or highly persuasive authority for countries across Europe. However, it will be seen that in one attempt to minimise divergence, insufficient consideration of value pluralism and substantive fragmentation led to a problematic *outcome*.[4] In another attempt towards convergence, although the decision was beneficial to society, problematic *practices* emerged.[5] Within these examples, considerations of other court decisions were present but there were missed opportunities for further dialogue. It is suggested that responses to fragmentation, particularly in relation to the exceptions to patentability, must involve a deeper consideration of values, value pluralism and national diversity. The desire to remove fragmentation should not disengage institutions from important substantive and procedural considerations. Fragmentation may therefore be necessary unless harmonisation can be achieved in an appropriate and considered manner.

I. The Impact of the Biotech Directive

The EU has had some involvement in substantive patent law, the most significant being the implementation of the Biotech Directive in 1998. The finalisation of the Directive was far from straightforward. The first attempt, initially drafted in 1985, was rejected in 1995.[6] Difficulties arose due to controversy around ethical and

[2] Directive 98/44EC of the European Parliament and of the Council of 6 July 1998 on the legal protection of biotechnological inventions.

[3] Convention on the Grant of European Patents of 5 October 1973.

[4] Case C-34/10 *Oliver Brüstle v Greenpeace eV* ECLI:EU:C:2011:669 (*Brüstle*).

[5] G3/19 *Pepper (follow-up to 'Tomatoes II' and 'Broccoli II')* of 14.05.20.

[6] R Nott, '"You Did It!": The European Biotechnology Directive At Last' (1998) 20(9) *EIPR* 347, 347.

social concerns over patenting biotechnological inventions, specifically the appropriateness and safety of genetically engineered products, as well as concerns over animal suffering and patenting 'life'.[7] Following a speedy process, the proposal was redrafted and enacted a few years later.[8]

However, these concerns did not fade away on enactment. Shortly thereafter, an action for annulment was brought by the Netherlands to the CJEU.[9] The arguments put forward were based on the legal basis of the Directive, issues of subsidiarity and legal certainty, and the consistency of the Directive with international law and fundamental rights. However, the action failed on all grounds.[10] The CJEU found that the harmonisation provided by the Biotech Directive was justified and could only be achieved through Community action and not by Member States alone, thereby rejecting the subsidiarity argument.[11] The Directive was found to safeguard human dignity and integrity, and to be consistent with international law.[12] Further, while the wording of the Directive provided scope for manoeuvre for Member States with regard to interpretation, it did not lack legal certainty.[13] This final aspect of the case is important and highly relevant as it displays the importance of national interpretations and the possibility of differing views remaining on the subject matter involved.

A. Legislative Harmonisation

Prior to the implementation of the Biotech Directive, there were numerous diverging national laws relating to the patentability of biotechnological inventions; for example, the Netherlands denied protection completely.[14] The Directive was introduced to strengthen the biotechnology industry in Europe and to ensure a harmonised approach towards the patentability of biotechnological inventions throughout the EU. It explains how substantive patent law provisions relate to biotechnological inventions and expands in certain areas. Given the difficulties with implementation, the provisions remain somewhat ambiguous and leave scope for manoeuvre for Member States. As stated by Jan Krauss and Toshiko Takenaka

[7] R Gold and A Gallochat, 'The European Biotech Directive: Past as Prologue' (2001) 7(3) *European Law Journal* 331, 337. For an excellent overview of the debates and discussions surrounding the finalisation of the Biotech Directive, see S Parthasarathy, *Patent Politics: Life Forms, Markets & the Public Interest in the United States & Europe* (University of Chicago Press 2017) chapter 2.

[8] Nott, '"You Did It!"' 347.

[9] Case C-377/98 *Netherlands v European Parliament and Council of the European Union* ECLI:EU:C:2001:523 (*Netherlands*).

[10] For more detail on the arguments raised by the Netherlands, see, for example, A Scott, 'The Dutch Challenge to the Bio-Patenting Directive' (1999) 21(4) *EIPR* 212 and S Moore, 'Challenge to the Biotechnology Directive' (2002) 24(3) *EIPR* 149.

[11] *Netherlands*, para 32.

[12] ibid paras 71, 79 and 20.

[13] ibid para 39.

[14] G Laurie, 'Intellectual Property Protection of Biotechnological Inventions and Related Materials' (2003) 4 *Innogen Working Paper*, 9.

in relation to the isolation of DNA sequences, 'The texts of the Biotech Directive represent compromises and thus include a lot of ambiguity in key terms defining the scope of protection'.[15]

EU Member States were obliged to transpose the provisions of the Biotech Directive into national law; however, the provisions did not have to be implemented directly, word for word. According to EU law, the national measure must only achieve the objectives set by a directive, which allows Member States to consider specific national characteristics when transposing the law.[16] Reflecting the implementation of the EPC into national laws, some Member States have introduced the substantive patent law of the Biotech Directive into their own national legislation using different terminology.[17] These provisions can then be interpreted in different ways.

The implementation of the Biotech Directive also had a significant effect on the European (EPC) patent system. Rather than directly competing with the Biotech Directive, the EPOrg considered that the area of biotechnological innovation was so important to industry that a coordinated approach was necessary. In 1999, only one year after its introduction, the Biotech Directive was incorporated into the Implementing Regulations to the EPC, which state in Chapter V:

> For European patent applications and patents concerning biotechnological inventions, the relevant provisions of the Convention shall be applied and interpreted in accordance with the provision of this Chapter. Directive 98/44/EC of 6 July 1998 on the legal protection of biotechnological inventions shall be used as a supplementary means of interpretation.[18]

The aim was to ensure that EU Member States complied with their duty to bring national laws in line with the Directive. However, from a political perspective, the EPC had little choice in the matter since most of its Contracting States are also EU Member States.[19] This had the effect of strengthening the biotechnology industry across Europe, but also put a greater focus on ethical considerations at EU level, as well as at the EPO.

[15] J Krauss and T Takenaka, 'Construction of an Efficient and Balanced Patent System: Patentability and Patent Scope of Isolated DNA Sequences under US Patent Act and EU Biotech Directive' in C Geiger (ed), *Constructing European Intellectual Property: Achievements and New Perspectives* (Edward Elgar 2013) 256.

[16] Article 288 TFEU: 'A directive shall be binding, as to the result to be achieved, upon each Member State to which it is addressed, but shall leave to national authorities the choice of form and methods'.

[17] For a detailed discussion on the introduction of Article 6(2)(c) Biotech Directive into national law, see Å Hellstadius, 'A Comparative Analysis of the National Implementation of the Directive's Morality Clause' in A Plomer and PLC Torremans (eds), *Embryonic Stem Cell Patents: European Law and Ethics* (Oxford University Press 2009). For the differences between the Biotech Directive and the UK implementation, see Laurie, 'Intellectual Property Protection' 12.

[18] Chapter V, Rule 26(1) Implementing Regulations to the EPC 2000.

[19] This action was taken by the Administrative Council and was criticised as an overstep at the time, as elaborated upon in A Bakardjieva Engelbrekt, 'Institutional and Jurisdictional Aspects of Stem Cell Patenting in Europe (EC and EPO): Tensions and Prospects' in A Plomer and PLC Torremans (eds), *Embryonic Stem Cell Patents: European Patent Law and Ethics* (Oxford University Press 2009) 255–57.

Substantive law regarding biotechnological inventions was therefore essentially harmonised across Europe, not only the EU. However, institutional and substantive fragmentation remain a concern since interpretations can still vary depending on the tribunal in question.

B. Institutional Addition

Additionally, the introduction of the Biotech Directive expanded the jurisdiction of the CJEU in the patent field, thus increasing the possibility for institutional fragmentation. Prior to the introduction of the Directive, the CJEU had only very limited jurisdiction regarding substantive patent law. Once the Biotech Directive was introduced, EU Member States were required to refer questions on its interpretation to the CJEU.[20] Accordingly, the CJEU has jurisdiction to give preliminary rulings on the interpretation of these aspects of substantive patent law, rulings which must then be incorporated by the national court in its ultimate decision and must also be considered by all EU Member States. Its decisions are not binding on the Boards of Appeal of the EPO, but they are of persuasive authority.[21] With the incorporation of the Biotech Directive into the Implementing Regulations of the EPC, the Boards of Appeal and the Enlarged Board of Appeal also provide interpretations of provisions relating to biotechnological inventions. Crucially, the decisions of both the CJEU and the Enlarged Board of Appeal are either of binding or highly persuasive authority for countries across Europe and so are especially significant.

The involvement of the CJEU in substantive patent law is a complicated matter and involves both benefits and shortcomings. First, another institution is now tasked with the interpretation of substantive patent law, increasing the risk of divergence. Second, a formal dialogue between some patent law tribunals in the European patent system has been initiated. This is a positive step for harmonisation in theory; however, in practice, the decisions of the CJEU in intellectual property law, and specifically in patent law, have been criticised extensively for taking interpretations of the law too far.[22] Finally and relatedly, the CJEU has been criticised for being limited in its ability to interpret substantive patent law provisions because it is a generalist court.[23] By contrast, it has been argued convincingly

[20] Article 267 TFEU. For more on this topic see, for example, RJ Aerts, 'The Patenting of Biotechnological Inventions in the EU, the Judicial Bodies Involved, and the Objectives of the EU Legislator' (2014) 36(2) *EIPR* 88.

[21] EPO, Guidelines for Examination, March 2021, G.II.5.2.

[22] For a critique of CJEU decisions in intellectual property law, see, for example, R Jacob, 'The Relationship between European and National Courts in Intellectual Property Law' in A Ohly and J Pila (eds), *The Europeanization of Intellectual Property Law: Towards a European Legal Methodology* (Oxford University Press 2013) 198.

[23] See, for example, D Smyth, 'Patent Law Decisions from Supreme Courts: How Can Non-specialist Judges Decide this Field of Law?' (2014) 9(1) *JIPLP* 31. Criticisms of this kind were one of the main reasons for the removal of the original Articles 6–8 from the text of the Unitary Patent Regulations, which contained most of the substantive patent law therein. Discussed in detail in Chapter 2.

that a generalist perspective is necessary to consider rights other than those relating to patents, such as human dignity,[24] thus limiting (though not excluding) the possibility of substantive fragmentation.

These factors will now be considered in detail in relation to the interpretation of the exceptions to patentability.

II. Interpretations of the Exceptions to Patentability

The following section will consider the interpretation of two exceptions to patentability, specifically those in relation to, first, uses of human embryos for industrial or commercial processes and, secondly, essentially biological processes.[25] These two areas are the most relevant to this book because of the attempts that have been made by the institutions involved to respond to fragmentation and promote convergence across Europe. However, decisions in each area involved concerning aspects – one in terms of outcome, and one in terms of process. These provisions have also both been interpreted multiple times by multiple institutions at the highest possible levels of the European patent system. In each area, the relevant case law will be considered and then evaluated with reference to the factors previously mentioned.

A. Uses of Human Embryos for Industrial or Commercial Purposes

Article 6 of the Biotech Directive excludes certain subject matter from patentability. It states:

> (1) Inventions shall be considered unpatentable where their commercial exploitation would be contrary to *ordre public* or morality; however, exploitation shall not be deemed to be so contrary merely because it is prohibited by law or regulation.
>
> (2) On the basis of paragraph 1, the following, in particular, shall be considered unpatentable:
>
> (a) processes for cloning human beings;
> (b) processes for modifying the germ line genetic identity of human beings;
> (c) uses of human embryos for industrial or commercial purposes;
> (d) processes for modifying the genetic identity of animals which are likely to cause them suffering without any substantial benefit to man or animal, and also animals resulting from such processes.

[24] J Schovsbo, T Riis and CS Petersen, 'The Unified Patent Court: Pros and Cons of Specialization – Is There a Light at the End of the Tunnel (Vision)?' (2015) 46(3) *IIC* 271; J Pila, 'An Historical Perspective I: The Unitary Patent Package' in J Pila and C Wadlow (eds), *The Unitary EU Patent System* (Hart Publishing 2014).

[25] Some of the material in this section was first published by Sweet & Maxwell in *Intellectual Property Quarterly* in K Walsh, 'The Unitary Patent Package, the Court of Justice of the European Union, and Brexit: (Ir)reconcilable?' (2019) 2 *IPQ* 91 and is reproduced by agreement with the publishers.

Article 6(2)(c) prohibits the patenting of inventions that involve the use of human embryos for industrial or commercial purposes and has been controversial ever since it was adopted.[26] It has been incorporated into the Implementing Regulations to the EPC in Rule 28 and linked to Article 53(a) EPC, which prevents the patentability of inventions whose commercial exploitation would be contrary to *ordre public* or morality. In almost identical terms to the Biotech Directive, Rule 28(1) states:

> Under Article 53(a), European patents shall not be granted in respect of biotechnological inventions, which, in particular, concern the following:
>
> …
>
> (c) uses of human embryos for industrial or commercial purposes.[27]

This exception has been interpreted by numerous national courts, the Boards of Appeal and the Enlarged Board of Appeal, and twice by the CJEU.

i. WARF

The first key decision relating to the interpretation of this exception, in this case Rule 28(1)(c), was handed down by the Enlarged Board of Appeal in G2/06,[28] also known as the *WARF* decision.[29] The question referred to the Enlarged Board was whether Rule 28(1)(c) forbids the patenting of an invention that concerns, inter alia, human embryonic stem cell cultures, which 'at the filing date could be prepared exclusively by a method which necessarily involved the destruction of the human embryos from which they were derived'.[30]

In its interpretation, the Enlarged Board considered Article 6(2)(c) of the Biotech Directive and observed that neither the EU nor the EPC legislator had chosen to define the term 'embryo', assuming that they had been aware of the varying

[26] A Plomer, 'After *Brüstle*: EU Accession to the ECHR and the Future of European Patent Law' (2012) 2(2) *Queen Mary Journal of Intellectual Property* 110. For an analysis of the patenting of human stem cells in the period prior to the case law that will subsequently be discussed, see G Laurie, 'Patenting Stem Cells of Human Origin' (2004) 26(2) *EIPR* 59.

[27] Chapter V, Rule 28(c) Implementing Regulations to the EPC 2000.

[28] G2/06 *Use of embryos/WARF* of 25.11.2008 (*WARF*). For a detailed analysis of the proceedings before the Enlarged Board of Appeal in this case, see S Sterckx, 'The WARF/Stem Cells Case before the EPO Enlarged Board of Appeal' (2008) 30(12) *EIPR* 535 and S Sterckx, 'The European Patent Convention and the (Non-) Patentability of Human Embryonic Stem Cells – the WARF case' (2008) 4 *IPQ* 478.

[29] The scope of application of the exclusion's reference to 'industrial or commercial use' was first addressed by the Opposition Division of the EPO in relation to EP0695351, also known as the *Edinburgh* case. The decision of the Opposition Division can be found on the European Patent Register, Grounds for the decision (Annex), dated 21.07.2003. See M Rowlandson, 'WARF/Stem Cells (G2/06): The Ordre Public and Morality Exception and Its Impact on the Patentability of Human Embryonic Stem Cells' (2010) 32(2) *EIPR* 67.

[30] *WARF*, Question 2.

definitions in national laws and deliberately refrained from defining the term.[31] It was decided that since the aim of preventing the commercialisation of embryos was to protect the fundamental right of human dignity, the Enlarged Board of Appeal presumed that neither the exclusion nor the term 'embryo' ought to be construed restrictively.[32]

Proceeding from this basis, it was decided that Rule 28(1)(c) prohibits the patenting of products that at the time of filing can only be prepared by methods involving the destruction of human embryos.[33] Considering that the definition of human embryo differs depending on the country in question, rather than attempt to define it, the Enlarged Board stated that 'what is an embryo is a question of fact in the context of any particular patent application'.[34]

ii. Brüstle

The next key decision, this time directly on the interpretation of Article 6(2)(c) of the Biotech Directive, was the *Brüstle* decision.[35] The German Court made a reference for a preliminary ruling by the CJEU.[36] The patent in question related to neural precursor cells and the processes used to produce them by means of embryonic stem cells. Several questions were put forward, including a request to elaborate on the meaning of the term 'human embryo' for the purpose of Article 6(2)(c).[37]

Instead of following the approach of the Enlarged Board of Appeal to this issue in *WARF*, the CJEU decided that the term must be regarded 'as designating an autonomous concept of EU law' for the purposes of the application of the Directive, and must be 'interpreted in a uniform manner throughout the territory of the Union'.[38] It went on to define 'human embryo' having regard to the fundamental rights underpinnings of the exception as 'any human ovum after fertilisation, any non-fertilised human ovum into which the cell nucleus from a mature human cell has been transplanted and any non-fertilised human ovum whose division and further development have been stimulated by parthenogenesis'.[39] This is a

[31] *WARF*, Reasons, Point 20 and European Patent Office, *Case Law of the Boards of Appeal of the European Patent Office* (9th edn, Druckerei CH Beck 2019) I, B, 2.1.1.

[32] *WARF*, Reasons, Point 20. The decision in *WARF* has subsequently been followed by the Boards of Appeal of the EPO in cases such as T522/04 *Stem Cells/CALIFORNIA* of 28.05.2009 and T2221/10 *Culturing stem cells/TECHNION* of 04.02.2014.

[33] *WARF*, Order, Point 2.

[34] *WARF*, Reasons, Point 20. For a discussion on the legal nature of the interpretation of the Biotech Directive provisions by the Boards of Appeal of the EPO after Opinion 1/09, see Aerts, 'The Patenting of Biotechnological Inventions'.

[35] Case C-34/10 *Oliver Brüstle v Greenpeace eV* ECLI:EU:C:2011:669.

[36] Decision of the Bundesgerichtshof, 17 December 2009 – Xa ZR 58/07 '*Neurale Vorläuferzellen (Neural precursor cells)*'.

[37] For more detailed commentary on the CJEU ruling in this case, see, for example, M Ines Schuster, 'The Court of Justice of the European Union's Ruling on the Patentability of Human Embryonic Stem-cell-related Inventions (Case C-34/10)' (2012) 43(6) *IIC* 626.

[38] *Brüstle*, para 26.

[39] ibid para 38.

significantly broad definition and restricted patentability in most countries where the definition of human embryo was far less expansive.[40]

iii. ISCC

Brüstle was not the last instalment in this narrative. A question on the interpretation of Article 6(2)(c), specifically regarding the previous interpretation of the term 'human embryo', was referred to the CJEU by the UK.[41] In Case C-364/13 *International Stem Cell Corporation (ISCC)*,[42] the referring Court asked:

> Are unfertilised human ova whose division and further development have been stimulated by parthenogenesis, and which, in contrast to fertilised ova, contain only pluripotent cells and are incapable of developing into human beings, included in the term 'human embryos' in Article 6(2)(c) of Directive 98/44/EC on the legal protection of biotechnological inventions?

The CJEU clarified its earlier decision in *Brüstle* and decided that an unfertilised human ovum whose division and further development have been stimulated by parthenogenesis does not constitute a 'human embryo' if it does not, in itself, 'have the inherent capacity of developing into a human being'.[43] The effect of the decision is that rather than the definition of 'human embryo' concerning the capability of the ovum to *commence* the development into a human being (as in *Brüstle*), it must have the inherent capacity of *developing into* a human being. Overall, the *ISCC* decision has been welcomed and has somewhat reopened the doors of commercialising research through patents in this area.[44]

iv. Evaluation

There is much to evaluate from these responses to fragmentation. First is the criticism that the CJEU went too far in *Brüstle* in a push towards convergence by defining human embryo as it did for the purposes of the Biotech Directive. Second is the related question as to whether, as a generalist institution, the CJEU has the expertise to make decisions in technical and specialist areas such as patent law, and if not, whether this is a problem. Finally, the institutional interactions and

[40] SHE Harmon, G Laurie and A Courtney, 'Dignity, Plurality and Patentability: The Unfinished Story of Brustle v Greenpeace' (2013) 38(1) *European Law Review* 92, 97.

[41] *International Stem Cell Corporation v Comptroller General of Patents* [2013] EWHC 807 (Ch).

[42] Case C-364/13 *International Stem Cell Corporation v Comptroller General of Patents, Designs and Trade Marks* ECLI:EU:C:2014:2451 (*ISCC*).

[43] ibid para 28.

[44] See, for example, S Moore and A Wells, 'Clarification of European Law Relating to Stem Cell Patents' (2015) 37(4) *EIPR* 258; E O'Sullivan, 'International Stem Cell Corp v Comptroller General of Patents: The Debate Regarding the Definition of the Human Embryo Continues' (2014) 36(3) *EIPR* 155. O'Sullivan welcomes this clarification but questions whether it entirely opens the doors for the patentability of inventions involving parthenotes.

considerations that occurred within these cases, including missed opportunities for dialogue, can be assessed.

a. Convergence Overextended

In the *Brüstle* decision, the CJEU decided that 'human embryo' ought to be defined as an autonomous concept for the purposes of the Biotech Directive and thus applicable in all EU Member States. This unified the meaning of the term but the definition implemented was problematic.[45]

The *Brüstle* decision importantly introduced a consideration of fundamental rights into patent law and promoted a harmonised approach to patentability in this context; however, it did not adequately consider the practice of its Member States or decisions on similar concepts from other areas of law. Due to the latter, as well as incorrect scientific evidence, the CJEU implemented a definition that was too expansive. This had to be later clarified in *ISCC*.

Focusing on the *Brüstle* decision raises a question as to whether the identification of terms as autonomous concepts of EU law is an appropriate action for the CJEU to take in circumstances involving patents and morality or public policy. Laudably, the CJEU considered the intention of the legislator to protect fundamental rights and human dignity. It provided a uniform definition to promote legal certainty in the area. The push towards convergence was motivated by the purpose of the Biotech Directive and EU law generally to harmonise the protection of such inventions and ensure the smooth functioning of the internal market. The role of the CJEU in promoting a harmonised approach cannot be underestimated.

However, it is also important that it does so with full consideration of the various perspectives that exist. While the CJEU may have the competence to define terms as autonomous concepts of EU law, and the resulting harmonisation provides legal certainty, it has been argued that the way it has been done in this context is moving from the realm of judicial interpretation into that of judicial activism.[46] At the very least, the expansive nature of the chosen definition was problematic. As a result, the decision was rightly criticised as one that went too far by overly simplifying and giving an 'incomplete analysis of the human rights situation'.[47] By defining 'human embryo' expansively and as an autonomous concept of EU law, the CJEU did not sufficiently acknowledge the fact that various definitions

[45] S Burke, 'Interpretative Clarification of the Concept of "Human Embryo" in the Context of the Biotechnology Directive and the Implications for Patentability: Brüstle v Greenpeace eV (C-34/10)' (2012) 34(5) *EIPR* 346, 349; A Odell-West, 'Invention and the Human Embryo' (2020) 1 *IPQ* 1.

[46] A Faeh, 'Judicial Activism, the Biotech Directive and Its Institutional Implications: Is the Court Acting as a Legislator or a Court When Defining the "Human Embryo"?' (2015) 40(4) *European Law Review* 613.

[47] A Ohly, 'European Fundamental Rights and Intellectual Property' in A Ohly and J Pila (eds), *The Europeanization of Intellectual Property Law: Towards a European Legal Methodology* (Oxford University Press 2013) 159. For a brief outline of the criticisms of *Brüstle*, see S Parker and P England, 'Where Now for Stem Cell Patents?' (2012) 7(10) *EIPR* 738, 743.

existed in many Member States and, in doing so, 'ignored considerations of value diversity'.[48] Aurora Plomer argues that imposing uniform exclusions based on human dignity, where reality points to diversity, threatens not only the autonomy of Member States, but also the integrity of the EU.[49]

Of the utmost relevance here is that in *Brüstle*, the CJEU distanced itself from the broader social context of the situation, stating that

> although, the definition of human embryo is a very sensitive social issue in many Member States, marked by their multiple traditions and value systems, the Court is not called upon, by the present order for reference, to broach questions of a medical or ethical nature, but must restrict itself to a legal interpretation of the relevant provisions of the Directive.[50]

However, it is not possible to separate the legal and social context here. The Court was making a value-based judgment which must be acknowledged, and that context must be sufficiently considered. Had it been, there may have been a hesitance in defining this term as it did, which would have allowed fragmentation to persist but would also have shown respect to the autonomy of Member States.

Previously, in the *Omega* case, the CJEU had emphasised the need to ensure a margin of appreciation to EU Member States regarding the meaning and requirements of human dignity.[51] Furthermore, as mentioned, the CJEU had held in the *Netherlands* case that provisions of the Biotech Directive should allow Member States a wide scope for manoeuvre and discretion in their application.[52] The Court had said that Member States are 'better placed' to understand the social and cultural context regarding the use of certain patents.[53]

The CJEU should have followed this precedent and shown restraint in *Brüstle*, leaving some room for manoeuvre for national courts. Requiring Member States to bypass the legislature by adopting a definition of 'human embryo' that is different

[48] As mentioned in J Pila, 'A Constitutionalized Doctrine of Precedent and the *Marleasing* Principle as Bases for a European Legal Methodology' in A Ohly and J Pila (eds), *The Europeanization of Intellectual Property Law: Towards a European Legal Methodology* (Oxford University Press 2013) 236, citing L Azoulai, 'The Europeanisation of Legal Concepts' in U Neergaard and R Nielsen (eds), *European Legal Method: In a Multi-Level EU Legal Order* (DJØF Publishing 2012). See also K Walsh and N Hawkins, 'Expanding the Role of Morality and Public Policy in European Patent Law' in PLC Torremans (ed), *Intellectual Property Law and Human Rights* (4th edn, Wolters Kluwer 2020).

[49] Plomer, 'After Brüstle' 125; A Plomer, 'Human Dignity, Human Rights, and Article 6(1) of the EU Directive on Biotechnological Inventions' in A Plomer and PLC Torremans (eds), *Embryonic Stem Cell Patents: European Law and Ethics* (Oxford University Press 2009). Relatedly, this was also one of the reasons that the European Court of Human Rights decided not to define when the right to life begins. It was stated that the issue of 'when the right to life begins comes within the margin of appreciation which the Court generally considered that states should enjoy' themselves: *Vo v France* App no 53924/00 (ECtHR 8 July 2004), para 82; *Evans v UK* App no 6339/05 (ECtHR, 7 March 2006), para 46.

[50] *Brüstle*, para 30.

[51] Case C-36/02 *Omega Spielhallen- und Automatenaufstellungs-GmbH v Oberbürgermeisterin der Bundesstadt Bonn* ECLI:EU:C:2004:614 (*Omega*).

[52] This point seemed to have been forgotten in *Brüstle*, as noted in Harmon, Laurie and Courtney, 'Dignity, Plurality and Patentability'.

[53] *Netherlands*, para 38.

from the definitions in many EU Member States has important implications for other areas of law and social policy.[54] Restraint should have been shown by either allowing Member States full discretion to consider the term on a case-by-case basis, or providing a less expansive definition that would allow Member States some discretion in application.[55] Additional guidance, alongside a general ruling, could have been provided to ensure that patent law was being considered in a broader context.[56]

As mentioned, the problematic nature of the definition provided in *Brüstle* required clarification in *ISCC*. The main reason for this clarification was because in *Brüstle*, the CJEU had based its findings on incorrect observations that the ovum in question would be capable of full development.[57] Had this been known at the time, the decision in *Brüstle* may have been very different. Some commentators are of the opinion that this clarification in *ISCC* is a step in the right direction,[58] but it does not take away from the fact that the CJEU may have defined subject matter that it ought to have left to the discretion of national courts.

Overall, the CJEU's decision in the *Brüstle* case raises important questions regarding the role of the CJEU in the areas of both patent law and fundamental rights. This case law shows how interpretation resulted in a unitary understanding of requirements for all EU Member States where one does not exist. Allowing for fragmentation to persist, rather than providing an expansive uniform definition, would have been more appropriate here because it would have allowed for considerations of diversity, value pluralism and substantive fragmentation.

Importantly, adopting such a response to fragmentation would not prevent progress towards integration where possible. In Chapter 3, it was seen that in supranational law-making a small space for fragmentation can remain to allow progress towards integration by a group of states when it would not be possible otherwise.[59] The differences that require such an approach are often based on contrasting values. Although this raises concerns over different laws being applicable in different states, the idea is that those outside the group will eventually join. The same idea can be applied to supranational decision-making. In areas where significant value pluralism exists, and an answer is not apparent from the legislation concerned, supranational decision-makers could allow a level of

[54] J Pila and PLC Torremans, *European Intellectual Property Law* (2nd edn, Oxford University Press 2016) 144.

[55] The latter point has also been raised in Plomer, 'Human Dignity'.

[56] Such restraint is also shown by supranational courts in the international legal system, including the ICJ. Caution is perceived in areas where there is a lack of state consensus: P Webb, *International Judicial Integration and Fragmentation* (Oxford University Press 2013) 181.

[57] *ISCC*, paras 31 and 32.

[58] See T Minssen and A Nordberg, 'The Evolution of the CJEU's Case Law on Stem Cell Patents: Context, Outcome and Implications of Case C-364/13 *International Stem Cell Corporation*' (2015) 5 *Nordic Intellectual Property Law Review* 493; A Nordberg and T Minssen, 'A "Ray of Hope" for European Stem Cell Patents or "Out of the Smog into the Fog"? An Analysis of Recent European Case Law and How it Compares to the US' (2016) 47 *IIC* 138.

[59] Specifically the use of the enhanced cooperation process in EU law-making.

fragmentation to persist while progress towards integration is being made on a more local level, if possible and appropriate. Progress could be achieved through general rulings and additional guidance being given by the supranational institutions, judicial dialogue and cooperation, and gradual developments within states. If Member States maintain some discretion in certain areas and a national court is required to make a decision, considerations of other court decisions would be encouraged. Responding to fragmentation through judicial dialogue and cooperation can allow such progress towards convergence while also considering value pluralism.

b. Generalist v Specialist Decision-making

The debate following the *Brüstle* judgment was extensive. Another central theme was that as a generalist court, the CJEU did not have the expertise necessary to make decisions on cases concerning patent law. The main argument in this regard was that, in an area as specialised as patent law, a generalist court lacks the technical understanding that is necessary to interpret provisions of patent law and the subject matter that is at issue in particular cases. However, others have persuasively emphasised that this is exactly what patent law needs – the overview of a generalist court in order to take into account fundamental rights such as human dignity and to avoid the development of 'tunnel vision' in specialist courts.[60] As stated by Justine Pila, 'patent law does not belong exclusively to the worlds of commerce, industry, and technology, but rather has other social and cultural dimensions which must be considered by the legislature and courts when developing and applying it'.[61]

That the decision in *Brüstle* required clarification could support the argument that specialist courts are necessary in this field; however, the decision was based on incorrect evidence and the importance of a broader perspective cannot be underestimated.[62] Patent institutions are predominantly focused on granting patents and have extended patent protection with less attention given to the place of patent law in the legal system overall.[63] Specialist patent courts would likely operate similarly.

[60] Schovsbo, Riis and Petersen, 'The Unified Patent Court'; and A Ohly, 'Concluding Remarks: Postmodernism and Beyond' in A Ohly and J Pila (eds), *The Europeanization of Intellectual Property Law: Towards a European Legal Methodology* (Oxford University Press 2013) 264; A Strowel and H-E Kim, 'The Balancing Impact of General EU Law on European Intellectual Property Jurisprudence' in A Ohly and J Pila (eds), *The Europeanization of Intellectual Property Law: Towards a European Legal Methodology* (Oxford University Press 2013) 122.

[61] Pila, 'Constitutionalized Doctrine of Precedent' 228.

[62] Ohly, 'European Fundamental Rights' 159.

[63] For example, many patent offices, including the EPO, have introduced the possibility of second medical use patents, which allow protection for new uses of known products. However, second medical use patents can have a negative impact on society when one considers the possibility of doctors or medical institutions being sued for prescribing a drug that could be taken for the new use. This could be considered as a direct or indirect infringement depending on the law of the Member State in question. For more on second medical use, see P England, 'Infringement of Second Medical Use Patents in

This specialist focus can also result in substantive fragmentation, that is a divide between patent law and other areas of law.[64] It is therefore submitted that by having the oversight of a generalist court, the risks associated with substantive fragmentation are reduced and important social and ethical aspects can be considered.[65] This is possible because a generalist court ensures that patent law is interpreted having regard to other legal principles, be they principles of competition law, contract law, fundamental rights, or otherwise. This is also core in the response to fragmentation in international law.

Overall, as a generalist institution, the CJEU adds something that would otherwise be missing from the European patent system – a consideration of where the protection of inventions sits within society generally, and not as a specialist subject. This is particularly important in light of the limitations on the public interest that patent rights can cause. Moving forward in patent law, it must also place more attention on considerations of value pluralism and interpretations of similar concepts in other fields of law. It must acknowledge, and more importantly consider, the social context of its decisions rather than avoid this responsibility.

c. Institutional Interactions

Finally, in CJEU and EPO cases involving the interpretation of the exception relating to uses of human embryos for industrial or commercial processes, reflections on other court decisions were evident, but it is argued that there were missed opportunities for further consideration.

In *Brüstle*, the CJEU relied on the *WARF* decision in relation to another aspect of the case. The second question referred by the German Court was whether the concept 'uses … for industrial or commercial purposes' also covers use for the purpose of scientific research.[66] It was held, in an identical manner to that of the Enlarged Board of Appeal in *WARF*, that

> although the aim of scientific research must be distinguished from industrial or commercial purposes, the use of human embryos for the purposes of research, which constitutes the subject matter of a patent application, cannot be separated from the patent itself and the rights attaching to it.[67]

Europe and the UPC' (2016) 7 *GRUR Int* 714; K Rüting, 'A New Scenario for Infringement of Second Medical Use Patents: Are Generics Liable when They Participate in Discount Contract Tenders?' (2016) 1 *epi Information* 25. For more on the expanding nature of patent rights, see S Thambisetty, 'The Institutional Nature of the Patent System: Implications for Bioethical Decision-Making' in C Lenk, N Hoppe and R Andorno (eds), *Ethics and Law of Intellectual Property: Current Problems in Politics, Science and Technology* (Ashgate 2007).

[64] This has also been discussed in L Bently and B Sherman, 'The Ethics of Patenting: Towards a Transgenic Patent System' (1995) 3 *Medical Law Review* 275.

[65] Although this will reduce the risks of substantive fragmentation, it will not exclude it entirely. For example, in the *Brüstle* case, the CJEU did not consider how similar concepts were being interpreted by courts in other fields. If required, the CJEU could also be supported by technical experts.

[66] *Brüstle*, para 39.

[67] ibid para 45.

The practice of taking opinions of the CJEU into account, as well as those of national courts, was also encouraged by the Boards of Appeal in other cases relating to embryonic stem cells. In T1441/13 *Embryonic stem cells, disclaimer/ASTERIAS*, the Board stated:

> Although the Boards of Appeal are only bound by the European Patent Convention and the Implementing Regulations as part of the Convention according to Article 23(3) EPC, the decisions taken by the CJEU and the Supreme Courts of EPC Contracting States on the interpretation of shared or common legislative terms and concepts are certainly of relevance for, and may be considered by, the Boards of Appeal to arrive at their decisions.[68]

Furthermore, in T2221/10 *Culturing stem cells/TECHNION*, the Board of Appeal followed the *WARF* decision and also aligned the EPO with the reasoning of *Brüstle*.[69] However, a word of caution is necessary. This incorporation of the *Brüstle* decision has also been considered restrictive, and its application at the EPO led to further constraints.[70] When responding to fragmentation with judicial dialogue and cooperation in these areas (and more generally), the court considering other viewpoints must do so critically with the public interest in mind. Convergence towards a certain decision may not always be desirable.

Generally, these attempts further reinforce the fact that the various tribunals are considering the decisions of others to promote judicial dialogue and cooperation in the European patent system.[71] This is all further evidence that judicial cooperation is happening and that the institutions of the European patent system are willing to take account of one another's judgments, even when they are not required to do so.

However, there were also some missed opportunities in this area. On the meaning of the term 'human embryo' the Enlarged Board of Appeal in *WARF* decided not to provide a definition. Rather than following the reasoning of the Enlarged Board for doing so, the CJEU clearly went in another direction in *Brüstle*. Had more consideration been given to this reasoning by the CJEU, perhaps the same approach would have been taken, leaving some room for manoeuvre for Member States in determining the answer to this question on a case-by-case basis.

Another relevant point arose in the *WARF* decision relating to the interaction of the various tribunals in the European patent system. Similar to the attempted referral by the UK Court of Appeal to the Enlarged Board of Appeal in *Aerotel* discussed in the previous chapter,[72] the appellant in *WARF* requested that the

[68] T1441/13 *Embryonic stem cells, disclaimer/ASTERIAS* of 09.09.2014.

[69] T2221/10 *Culturing stem cells/TECHNION* of 04.02.2014. For more on this issue, see A Mahalatchimy, E Rial-Sebbag, A-M Duguet, A Cambon-Thomsen and F Taboulet, 'Exclusion of Patentability of Embryonic Stem Cells in Europe: Another Restriction by the European Patent Office' (2015) 37(1) *EIPR* 25.

[70] A Norberg, 'Patents, Morality and Biomedical Innovation in Europe: Historical Overview, Current Debates on Stem Cells, Gene Editing and AI, and *De Lege Ferenda* Reflections' in D Gervais (ed), *Fairness, Morality and Ordre Public in Intellectual Property* (Edward Elgar 2020) 257.

[71] For more on the institutional and jurisdictional aspects of stem cell patenting, see, for example, Bakardjieva Engelbrekt, 'Institutional and Jurisdictional Aspects'.

[72] *Aerotel Ltd v Telco Holdings Ltd & Macrossan's Patent Application* [2006] EWCA Civ 1371.

Enlarged Board refer a number of questions to the CJEU.[73] However, the Enlarged Board decided that 'neither the EPC nor the Implementing Regulations make any provision for a referral' to the CJEU and that 'their powers were limited to those given in the EPC'.[74] The Enlarged Board also went on to say that the identical nature of the wording of both provisions could not lead to the conclusion that the CJEU has jurisdiction to decide matters for the EPO under the EPC.[75]

These points are accurate; however, this was another missed opportunity. To have a non-binding opinion from the CJEU on the matter would have been a positive step towards further judicial dialogue and cooperation.[76] The Enlarged Board of Appeal would not have been obliged to follow the CJEU but could have taken its opinion into account in its own decision. Whether the CJEU would or could have accepted the referral is another question entirely. Its preliminary reference procedure is for EU Member States, but this would have been a useful opportunity for the EPO to explore whether it was possible to seek a non-binding opinion within the current institutional framework.

d. Conclusion

In sum, the interpretation of the exception related to uses of human embryos for industrial or commercial purposes has highlighted some positive practices of judicial dialogue and cooperation, but also some concerns relating to considerations of value pluralism and substantive fragmentation. In an attempt towards convergence in *Brüstle*, the CJEU importantly acknowledged the human dignity underpinnings of the exception and mentioned the differences that existed in Members States but failed to sufficiently incorporate this value pluralism in its decision. Had this been a key factor in the decision-making process and had the CJEU considered in more depth the decision of the Enlarged Board of Appeal in *WARF*, some discretion may have been left to national courts.

In this situation, it can be argued that a level of fragmentation ought to have been preserved, given the context of the decision. More broadly, perhaps decisions where diverse ethical and social considerations exist should always include a level of discretion for individual national courts. In doing so, progress can still be made towards convergence using mechanisms such as judicial dialogue and cooperation where possible and desirable.

There were also some missed opportunities in these cases where lines of communication could have been explored, and considerations of earlier jurisprudence of the same and other institutions could have had an impact on later decisions. Further considerations of this kind will highlight where similarities

[73] *WARF*, Reasons, Points 2–11.

[74] ibid, Point 3.

[75] ibid, Point 8.

[76] The lack of a referral mechanism in this area has also been noted in RJ Aerts, 'A Switch on a Switch on a Switch: The Status of Harmonisation of Biotech Patent Law in Europe' (2019) 41(9) *EIPR* 541, 544.

and differences exist, which can also assist in determining whether a common approach can be introduced.

B. Essentially Biological Processes

Article 4 of the Biotech Directive also excludes specific subject matter from patentability. It states:

> (1) The following shall not be patentable:
>
> ...
>
> (b) essentially biological processes for the production of plants or animals.

An almost identical provision appears in Article 53(b) EPC. This exception has been the subject of considerable debate and divergent interpretations, predominantly within the same institution. Earlier Board of Appeal case law has dealt with the meaning of essentially biological processes, though not without criticism.[77] However, a question remained in relation to the patentability of products resulting from essentially biological processes. This aspect of the exception has been interpreted multiple times by the Enlarged Board of Appeal and inputs from the Administrative Council of the EPOrg and the European Commission have also had an impact.

i. G2/13 and G2/12 (*Broccoli II and Tomatoes II*)

The *Broccoli II and Tomatoes II* decision was the first key case dealing with the patentability of products resulting from essentially biological processes.[78] It had previously been decided that the subject matter of the inventions concerned involved essentially biological processes and so the claims were redrafted to focus on the resulting products. On remittance, the Board of Appeal referred further questions to the Enlarged Board of Appeal on whether these products were patentable. The Enlarged Board, very narrowly interpreting the exception, decided that they were.

This decision raised some concern. In many countries across Europe, such products were not patentable and the decision of the Enlarged Board to the contrary was inconsistent with Contracting State practice and laws. Subsequently, the European Commission released a Notice to the effect that products resulting from essentially biological processes should not be patentable.[79]

[77] G2/07 *Broccoli/PLANT BIOSCIENCE* of 09.12.10 and G1/08 *Tomatoes/STATE OF ISRAEL* of 09.12.10. For more detail on this case, see S Sterckx and J Cockbain, *Exclusions from Patentability: How Far Has the European Patent Office Eroded Boundaries?* (Cambridge University Press 2012) chapter 6; J Pila, 'Article 53(b) EPC: A Challenge to the Novartis Theory of European Patent History' (2009) 72 *MLR* 436.

[78] G2/13 of 25.03.13 and G2/12 of 25.03.15 (*Broccoli II and Tomatoes II*).

[79] Commission Notice on certain articles of Directive 98/44/EC of the European Parliament and of the Council on the legal protection of biotechnological inventions (2016/C 411/03).

Shortly thereafter, the Administrative Council of the EPOrg decided to amend the Rules relating to the EPC to align with the Commission Notice. With a significant majority (35/37), Rule 27 was amended, and a new subsection was added to Rule 28 stating that 'under Article 53(b), European patents shall not be granted in respect of plants or animals exclusively obtained by means of an essentially biological process'.[80] This amendment is clearly contradictory to the decision of the Enlarged Board in *Broccoli II and Tomatoes II* and its validity has been questioned. The Administrative Council can amend the Rules relating to the EPC by qualified majority. However, this change arguably amended the Convention by altering the interpretation of Article 53(b) EPC, and amending the Convention requires unanimity.[81] By approving this as a change to the Rules, the Administrative Council was effectively bypassing the requirement for unanimity.

ii. T1063/18 *Extreme Dark Green, Blocky Peppers*

Following the amendments to Rules 27 and 28, an appeal related to the patentability of products resulting from essentially biological processes came before the Boards of Appeal.[82] In deciding on the patentability of an extremely dark green blocky pepper, the Board followed the precedent set by the Enlarged Board of Appeal in *Broccoli II and Tomatoes II*, stating that the amendment made to the Rules was beyond the competence of the Administrative Council and therefore void.

The Board determined that the amendment altered the meaning of Article 53(b) EPC and relied on Article 164(2) EPC, which states that 'in case of conflict between the provisions of the Convention and those of the Implementing Regulations, the provisions of the Convention shall prevail'. Products resulting from essentially biological processes were patentable once more.

As expected, this decision caused alarm at the EPO. It was agreed, following meetings between Contracting States, the Committee of Experts on Patents, and the European Commission, that the President of the EPO would refer another question on Article 53(b) EPC to the Enlarged Board of Appeal.[83] However, there were concerns in the patent law community over the admissibility of said referral.[84] The President can refer questions to the Enlarged Board in circumstances of conflicting EPO case law.[85] The Board in this case was in fact following previous case law and therefore, it appeared that no conflict existed.

[80] Rule 28(2) Implementing Regulations to the EPC.

[81] See K Walsh, 'Invoking the Public Interest in the European Patent System' in N Hawkins (ed), *Patenting Biotechnological Innovation: Eligibility, Ethics and Public Interest* (Edward Elgar 2022).

[82] T1063/18 *Extreme dark green, blocky peppers/SYNGENTA* of 05.12.2018.

[83] 'Referral of a point of law to the Enlarged Board of Appeal by the President of the European Patent Office (Article 112(1)(b) EPC) – G3/19' available at http://documents.epo.org/projects/babylon/eponet.nsf/0/09D15FA10C1A3A55C125856C0057B988/$File/Referral%20under%20Art.%20112(1)(b)%20EPC_G%2003-19.pdf (President's Referral).

[84] As evidenced by a number of the amicus curiae briefs filed for G3/19, available at www.epo.org/law-practice/case-law-appeals/eba/number.html.

[85] Article 112 EPC.

iii. G3/19 *Pepper (follow-up to 'Tomatoes II' and 'Broccoli II')*

In a surprise to many, the Enlarged Board found that the referral was admissible on the basis of conflicting decisions – previous Board of Appeal decisions had held that the Rules can have an impact on the interpretation of an Article, whereas in T1063/18 *Extreme dark green, blocky peppers*, the Board decided that they did not.[86]

As a result, the Enlarged Board once again contributed to the interpretation of Article 53(b) EPC. Pertinently, on whether the Administrative Council had the competence to introduce Rule 28(2), the Enlarged Board was restrained. Rather than directly addressing the matter, which was raised in the first question, the questions were rephrased to place focus on what the Enlarged Board believed to be 'the real purpose of the President's referral' – to reinterpret whether products resulting from essentially biological processes were patentable.[87] The reason outlined for limiting the question in this way was because the phrasing of the first question was deemed to be a broader institutional topic, which might, if answered, give the Administrative Council 'carte blanche to deviate from established case law'.[88]

In answering its rephrased question, the Enlarged Board abandoned the approach taken in *Broccoli II and Tomatoes II* and decided that products resulting from essentially biological processes were not patentable (again). A dynamic interpretation was undertaken and the Enlarged Board considered that the introduction of Rule 28(2) had significantly altered the situation underlying *Broccoli II and Tomatoes II*.[89] Developments in the area since then and current practices in Contracting States led the Enlarged Board to decide that the changes introduced by Rule 28(2) were representative of how the law had evolved, validating the decision.

iv. Evaluation

Corresponding and distinct points of analysis to those above also arise in relation to the response to fragmentation surrounding this exception. First, institutional interactions and considerations of alternative views are clearly apparent, however in this situation problematic practices have emerged in the push towards convergence. Second, a situation has arisen where most of the institutions interpreting this provision are specialist, and a generalist perspective has not yet been conveyed. Each of these points will be considered in turn.

a. Institutional Interactions and Convergence Overreach

In the interpretation of this exception, the institutions of the European patent system are clearly taking notice of alternative decisions and perspectives.

[86] G3/19 *Pepper (follow-up to 'Tomatoes II' and 'Broccoli II')* of 14.05.20 (G3/19), VI.5.1, 5.2.
[87] ibid II.4.
[88] ibid II.5.
[89] ibid XXXVI.3, XXVI.4.

Attempts are being made to remove the possibility of fragmentation. However, there are also some problematic aspects in the practices that have been used to do so.

In this attempt towards convergence, the Administrative Council observed a non-binding European Commission Notice and introduced Rule 28(2), significantly changing the interpretation of Article 53(b) EPC. The intention here was laudable and the decision that products resulting from essentially biological processes should not be patentable is one that is more beneficial from a societal perspective than the alternative. Not allowing patents on products resulting from essentially biological processes allows farmers more freedom, which in turn has a beneficial impact on food security and crop development.[90] It also reflects practices and understandings in many countries across Europe.[91] However, given the impact on Article 53(b) EPC, these changes ought to have been achieved through unanimity rather than by qualified majority and so the route taken towards convergence is problematic. This is not the first time the Administrative Council has been criticised for 'legislating in disguise'.[92] As elaborated on by Antonia Bakardjieva Engelbrekt, at the time, questions arose around the competence of the Administrative Council to make the decision to incorporate the Biotech Directive into the Implementing Regulations as a means of supplementary interpretation rather than as an amendment to the Convention.[93]

In G3/19, the Enlarged Board of Appeal had the opportunity to address this issue in relation to products resulting from essentially biological processes but decided against it. The Enlarged Board considered its own precedent and completely changed its approach based in no small part on a consideration of practices in many Contracting States. This displays how, even within an institution, approaches towards interpretation can differ and alter based on new evidence, developing practices, and a consideration of alternative viewpoints. However, little consideration was given to the validity of the Administrative Council's actions. In the lead-up to this decision, alternative routes were suggested that would achieve the same result but in a more favourable manner.[94] Regardless, Rule 28(2) was upheld and will remain.

Although the decision itself is a positive step, and changes were made as a result of cooperation and in a push towards convergence, the manner by which these steps were taken is problematic. It is important that in the desire to remove fragmentation, appropriate use of process is upheld.

[90] In general, see chapters in F Girard and C Frison (eds), *The Commons, Plant Breeding and Agricultural Research: Challenges for Food Security and Agrobiodiversity* (Routledge 2018).

[91] G3/19, XV.3.1–XV.3.2

[92] Bakardjieva Engelbrekt, 'Institutional and Jurisdictional Aspects' 256.

[93] ibid 255–57.

[94] CIPA, 'Patenting of Plants in Europe Position Paper' (2019) *Chartered Institute of Patent Attorneys* available at www.cipa.org.uk/news/patenting-of-plants-in-europe/.

b. Specialist Institution Perspective

Above, it was concluded that the generalist perspective is a necessary one for responding to the possibility of substantive fragmentation, owing to its consideration of patent law in a broader context. One of the concerns with specialist-only institutions is that such considerations might be lacking and that there would be a preoccupation with granting patents. In the interpretation of this exception, most decisions and actions have been taken by specialist institutions.

Surprisingly, therefore, the final decision in this instance is one that prevents patents in a particular area, which, as mentioned, is positive from a societal perspective. However, these issues were not even mentioned in the G3/19 decision. The reason for the decision has been criticised as one that is entirely political.[95] It is important to ensure that societal issues are given adequate consideration within decisions by all institutions in the European patent system, both national and supranational. Doing so will ensure that all views are taken into account when determining whether convergence is possible or beneficial.

It is also worth noting that the CJEU has not yet been presented with a question on Article 4 of the Biotech Directive. The European Commission Notice was not binding, and it was acknowledged that only the CJEU could provide an interpretation of Article 4 that was binding on EU Member States. This is something to bear in mind moving forward because the CJEU could take the opposite view on the patentability of products resulting from essentially biological processes.

c. Conclusion

In sum, the interpretation of the exception related to essentially biological processes has highlighted some positive interactions, but also some areas where, in the response to fragmentation, pushing towards convergence has resulted in problematic practices. The decision to amend the interpretation of Article 53(b) EPC ought to have been unanimous. Although other court and institutional practices are being considered by the Enlarged Board of Appeal, where appropriate there needs to be scope for disagreement with other institutions or bodies within the same institution. The Enlarged Board missed an opportunity to reject the questionable implementation of Rule 28(2).

With the implementation of Rule 28(2), this now needs to be considered and followed by all EPC Contracting States, not only EU Member States. Although many countries already have such practices and agree with the provision, this change required a unanimous decision. In this situation, fragmentation ought to have been accepted since convergence could not be achieved by the appropriate means.

[95] For more on the political nature of this decision, see Walsh, 'Invoking the Public Interest'.

The social and public policy issues that are directly relevant to the decision-making process must also be considered in detail. In G3/19, the social context of the decision was not even mentioned, and although the outcome is in the public interest, the institutions involved must engage with these discussions on a deeper level.

III. Impact of the Unitary Patent Package

Responses to fragmentation, institutional interaction, caution around attempts towards convergence in areas with divergent viewpoints, and the nature of generalist and specialist decision-making must also be considered in relation to the forthcoming EU unitary patent system.

With the introduction of another specialised supranational decision-making authority, with part of its legal basis in EU law, the relationship between the UPC and other institutions in the European patent system will be of the utmost importance. This is true in all areas, but especially on the interpretation of the exceptions to patentability, where differing views are more prevalent.

Judicial dialogue and cooperation will be crucial.[96] The potential for fragmentation introduced by the UPC is significant. The UPC is an attempt at convergence in the European patent system; however, it will not remove the potential for fragmentation, it will add to it.[97] The decisions of the UPC will only be applicable for those participating in the UPP, excluding non-participating EU Member States and states outside the EU but within the European patent system. Additionally, the potential for fragmentation is increased in both the transitional period and because of the number of divisions that are expected, coupled with concerns over bifurcation.[98] An open dialogue among all decision-makers in the European patent system will be even more important; the UPC will have to consider existing precedent and pre-existing institutions will have to consider UPC jurisprudence.

It will also be important for the UPC to consider both substantive and procedural aspects in attempts towards convergence. It is possible that the UPC could interpret the exceptions to patentability (as well as other provisions) in a way that differs from all other institutions so far, or it could lean towards convergence. However, in practice, coming to a European-wide decision in relation to the exceptions to patentability will be difficult.

[96] As mentioned in Chapter 5, Federica Baldan and Esther van Zimmeren have discussed the role of the UPC in this regard in detail: F Baldan and E van Zimmeren, 'The Future Role of the Unified Patent Court in Safeguarding Coherence in the European Patent System' (2015) 52 *Common Market Law Review* 1529, 1573.

[97] For more in relation to morality in this context, see A McMahon, 'An Institutional Examination of the Implications of the Unitary Patent Package for the Morality Provisions: A Fragmented Future Too Far?' (2017) 48(1) *IIC* 42.

[98] See Chapter 2.

The tension that exists between cultures in the European patent system will remain. It is part of the reason for the length of time taken to come to an agreement on a EU unitary patent system. Considering the multinational composition of the panels, some commentators find it difficult to see how the UPC would do much better than the current systems against the 'obstacles to uniform interpretation of differing patent cultures and language barriers'.[99] However, the composition of the UPC panels could be one of the most beneficial aspects of the forthcoming system.[100] Judges from different Member States sitting on the same panel will have to come to a compromise. At times, this will be on issues where there has been divergence between their countries. This could introduce a more inclusive UPC precedent and ensure a broader consideration of national and EPO jurisprudence, including value pluralism.[101]

Adding to the beneficial impact of a multinational composition of panels, judges of the UPC can retain positions as judges in their national courts. Consequently, practices developed in the interpretation of substantive patent law on a UPC panel could filter into the respective judge's national decisions, making progress towards convergence through judicial dialogue and cooperation. UPC decisions will likely be highly persuasive throughout Europe; however, a critical consideration will be required when deciding whether to follow the UPC, particularly for the Boards of Appeal and states outside the EU and UPP.

It has also been argued that the specialist nature of the UPC panels could lead to a 'very closed legal culture', predominantly focused on patents, and so a balancing act is required to ensure this does not occur.[102] Adding to this closed legal culture is the fact that dissenting opinions will only be given in exceptional circumstances.[103] Federica Baldan and Esther van Zimmeren convincingly argue that these should be more prevalent and would add to the discussion to ensure an autonomous body of law.[104]

A significant factor here will be the future relationship between the UPC and the CJEU. The provisions of the UPCA ensure the UPC's respect for the

[99] J Smits and W Bull, 'The Europeanization of Patent Law: Towards a Competitive Model' in A Ohly and J Pila (eds), *The Europeanization of Intellectual Property Law: Towards a European Legal Methodology* (Oxford University Press 2013) 50.

[100] Also discussed by Baldan and van Zimmeren, 'The Future Role of the Unified Patent Court' 1573.

[101] The potential benefits of UPC judges also being neutral decision-makers has been highlighted in A Alba Betancourt, 'Cross-Border Patent Disputes: Unified Patent Court or International Commercial Arbitration?' (2016) 32(82) *Utrecht Journal of International and European Law* 44, 48–49. For more on a European precedent see Pila, 'Constitutionalized Doctrine of Precedent' 228.

[102] CS Petersen and J Schovsbo, 'On Law and Policy in a European and European Union Patent Court (EEUPC) – What Will It Do to Patent Law and What Will Patent Law Do to It?' in H Koch, K Hagel-Sørensen and JHH Weiler (eds), *Europe: The New Legal Realism* (Djøf Forlag 2010) 630. See also CS Petersen, T Riis and J Schovsbo, 'The Unified Patent Court (UPC) in Action: How Will the Design of the UPC Affect Patent Law?' in RM Ballardini, M Norrgård and N Bruun (eds), *Transitions in European Patent Law: Influences of the Unitary Patent Package* (Kluwer 2015).

[103] Article 78(2) UPCA.

[104] Baldan and van Zimmeren, 'The Future Role of the Unified Patent Court' 1573.

primacy of EU law and its cooperation with the preliminary reference procedure in order to ensure the correct application and uniform interpretation of Union law, among other matters.[105] Jan Smits and William Bull remark that this has been interpreted as a 'major limitation' on the UPC and note the potential impact it could have on patent litigation.[106] There have been multiple criticisms raised relating to the role of the CJEU in relation to the UPC. Expanded on in detail elsewhere, the main criticisms relate to the possibility of the CJEU taking an over-active role in the UPP and that, as a generalist court, it does not have the expertise required to make decisions in the patent field; however, as noted above, the generalist overview of the CJEU is exactly what is required in the European patent system to add a consideration of patent law in a broader context and to reduce the risk of substantive fragmentation; so too with the introduction of the UPC.[107]

The UPC could be seen as a hybrid court in this context – one that is specialist enough to deal with the technical subject matter that comes before it, but also required to refer questions on EU law to the CJEU, thereby adding a generalist perspective. The result might be expected to safeguard the interpretation of substantive patent law, while also ensuring that patent law takes account of issues of public policy. However, this would be highly dependent on the UPC referring questions to the CJEU in the first place, which may be avoided unless absolutely necessary.

It is important to prevent decisions of the UPC proceeding with 'tunnel vision' as a result of becoming too specialised, and to emphasise the importance of patent law being seen in a broader context.[108] As noted above, convergence cannot be pursued at the expense of substantive and procedural considerations. Courts will have to proceed with these factors in mind.

[105] Articles 20–23 UPCA.

[106] Smits and Bull, 'The Europeanization of Patent Law' 52.

[107] Elaborated on in Walsh, 'The Unitary Patent Package'; Smits and Bull, 'The Europeanization of Patent Law' 52. For the role of the CJEU throughout the history of attempts at unitary patent protection, see S Luginbuehl and T Kandeva, 'The Role of the European Court of Justice in the European Patent Court System' in C Geiger, CA Nard and X Seuba (eds), *Intellectual Property and the Judiciary* (Edward Elgar 2018).

[108] Schovsbo, Riis and Petersen, 'The Unified Patent Court' 273. See also CS Petersen and J Schovsbo, 'Decision-making in the Unified Patent Court: Ensuring a Balanced Approach' in C Geiger, CA Nard and X Seuba (eds), *Intellectual Property and the Judiciary* (Edward Elgar 2018) and A Plomer, 'The EPO as Patent Law-maker in Europe' (2019) 25(1) *European Law Journal* 57. For a comparison with the US and Japan, see RC Dreyfuss, 'An International Perspective I: A View from the United States' in J Pila and C Wadlow (eds), *The Unitary EU Patent System* (Hart Publishing 2015) 157; KM O'Malley and BMG Lynn, 'The Proposed Structure and Function of the Unified Patent Court: Lessons from the American Judicial Experience' in C Geiger, CA Nard and X Seuba (eds), *Intellectual Property and the Judiciary* (Edward Elgar 2018); and T Takenaka, 'The Best Practice for Patent Judiciary: Lessons from Another Experiment on Specialised Adjudications for Patent Cases in Japan' in C Geiger, CA Nard and X Seuba (eds), *Intellectual Property and the Judiciary* (Edward Elgar 2018).

IV. Considering Diversity and Value Pluralism when Responding to Fragmentation

This chapter has investigated responses to fragmentation by supranational institutions in the area of exceptions to patentability. Through an investigation of the interpretation of two exceptions, it has been shown that in certain circumstances the push towards convergence can go too far.

In one situation, although somewhat clarified by later case law, in defining human embryo expansively for all EU Member States, the CJEU did not sufficiently consider relevant practices in its Member States. Allowing some flexibility, some fragmentation, would have considered the existing value pluralism and allowed for national diversity where appropriate. At the very least, these factors deserved a much more detailed consideration. In another area, the push towards convergence by the Administrative Council of the EPOrg on the patentability of products resulting from essentially biological processes, maintained by the Enlarged Board, led to changes being implemented by qualified majority rather than by unanimity. These responses to fragmentation raise concerns. While the intentions are laudable, it must be recognised that fragmentation may be necessary unless convergence can be achieved by the most appropriate means and consensus built in a way that is accepted by all involved.

In both situations, interactions between institutions are apparent, but there were missed opportunities and imperfect implementations. These interactions are also praiseworthy, but changes cannot be introduced without a critical consideration of the consequences, and in certain circumstances convergence may not be possible or desirable.

Moving forward, when responding to fragmentation, all institutions, national and supranational, should critically consider their own precedent and that of other courts and institutions when decision-making. Diversity will always exist in the European patent system. Only on consideration of the variety of viewpoints that exist can an informed decision be made on whether convergence is possible or desirable. It must be acknowledged that fragmentation may persist while societal or cultural differences remain. Judicial dialogue and cooperation can promote progress towards convergence on a case-by-case basis, but also leave open the possibility for fragmentation and, thus, a consideration of national diversity. At the same time, courts must also be aware of implementing decisions that are in the public interest and consider how similar concepts are being interpreted in other areas of law.

In addition to fragmentation being inherent and capable of being harnessed by certain informal and formal mechanisms, acknowledging fragmentation can also provide for a consideration of the multiple values that exist in supranational legal regimes, including the European patent system.

Conclusion: Fragmentation and the European Patent System

Fragmentation is a consistent and significant issue that has been at the core of many criticisms of the European patent system. However, until now, we have not paused to comprehensively consider the concept, and ask what the consequences might be for the European patent system and for substantive patent law if fragmentation is, and remains, a significant feature.

This book has considered current perceptions of and responses to fragmentation in the European patent system. It argues that fragmentation can and should be perceived in a more nuanced manner and, as a result, responded to in a more effective way. It can be concluded that, while fragmentation is a central feature of the existing European patent system and is likely to be a central feature of the forthcoming EU unitary patent system, it is also something that can never be removed entirely.

Fragmentation is an inherent feature of the European patent system because of the way legislation has been introduced. No system has replaced the last, and rather than unifying the area, law-making in the form of international agreements and directives has ensured a level of fragmentation. Additionally, multiple institutions exist to interpret the same laws, which can lead, and has led, to divergent decisions on the same invention and different interpretations of the same laws. With or without an EU unitary patent system, fragmentation will remain. When responding to fragmentation, this must be considered.

Furthermore, the goals of European harmonisation and integration cannot be pursued entirely at the expense of national diversity, particularly in relation to areas where a plurality of values exist, such as with the exceptions to patentability. In some situations, attempts towards harmonisation have resulted in unnecessarily broad definitions of terms. In other attempts towards convergence, problematic practices have emerged. It must therefore be recognised that fragmentation may be necessary unless consensus in these areas is built in an appropriate and considered manner.

For these reasons, the fragmentation that exists within the current and future European patent system should be perceived as an inherent aspect. Attention should be placed on better understanding its challenges and responding to it in a more effective manner.

There are multiple routes to patent protection available in Europe: first, the national route, through individual national patent systems;[1] second, the European (EPC) route to patent protection;[2] and third, the PCT route to patent protection through an initial international application, which must then enter the national or regional stage.[3] The common feature of each route is that, if the applicant is ultimately successful, the result is effectively a national patent – that is, a patent that is validated and litigated in the territory for which it is granted.

Many criticisms of the current routes to patent protection arise due to their fragmented nature, and numerous problems have been identified. The risks that have been associated with fragmentation in the current European patent system involve different types of fragmentation. Territorial fragmentation means that it is not currently possible to have a single patent granted that covers all countries in Europe, which risks patents being granted in some countries and not others due to, for example, differing examination standards. Institutional fragmentation can occur because patents are still mostly enforced at the national level, which risks differences in the interpretation of substantive patent law provisions by various national and European courts and tribunals, and divergence in decisions of various institutions regarding the same patent. Substantive fragmentation can occur when separate regimes interpret similar concepts in different ways, which risks concepts that arise in patent law being interpreted without the consideration of similar interpretations in other areas of law (such as the meaning of human dignity in human rights law). Procedural fragmentation, resulting from offices and courts operating using different processes, can also have an impact on each of these forms of fragmentation.

These risks are a reality. Differences in the interpretation of substantive patent law are apparent from the approach taken by some national courts when compared to the approach taken by the Boards of Appeal of the EPO, such as in relation to the requirements for an invention and inventive step. Divergent decisions are also apparent, with the most well-known example being *Improver v Remington*.[4] In this case, and many others, national courts across Europe have come to different conclusions on patent validity and infringement when dealing with the same invention.

Furthermore, although the provisions of the EPC have been implemented into the laws of its 38 (current) Contracting States, they have not been implemented using the exact same wording as the EPC. This can lead, and has led, to differences in the interpretation of substantive patent law. Additionally, the EU has implemented the Biotech Directive,[5] which contains substantive EU patent law

[1] For example, Patents Act 1977 (UK); Patentgesetz in der Fassung der Bekanntmachung vom 16. Dezember 1980 (BGBI. 1981 I S. 1), das zuletzt durch Artikel 1 des Gesetzes vom 30. August 2021 (BGBI. I S. 4074) geändert worden ist (German Patents Act).

[2] Convention on the Grant of European Patents of 5 October 1973, amended in 2000.

[3] Patent Cooperation Treaty 1970.

[4] *Improver Corp v Remington Consumer Product Ltd* [1990] FSR 181.

[5] Council Directive 98/44/EC of the European Parliament and of the Council of 6 July 1998 on the legal protection of biotechnological inventions [1998] OJ L 213/13.

provisions on inventions relating to biotechnology, which are applicable to all EU Member States. These provisions are also considered by the Boards of Appeal, owing to their inclusion in the Implementing Regulations to the EPC as a supplementary means of interpretation. Here, too, provisions are not always directly transposed and scope for divergence remains. The implementation of the Biotech Directive has also included the CJEU more substantially in the European patent system, increasing the potential for institutional fragmentation.

The current European patent system is thus clearly fragmented. There are various ways in which substantive patent law can be interpreted and a number of different institutions to carry out that role, which can create divergence in the interpretation and application of that law. To minimise fragmentation and the risks associated with it, multiple attempts have been made to introduce a unitary patent right and court system to adjudicate on such rights. However, over 70 years after the idea was first contemplated, the idea for a European unitary patent system is only just being realised. The difficulties faced have been plentiful and each attempt to introduce a unitary patent system in Europe has been met with fierce debate and criticism.

For the UPP, which will establish the EU unitary patent system, this tradition has continued.[6] Once established, it will introduce, for the first time, a unitary patent for all participating EU Member States, and the UPC to deal with disputes and provide cross-border decisions on both infringement and validity. It has been seen that rather than increasing harmonisation, the proposed system will add another layer onto the existing layers of the European patent system and thus add to its existing fragmentation. It will increase all types of fragmentation that currently exist.

Concerns exist relating to the patchwork of laws from which the UPP derives its substance, and that territorial fragmentation will increase because this system will not replace but add to the European patent system. This could be exacerbated by its potentially stagnated process of ratification and implementation, which will result in the UPP being applicable in different territories at different times. There is also a fear that owing to the potential cost of the system, its users will ultimately be limited. The UPP will also introduce to the European patent system an additional institution with numerous divisions, significantly increasing the potential for institutional fragmentation both inside and outside the new system. Shared jurisdiction during the transitional period will add to this, as will the procedural intricacies that are expected on implementation.

[6] The package consists of Regulation (EU) 1257/2012 of the European Parliament and of the Council of 17 December 2012 implementing enhanced cooperation in the area of the creation of unitary patent protection [2012] OJ L 361/1; Regulation (EU) 1260/2012 of the European Parliament and of the Council of 17 December 2012 implementing enhanced cooperation in the area of the creation of unitary patent protection with regard to the applicable translation arrangements [2012] OJ L 361/89; and Agreement 2013/C on a Unified Patent Court [2013] OJ L 175/01.

Just as fragmentation is a central feature of the existing European patent landscape, so too will it continue to be a central feature of the forthcoming EU unitary patent system. The almost universal assumption has been that fragmentation is a shortcoming of the current system and that it will be a shortcoming of the forthcoming system. Indeed, as noted previously, fragmentation can have serious negative consequences, and there are aspects of the forthcoming system that could and should be improved. Importantly, however, all risks associated with fragmentation cannot be solved with the addition of an EU unitary patent system. There will never be a truly unitary patent system in Europe. There will always be fragmentation and diversity.

Therefore, rather than concentrating on how to respond to fragmentation through a unitary patent system alone, attention ought to be directed towards understanding it more deeply and responding to it in a multifaceted manner. By perceiving fragmentation in a more nuanced way our response to it can similarly change. Perspectives of fragmentation in the European patent system can change and alternative perspectives have been evidenced outside the patent system. Looking at the evolution of EU law-making, and the way fragmentation is responded to in the international legal system, has given reason to pause and reflect.

Methods of EU law-making have developed alongside the aims and motivations of the EU owing to its expansion. Today, mechanisms exist that allow integration to be pursued for Member States that are able and willing to do so without the full participation of all Member States. Differentiated integration allows for a level of divergence, or fragmentation, in Member State laws, but it also allows progress towards integration where it would not have been achieved otherwise. For example, enhanced cooperation was used for the forthcoming EU unitary patent system. Although there are some concerns about its use in this instance, as a concept it is favourable. Fragmentation has a place in EU law-making. The necessity of such mechanisms was clearly foreseen and, as long as Member States are not excluded from joining the integration effort in the future, progress towards harmonisation can be achieved, but not at the expense of national diversity.

National diversity has always been a key factor in establishing European and international agreements and legislation. For the European patent system, pure unification, meant as one system to replace all others, has never been an achievable goal for European law-makers, even if it were considered desirable.[7] Provisions have been made to ensure that national diversity and value pluralism are considered. In the European patent system, this can be seen in the implementation of the EPC and the Biotech Directive. Rather than imposing specific terms and conditions on countries, including those involving fundamental rights and other matters on which there is no consensus, these laws could be implemented by each country in a way that was deemed appropriate for that region.

[7] J Pila, 'The European Patent: An Old and Vexing Problem' (2013) 62(4) *ICLQ* 917.

Fragmentation is also perceived differently in the international legal system. While previously it had been feared, fragmentation is now seen as an inherent aspect of the international legal system. More recently, it has been viewed in neutral and positive terms, frequently aligned with diversity and flexibility. Importantly, interpretative mechanisms, such as the rules on interpretation contained in the Vienna Convention[8] and methods such as systemic integration and judicial dialogue and cooperation, are regarded as effective means for reducing the risks associated with fragmentation. As a result, the fear of fragmentation has diminished, and international legal scholars now speak in more neutral terms of its capacity to be harnessed and its promotion of diversity instead. In order to respond to fragmentation, particularly fragmentation within regimes, persuasive suggestions have been made that place a strong emphasis on structured judicial dialogue, a prominent yet not hierarchical role for a central court, and a shared responsibility for integration by all stakeholders.[9]

Fragmentation, as an inherent aspect of a supranational legal system, need not therefore be feared. If it is responded to appropriately, it does not raise such significant concerns and can consider national diversity and value pluralism. Perceptions of, and responses to, fragmentation in the European patent system could and should alter similarly. Given current practices, this is entirely possible.

In examining how substantive patent law is currently interpreted, it has been shown that similar responses to fragmentation appear to be emerging, particularly around judicial cooperation and dialogue. Judges from all institutions are increasingly taking each other's judgments into account. If diverging from a previous interpretation, the reasons for doing so are sometimes explained. There are provisions in some national legislation to ensure that the provisions of international agreements are considered.[10] The Boards of Appeal use the Vienna Convention for the interpretation of treaties, despite the absence of any legal obligation to do so. Furthermore, judges meet at various events to discuss current trends and issues in patent law and each other's judgments. It can be seen from these measures that the fragmentation that exists in the European patent system is being addressed along the same lines as in the international legal system, albeit informally and irregularly. Areas of continued divergence and areas of convergence are apparent, but where possible and appropriate, judicial cooperation can lead to harmonisation. However, it is argued that these methods should be recognised, structured and promoted further to make our response to fragmentation more effective.

Additionally, in certain circumstances, responding to fragmentation can be more complicated. When considering the exceptions to patentability particularly, caution is required in attempts to harmonise and converge because of the public

[8] Vienna Convention on the Law of Treaties (Vienna, 23 May 1969, 1155 UNTS 331).

[9] P Webb, *International Judicial Integration and Fragmentation* (Oxford University Press 2013) 208–28.

[10] For example, section 130(7) Patents Act 1977 (UK).

policy concerns underlying their inclusion in substantive patent law. Additionally, similar concepts are also interpreted by institutions outside the patent system and so the potential for substantive fragmentation is increased. Attempts at harmonisation can go too far and in these situations allowing some divergence or some fragmentation may be the more appropriate response unless consensus can be built appropriately. For example, when interpreting the exception to patentability concerning uses of human embryos for industrial or commercial purposes, the CJEU expansively defined, as an autonomous concept of EU law, the term 'human embryo', and held the fundamental right of human dignity to require an expansive reading.[11] While this is an important consideration and the role of the CJEU as a harmonising body is crucial, there is no consensus on these issues in Europe and these differences were not adequately considered by the CJEU. Substantial controversy ensued, although this was somewhat clarified in later case law.[12] The lesson here is that some level of fragmentation, or in other words, allowing for some national diversity and value pluralism, is necessary unless consensus can be built appropriately. This approach would allow for a consideration of reasonable differences that exist between countries in Europe, while promoting harmonisation in the areas in which this can be achieved.

In a push towards convergence at the EPO, problematic practices emerged on the interpretation of the exception relating to essentially biological processes and the products resulting therefrom. Without the required unanimous decision, the Administrative Council amended a pre-existing rule and inserted a new rule in the Implementing Regulations to the EPC, altering the interpretation of an EPC article. When this came before the Enlarged Board of Appeal,[13] the focus was on whether a change in interpretation was necessary rather than on the appropriateness of the changes to these rules. Although the result that products resulting from essentially biological processes are not patentable is welcome, the manner in which it was achieved is problematic.

In these areas, because responding to fragmentation is more complicated, careful consideration of the similarities and differences in interpretations and opinions is required. This includes not only a consideration of interpretations within the European patent system, but also interpretations by institutions outside the patent system in relation to similar concepts. Progress towards integration can be facilitated where possible, but where consensus is not yet achievable or desirable, this must also be recognised. Appropriate consensus-building is of great importance, and widespread definitions and problematic practices that do not take this into account will be to the detriment of the European patent system and, furthermore, to the detriment of Europe. These considerations are necessary to maintain the respect and cooperation of the countries involved.

[11] Case C-34/10 *Oliver Brüstle v Greenpeace eV* ECLI:EU:C:2011:669.

[12] Case C-364/13 *International Stem Cell Corporation v Comptroller General of Patents, Designs and Trade Marks* ECLI:EU:C:2014:2451.

[13] G3/19 *Pepper (follow-up to 'Tomatoes II' and 'Broccoli II')* of 14.05.20.

Importantly, the methods used in the international legal system, and emerging in the European patent system, to respond to fragmentation can take this into account. For example, the point of judicial dialogue and cooperation is to consider differences of opinion, as well as developments in the field and new information, and to decide the most suitable way forward on this basis. It also allows for progress towards convergence, if deemed appropriate. Of course, as with any approach, there are evidently certain limitations to acknowledge, such as the risk of judicial law-making, bias towards certain viewpoints, lack of diversity in the judiciary, and differences in court procedures. However, this does not take away from the merits of the argument that all institutions in the European patent system need to consider the decisions and practices of all other institutions. These are additional factors that also need to feature in those considerations.

This approach will be all the more important on the implementation of the EU unitary patent system and the resulting increase in fragmentation. Under Article 24 of the UPCA, the sources of law upon which the UPC will base its decisions include Union law, the UPCA, the EPC, other international agreements applicable to patents and binding on all participating Member States, and finally, national law. The UPC is thus formally required to take all relevant patent laws into consideration. Therefore, the relationship between it and the pre-existing institutions of the European patent system will be of the utmost importance. The UPCA will further necessitate a dialogue (whether formal or informal) between all national courts, the members of the Boards of Appeal, the CJEU, and the various divisions of the UPC. As suggested above, there is also a place for a court with a prominent (though not hierarchical) role when responding to fragmentation. Whether the UPC could/should fill this role for the European patent system more broadly is questionable.

As the UPC will base its decisions on these various sources of law, it may have the effect of bringing the various interpretations of substantive patent law and jurisprudence of the relevant tribunals closer together, especially in the long term. The requirement to consider all sources of law could arguably be seen as supporting the wider introduction into the European patent system of the rules on interpretation from the international legal system, specifically from the Vienna Convention. The multinational composition of judicial panels may also facilitate convergence. This composition allows for judges from different participating Member States to come together and reach consensus on issues on which they may previously have had completely different opinions and approaches. This may eventually lead to further harmonisation. Most panels will consist of both legally qualified and technically qualified judges. In allowing these discussions to take place, a UPC ideology could begin to emerge, one that considers the opinions of all participating Member States. A UPC jurisprudence could develop based on interpretations of current precedent. Furthermore, having national judges sit on benches with judges from other participating Member States, and having a discussion regarding common, as well as controversial, issues will more than likely have a percolating effect. This new precedent might filter from the UPC panels into national courts, thus promoting harmonisation, yet allowing for national diversity where appropriate.

However, this precedent and these decisions will be binding on participating Member States only, and although likely to have a highly persuasive influence on the decisions of the Boards of Appeal, courts outside the UPP, and national courts more generally, a critical consideration of UPC jurisprudence will be required. The UPC will not be obliged to consider jurisprudence beyond its jurisdiction and there are significant concerns relating to its specialised nature. There are also various concerns relating to the UPP generally, especially for SMEs. The UPC will likely play a prominent role in the European patent system more broadly, but these concerns must be addressed and considered in decision-making both inside and outside the UPP. For now, judicial dialogue and cooperation between the current and future tribunals needs to be more structured, harnessed and promoted to ensure that fragmentation in the European patent system is responded to in an inclusive manner.

Overall, if recognised and developed further, the mechanisms that are being used in the European patent system to respond to fragmentation, like those seen in the international legal system, have the potential to promote convergence, both now and in the long term, while also remaining mindful of the appropriateness of some degree of national diversity and value pluralism. Fragmentation is and always will be an inherent part of the European patent system. Perceptions of fragmentation in the European patent system can and should therefore be revised. Altering our perceptions, and thus enhancing how we respond to fragmentation, would allow the patent system to move forward more effectively and become more focused on improving the system for all involved.

BIBLIOGRAPHY

Books

Andenas M and Bjorge E (eds), *A Farewell to Fragmentation: Reassertion and Convergence in International Law* (Cambridge University Press 2015)

Bently L, Sherman B, Gangjee D and Johnson P, *Intellectual Property Law* (5th edn, Oxford University Press 2018)

Brown A, Kheria S, Cornwell J and Iljadica M, *Contemporary Intellectual Property* (5th edn, Oxford University Press 2019)

Chalmers D, Davies G and Monti G, *European Union Law* (4th edn, Cambridge University Press 2019)

Cook T (ed), *The Patent Litigation Law Review* (2nd edn, Law Business Research 2018)

Correa CM, *Trade Related Aspects of Intellectual Property Rights: A Commentary on the TRIPS Agreement* (2nd edn, Oxford University Press 2020)

Craig C and de Búrca G, *EU Law: Text, Cases and Materials* (7th edn, Oxford University Press 2020)

Dashwood A, Dougan M, Rodger BJ, Spaventa E and Wyatt D, *Wyatt and Dashwood's European Union Law* (6th edn, Hart Publishing 2011)

Davis R, St Quintin T and Tritton G, *Tritton on Intellectual Property in Europe* (5th edn, Sweet & Maxwell 2020)

Dinan D, *Ever Closer Union* (4th edn, Palgrave Macmillan 2010)

Dunlop H, *European Unitary Patent and Unified Patent Court* (2nd edn, Chartered Institute of Patent Attorneys 2014)

Dutfield G and Suthersanen U, *Dutfield and Suthersanen on Global Intellectual Property Law* (2nd edn, Edward Elgar 2020)

European Patent Academy, *Patent Litigation in Europe: An Overview of National Law and Practice in the EPC Contracting States* (5th edn, European Patent Office 2019)

European Patent Office, *Case Law of the Boards of Appeal of the European Patent Office* (9th edn, Druckerei CH Beck 2019)

European Patent Office, *National Law Relating to the EPC* (20th edn, European Patent Office 2019)

Fisher M, *Fundamentals of Patent Law: Interpretation and Scope of Protection* (Hart Publishing 2007)

Gervais D, *The TRIPS Agreement; Drafting History and Analysis* (5th edn, Sweet & Maxwell 2021)

Girard F and Frison C (eds), *The Commons, Plant Breeding and Agricultural Research: Challenges for Food Security and Agrobiodiversity* (Routledge 2018)

Griset P, *The European Patent: A Success Story for Innovation* (Kösel Burch Altusried-Kuugzell 2013)

Grosse Ruse-Khan H, *The Protection of Intellectual Property in International Law* (Oxford University Press 2016)

Guellec D and Van Pottelsberghe de la Potterie B, *The Economics of the European Patent System* (Oxford University Press 2007)

Haedicke M and Timmann H, *Patent Law: A Handbook* (CH Beck 2013)

Ilardi A, *The New European Patent* (Hart Publishing 2015)

Jewess M, *Inside Intellectual Property: Best Practice in Intellectual Property Law, Management, and Strategy* (Chartered Institute of Patent Attorneys 2013)

Kur A, Dreier T and Luginbuehl S, *European Intellectual Property Law* (2nd edn, Edward Elgar 2019)

Llewelyn D and Aplin T, *Cornish Llewelyn & Aplin; Intellectual Property: Patents, Copyright, Trade Marks and Allied Rights* (9th edn, Sweet & Maxwell 2019)

Luginbuehl S, *European Patent Law: Towards a Uniform Interpretation* (Edward Elgar 2011)

McDonagh L, *European Patent Litigation in the Shadow of the Unified Patent Court* (Edward Elgar 2016)
Merges R, *Justifying Intellectual Property* (Harvard University Press 2011)
Moravcsik A, *The Choice for Europe: Social Purpose and State Power from Messina to Maastricht* (Cornell University Press 1998)
Murray K, *A Politics of Patent Law: Crafting the Participatory Patent Bargain* (Routledge 2013)
Okejidi RL and Bagley MA (eds), *Patent Law in Global Perspective* (Oxford University Press 2014)
Pagenberg J and Cornish W (eds), *Interpretation of Patents in Europe: Application of Article 69 EPC* (Heymanns 2007)
Parthasarathy S, *Patent Politics: Life Forms, Markets & the Public Interest in the United States & Europe* (University of Chicago Press 2017)
Paterson G, *The European Patent System: The Law and Practice of the European Patent Convention* (2nd edn, Sweet & Maxwell 2001)
Pila J, *The Requirement for an Invention in Patent Law* (Oxford University Press 2010)
—— *The Subject Matter of Intellectual Property* (Oxford University Press 2017)
Pila J and Torremans PLC, *European Intellectual Property Law* (2nd edn, Oxford University Press 2016)
Pila J and Wadlow C (eds), *The Unitary EU Patent System* (Hart Publishing 2015)
Seville C, *EU Intellectual Property Law and Policy* (Edward Elgar 2009)
Sterckx S and Cockbain J, *Exclusions from Patentability: How Far Has the European Patent Office Eroded Boundaries?* (Cambridge University Press 2012)
Stjerna IB, *The Parliamentary History of the European 'Unitary Patent': Verbatim Protocol of Selected Meetings in the European Parliament and its Legal Affairs Committee* (Tredition 2015)
Thumm N, *Intellectual Property Rights – National Systems and Harmonisation in Europe* (Springer Verlag 2000)
Van Empel M, *The Granting of European Patents* (Sijthoff 1975)
Webb P, *International Judicial Integration and Fragmentation* (Oxford University Press 2013)
Young MA (ed), *Regime Interaction in International Law: Facing Fragmentation* (Cambridge University Press 2015)

Book Chapters

Alter K, 'Explaining National Court Acceptance of European Court Jurisprudence: A Critical Evaluation of Theories of Legal Integration' in Slaughter A-M, Stone Sweet A and Weiler JHH (eds), *The European Courts and National Courts – Doctrine and Jurisprudence* (Hart Publishing 1998)
Azoulai L, 'The Europeanisation of Legal Concepts' in Neergaard U and Nielsen R (eds), *European Legal Method: In a Multi-Level EU Legal Order* (DJØF Publishing 2012)
Bakardjieva Engelbrekt A, 'Institutional and Jurisdictional Aspects of Stem Cell Patenting in Europe (EC and EPO): Tensions and Prospects' in Plomer A and Torremans PLC (eds), *Embryonic Stem Cell Patents: European Patent Law and Ethics* (Oxford University Press 2009)
Brinkhof J and Ohly A, 'Towards a Unified Patent Court in Europe' in Pila J and Ohly A (eds), *The Europeanization of Intellectual Property Law: Towards a Legal Methodology* (Oxford University Press 2013)
Broude T and Shany Y, 'The International Law and Policy of Multi-Sourced Equivalent Norms' in Broude T and Shany Y (eds), *Multi-Sourced Equivalent Norms in International Law* (Hart Publishing 2011)
Cornelisse G and Moraru M, 'Introduction: Judicial Dialogue on the Return Directive – Catalyst for Changing Migration Governance?' in Cornelisse G, Moraru M and De Bruycker P (eds), *Law and Judicial Dialogue on the Return of Irregular Migrants from the European Union* (Hart Publishing 2020)
de Witte B, Hanf D and Vos E, 'Introduction' in de Witte B, Hanf D and Vos E (eds), *The Many Faces of Differentiation in EU Law* (Intersentia 2001)

Deniau J, 'The Objectives and Constitutional Structure of the European Economic Community' in The British Institute of International and Comparative Law, *Legal Problems of the European Economic Community and the European Free Trade Association* (Stevens & Sons Limited 1961)

Dinwoodie G, 'The Europeanization of Trade Mark Law' in Ohly A and Pila J (eds), *The Europeanization of Intellectual Property Law: Towards a European Legal Methodology* (Oxford University Press 2013)

—— 'Diversifying Perspectives of the International Intellectual Property System' in Geiger C (ed), *The Intellectual Property System in a Time of Change: European and International Perspectives* (Lexis Nexis 2016)

Dreyfuss RC, 'An International Perspective I: A View from the United States' in Pila J and Wadlow C (eds), *The Unitary EU Patent System* (Hart Publishing 2015)

—— 'In Praise of an Incentive-Based Theory' in Dreyfuss RC and Ng ES-K (eds), *Framing Intellectual Property Law in the 21st Century: Integrating Incentives, Trade, Development, Culture, and Human Rights* (Cambridge University Press 2018)

Froschmaier F, 'Patents, Trade Marks and Licences within the Community' in The British Institute of International and Comparative Law, *Legal Problems of the European Economic Community and the European Free Trade Association* (Stevens & Sons Limited 1961)

Granata S, 'The Patent Mediation and Arbitration Centre: A Centre of Opportunities' in Geiger C, Nard CA and Seuba X (eds), *Intellectual Property and the Judiciary* (Edward Elgar 2018)

Greenwood C, 'Unity and Diversity in International Law' in Andenas M and Bjorge E (eds), *A Farewell to Fragmentation: Reassertion and Convergence in International Law* (Cambridge University Press 2015)

Hellstadius A, 'A Comparative Analysis of the National Implementation of the Directive's Morality Clause' in Plomer A and Torremans PLC (eds), *Embryonic Stem Cell Patents: European Law and Ethics* (Oxford University Press 2009)

Humphreys S, 'Structural Ambiguity: Technology Transfer in Three Regimes' in Young MA (ed), *Regime Interaction in International Law: Facing Fragmentation* (Cambridge University Press 2012)

Jacob R, 'The Relationship between European and National Courts in Intellectual Property Law' in Ohly A and Pila J (eds), *The Europeanization of Intellectual Property Law: Towards a European Legal Methodology* (Oxford University Press 2013)

Johnson A, 'Looking Forward: A User Perspective' in Pila J and Wadlow C (eds), *The Unitary EU Patent System* (Hart Publishing 2015)

Koskenniemi M, 'Hegemonic Regimes' in Young MA (ed), *Regime Interaction in International Law: Facing Fragmentation* (Cambridge University Press 2012)

Krauss J and Takenaka T, 'Construction of an Efficient and Balanced Patent System: Patentability and Patent Scope of Isolated DNA Sequences under US Patent Act and EU Biotech Directive' in Geiger C (ed), *Constructing European Intellectual Property: Achievements and New Perspectives* (Edward Elgar 2013)

Larsen TB, 'A "Bundle" of National Patents v a European Patent with Unitary Effect: A Jurisdictional Comparison' in Dinwoodie G (ed), *Intellectual Property and General Legal Principles: Is IP a Lex Specialis?* (Edward Elgar 2015)

Luginbuehl S, 'An Institutional Perspective I: The Role of the EPO in the Unitary (EU) Patent System' in Pila J and Wadlow C (eds), *The Unitary EU Patent System* (Hart Publishing 2015)

Luginbuehl S and Kandeva T, 'The Role of the European Court of Justice in the European Patent Court System' in Geiger C, Nard CA and Seuba X (eds), *Intellectual Property and the Judiciary* (Edward Elgar 2018)

Min E-J and Wichard JC, 'Cross-border Intellectual Property Enforcement' in Dreyfuss RC and Pila J (eds), *The Oxford Handbook of Intellectual Property Law* (Oxford University Press 2017)

Nollkaemper A, 'The Power of Secondary Rules to Connect the International and National Legal Orders' in Broude T and Shany Y (eds), *Multi-Sourced Equivalent Norms in International Law* (Hart Publishing 2011)

Norberg A, 'Patents, Morality and Biomedical Innovation in Europe: Historical Overview, Current Debates on Stem Cells, Gene Editing and AI, and *De Lege Ferenda* Reflections' in Gervais D (ed), *Fairness, Morality and Ordre Public in Intellectual Property* (Edward Elgar 2020)

O'Malley KM and Lynn BMG, 'The Proposed Structure and Function of the Unified Patent Court: Lessons from the American Judicial Experience' in Geiger C, Nard CA and Seuba X (eds), *Intellectual Property and the Judiciary* (Edward Elgar 2018)

Ohly A, 'Concluding Remarks: Postmodernism and Beyond' in Ohly A and Pila J (eds), *The Europeanization of Intellectual Property Law: Towards a European Legal Methodology* (Oxford University Press 2013)

—— 'European Fundamental Rights and Intellectual Property' in Ohly A and Pila J (eds), *The Europeanization of Intellectual Property Law: Towards a European Legal Methodology* (Oxford University Press 2013)

Pagenberg J, 'C – Conclusion and Proposals for Greater Harmonization' in Pagenberg J and Cornish W (eds), *Interpretation of Patents in Europe: Application of Article 69 EPC* (Heymanns 2007)

Payandeh M, 'Fragmentation within International Human Rights Law' in Andenas M and Bjorge E (eds), *A Farewell to Fragmentation: Reassertion and Convergence in International Law* (Cambridge University Press 2015)

Petersen CS, Riis T, and Schovsbo J, 'The Unified Patent Court (UPC) in Action: How Will the Design of the UPC Affect Patent Law?' in Ballardini RM, Norrgård M and Bruun N (eds), *Transitions in European Patent Law: Influences of the Unitary Patent Package* (Kluwer 2015)

Petersen CS and Schovsbo J, 'On Law and Policy in a European and European Union Patent Court (EEUPC) – What Will It Do to Patent Law and What Will Patent Law Do to It?' in Koch H, Hagel-Sørensen K and Weiler JHH (eds), *Europe: The New Legal Realism* (Djøf Forlag 2010)

—— 'Decision-making in the Unified Patent Court: Ensuring a Balanced Approach' in Geiger C, Nard CA and Seuba X (eds), *Intellectual Property and the Judiciary* (Edward Elgar 2018)

Pila J, 'A Constitutionalized Doctrine of Precedent and the *Marleasing* Principle as Bases for a European Legal Methodology' in Ohly A and Pila J (eds), *The Europeanization of Intellectual Property Law: Towards a European Legal Methodology* (Oxford University Press 2013)

—— 'An Historical Perspective I: The Unitary Patent Package' in Pila J and Wadlow C (eds), *The Unitary EU Patent System* (Hart Publishing 2014)

Pirker B, 'Interpreting Multi-Sourced Equivalent Norms: Judicial Borrowing in International Courts' in Broude T and Shany Y (eds), *Multi-Sourced Equivalent Norms in International Law* (Hart Publishing 2011)

Plomer A, 'Human Dignity, Human Rights, and Article 6(1) of the EU Directive on Biotechnological Inventions' in Plomer A and Torremans PLC (eds), *Embryonic Stem Cell Patents: European Law and Ethics* (Oxford University Press 2009)

Poiares Maduro M, 'Foreword' in Broude T and Shany Y (eds), *Multi-Sourced Equivalent Norms in International Law* (Hart Publishing 2011)

Schovsbo J, 'Constructing an Efficient and Balanced European Patent System: "Muddling Through"' in Geiger C (ed), *Constructing European Intellectual Property: Achievements and New Perspectives* (Edward Elgar 2013)

Seville C, 'The Emergence and Development of Intellectual Property Law in Western Europe' in Dreyfuss RC and Pila J (eds), *The Oxford Handbook of Intellectual Property Law* (Oxford University Press 2017)

Smits J and Bull W, 'The Europeanization of Patent Law: Towards a Competitive Model' in Ohly A and Pila J (eds), *The Europeanization of Intellectual Property Law: Towards a European Legal Methodology* (Oxford University Press 2013)

Strowel A and Kim H-E, 'The Balancing Impact of General EU Law on European Intellectual Property Jurisprudence' in Ohly A and Pila J (eds), *The Europeanization of Intellectual Property Law: Towards a European Legal Methodology* (Oxford University Press 2013)

Takenaka T, 'The Best Practice for Patent Judiciary: Lessons from Another Experiment on Specialised Adjudications for Patent Cases in Japan' in Geiger C, Nard CA and Seuba X (eds), *Intellectual Property and the Judiciary* (Edward Elgar 2018)

Thambisetty S, 'The Institutional Nature of the Patent System: Implications for Bioethical Decision-Making' in Lenk C, Hoppe N and Andorno R (eds), *Ethics and Law of Intellectual Property: Current Problems in Politics, Science and Technology* (Ashgate 2007)
Torremans PLC, 'An International Perspective II: A View from Private International Law' in Pila J and Wadlow C (eds), *The Unitary EU Patent System* (Hart Publishing 2015)
Tushnet R, 'Intellectual Property as a Public Interest Mechanism' in Dreyfuss RC and Pila J (eds), *The Oxford Handbook of Intellectual Property Law* (Oxford University Press 2017)
Ullrich H, 'Harmony and Unity of European Intellectual Property Protection' in Vaver D and Bently L (eds), *Intellectual Property in the New Millennium* (Cambridge University Press 2004)
Van Gerven W, 'Harmonisation Within and Beyond' in Van Empel M (ed), *'From Paris to Nice': Fifty Years of Legal Integration in Europe* (Kluwer Law International 2003)
Walsh K, 'Invoking the Public Interest in the European Patent System' in Hawkins N (ed), *Patenting Biotechnological Innovation: Eligibility, Ethics and Public Interest* (Edward Elgar 2022)
Walsh K and Hawkins N, 'Expanding the Role of Morality and Public Policy in European Patent Law' in Torremans PLC (ed), *Intellectual Property Law and Human Rights* (4th edn, Wolters Kluwer 2020)
Young MA, 'Fragmentation' in Carty T (ed), *Oxford Bibliographies in International Law* (Oxford University Press 2014)
—— 'Introduction: The Productive Friction between Regimes' in Young MA (ed), *Regime Interaction in International Law: Facing Fragmentation* (Cambridge University Press 2015)
—— 'Regime Interaction in Creating, Implementing and Enforcing International Law' in Young MA (ed), *Regime Interaction in International Law: Facing Fragmentation* (Cambridge University Press 2015)

Journal Articles and Research Papers

15th European Patent Judges' Symposium, [2011] *Special Edition*, OJ EPO 1
17th European Patent Judges' Symposium, [2015] *Supplementary Publication*, OJ EPO 5
Abi-Saab G, 'Fragmentation or Unification: Some Concluding Remarks' (1999) 31 *NYU Journal of International Law and Politics* 919
Aerts RJ, 'The Patenting of Biotechnological Inventions in the EU, the Judicial Bodies Involved, and the Objectives of the EU Legislator' (2014) 36(2) *EIPR* 88
—— 'A Switch on a Switch on a Switch: The Status of Harmonisation of Biotech Patent Law in Europe' (2019) 41(9) *EIPR* 541
Ajevski M, 'Special Issue: Fragmentation in International Human Rights Law – Beyond Conflict of Laws' (2014) 32(2) *Nordic Journal of Human Rights* 87
Alba Betancourt A, 'Cross-Border Patent Disputes: Unified Patent Court or International Commercial Arbitration?' (2016) 32(82) *Utrecht Journal of International and European Law* 44
Aoun W, '"Pith and Marrow is Dead … Long Live Pith and Marrow": The Doctrine of Equivalents after *Actavis*' (2022) 44(4) *EIPR Special Issue: Patents in a Changing Europe* 231
Arnold R, 'Harmonization of European Patent Law' (2019) 14(9) *JIPLP* 657
Baillie IC, 'Where Goes Europe? The European Patent' (1976) 58 *Journal of the Patent and Trademark Office Society* 153
Baker D, Jayadev A and Stiglitz J, 'Innovation, Intellectual Property and Development: A better set of approaches for the 21st Century' [2017] *Access IBSA: Innovation & Access to Medicines in India, Brazil & South Africa*
Baldan F and van Zimmeren E, 'The Future Role of the Unified Patent Court in Safeguarding Coherence in the European Patent System' (2015) 52 *Common Market Law Review* 1529
Barber N, 'Legal Pluralism and the European Union' (2006) 12(3) *European Law Journal* 306
Beier FK, 'Judicial Cooperation in European Patent Law' (1983) 6 *IIC* 707

Bellamy R and Kröger S, 'Differentiated Integration as a Fair Scheme of Cooperation' [2021] *Review of Social Economy* 1

Bently L and Sherman B, 'The Ethics of Patenting: Towards a Transgenic Patent System' (1995) 3 *Medical Law Review* 275

Benvenisti E and Downs GW, 'The Empire's New Clothes: Political Economy and the Fragmentation of International Law' (2007) 60(2) *Stanford Law Review* 595

Birss C, 'Unitary Rights and Judicial Respect in the EU – "Bringing Cool Back"' (2013) 3(3) *Queen Mary Journal of Intellectual Property* 195

Bjuggren PO, Domeij B and Horn A, 'Swedish Patent Litigation in Comparison to European' (2015) 5 *Nordisk Immateriellt Rättsskydd* 504

Boldrin M and Levine DK, 'The Case Against Patents' (2013) 27(1) *Journal of Economic Perspectives* 3

Booton D, 'The Construction of Patent Claims' (2020) 40 *Legal Studies* 651

Bossung O, 'The Return of European Patent Law to the European Union' (1996) 27(3) *IIC* 287

Brinkhof J, 'The Desirability, Necessity and Feasibility of Co-operation Between Courts in the Field of European Patent Law' (1997) 19(5) *EIPR* 226

Buergenthal T, 'Proliferation of International Courts and Tribunals: Is It Good or Bad?' (2001) 14(2) *Leiden Journal of International Law* 267

Burk DL and Lemley MA, 'Policy Levers in Patent Law' (2003) 89(7) *Virginia Law Review* 1575

Burke S, 'Interpretative Clarification of the Concept of "Human Embryo" in the Context of the Biotechnology Directive and the Implications for Patentability: Brüstle v Greenpeace eV (C-34/10)' (2012) 34(5) *EIPR* 346

Burley A-M and Mattli W, 'Europe before the Court: A Political Theory of Legal Integration' (1993) 47(1) *International Organization* 41

CIPA, 'Patenting of Plants in Europe Position Paper' [2019] *Chartered Institute of Patent Attorneys*

Cremers K, Ernicke M, Gaessler F, Harhoff D, Helmers C, McDonagh L, Schliessler P and Van Zeebroeck N, 'Patent Litigation in Europe' (2016) 44 *European Journal of Law and Economics* 1

Curtin D, 'The Constitutional Structure of the Union: A Europe of Bits and Pieces' (1993) 30 *Common Market Law Review* 17

de Búrca G, 'Europe's *Raison d'être*' [2013] *Public Law & Legal Theory Research Paper Series*, Working Paper No 13-09

England P, 'In? Out? What's It All About? Patent Opt-out and Withdrawal in the UPC' (2014) 9(11) *JIPLP* 915

—— 'Infringement of Second Medical Use Patents in Europe and the UPC' (2016) 7 *GRUR Int* 714

—— 'Parallel Patent Proceedings between the European Patent Office and UK Courts' (2015) 10(7) *JIPLP* 509

England P and Parker S, 'Obviousness in the New European Order' (2012) 7(11) *JIPLP* 805

Fabbrini F, 'Enhanced Cooperation under Scrutiny: Revisiting the Law and Practice of Multi-Speed Integration in Light of the First Involvement of the EU Judiciary' (2013) 40(3) *Legal Issues of Economic Integration* 197

Faeh A, 'Judicial Activism, the Biotech Directive and Its Institutional Implications: Is the Court Acting as a Legislator or a Court When Defining the "Human Embryo"?' (2015) 40(4) *European Law Review* 613

Fischer-Lescano A and Teubner G, 'Regime-Collisions: The Vain Search for Legal Unity in the Fragmentation of Global Law' (2004) 25 *Michigan Journal of International Law* 999

Fisher M, 'New Protocol, Same Old Story? Patent Claim Construction in 2007; Looking Back with a View to the Future' (2008) 2 *IPQ* 133

Fox N and Corbett W, 'UK and EPO Approaches to Excluded Subject Matter and Inventive Step: Are Aerotel and Pozzoli Heading for the Rocks?' (2014) 36(9) *EIPR* 569

Gandía Sellens MA, 'The Viability of the Unitary Patent Package After the UK's Ratification of the Agreement on a Unified Patent Court' (2018) 49 *IIC* 136

Gold R and Gallochat A, 'The European Biotech Directive: Past as Prologue' (2001) 7(3) *European Law Journal* 331

Gordon R and Pascoe T, 'Re The Effect of "Brexit" on the Unitary Patent Regulation and The Unified Patent Court Agreement' [2016] *Opinion*

Graham SJH and Van Zeebroeck N, 'Comparing Patent Litigation Across Europe: A First Look' (2014) 17 *Stanford Technical Law Review* 655

Graveson RH, 'The International Unification of Law' (1968) 16(1) *The American Journal of Comparative Law* 4

Griffiths J, 'What Is Legal Pluralism?' (1986) 24(1) *Journal of Legal Pluralism* 55

Hafner G, 'Pros and Cons Ensuing from Fragmentation of International Law' (2004) 25 *Michigan Journal of International Law* 849

Harhoff D, 'Research Paper: Challenges Affecting the Use and Enforcement of Intellectual Property Rights' [2009] *Economic Value of Intellectual Property*

Harmon SHE, Laurie G and Courtney A, 'Dignity, Plurality and Patentability: The Unfinished Story of Brustle v Greenpeace' (2013) 38(1) *European Law Review* 92

Helfer LR, 'Regime Shifting: The TRIPs Agreement and New Dynamics of International Intellectual Property Law Making' (2004) 29 *The Yale Journal of International Law* 1

Helmers C and McDonagh L, 'Patent Litigation in the UK' [2012] *LSE Legal Studies Working Papers* 12/2012

Hilty R, Jaeger T, Lamping M and Ullrich H, 'The Unitary Patent Package: Twelve Reasons for Concern' [2012] *Max Planck Institute for Intellectual Property & Competition Law Research Paper* No 12-12

Hugenholtz B, 'Harmonisation or Unification of European Union Copyright Law' (2012) 38(1) *Monash University Law Review* 4

Ines Schuster M, 'The Court of Justice of the European Union's Ruling on the Patentability of Human Embryonic Stem-cell-related Inventions (Case C-34/10)' (2012) 43(6) *IIC* 626

International Law Commission, 'Fragmentation of International Law: Difficulties arising from the diversification and expansion of International Law: Report of the Study Group of the International Law Commission, finalised by Martti Koskenniemi' [2006] A/CN.4/L.682

International Law Commission, 'Conclusions of the work of the Study Group on the Fragmentation of International Law: Difficulties arising from the Diversification and Expansion of International Law' (2006) 2(2) *Yearbook of the International Law Commission* 1

Jadeja N, Smith-Willis H and Hurdle H, 'Cast Back into the Sea of Uncertainty – A Doctrine of Equivalents in UK Law? The Supreme Court Ruling in *Actavis v Eli Lilly*' (2018) 13(7) *JIPLP* 564

Jaeger T, 'Back to Square One? An Assessment of the Latest Proposals for a Patent and Court for the Internal Market and Possible Alternatives' (2012) 43(3) *IIC* 286

—— 'What's in the Unitary Patent Package?' [2014] *Max Planck Institute for Intellectual Property & Competition Law Research Paper* No 14-08

—— 'Reset and Go: The Unitary Patent System Post-Brexit' (2017) 48(3) *IIC* 254

Jenks W, 'The Conflict of Law-Making Treaties' (1953) 30 *British Yearbook of International Law* 403

Johnson A, 'Unitary Patents and the Unified Patent Court – Part 3: Forum Shopping and Jurisdictional Battles' [2013] *Chartered Institute of Patent Attorneys* 1

Johnson P, 'The (Re-)emergence of the Doctrine of Equivalents' (2017) 12(10) *JIPLP* 817

Kaisi A, 'Finally a Single European Right for the EU? An Analysis of the Substantive Provisions of the European Patent with Unitary Effect' (2014) 36(3) *EIPR* 170

Kamba W, 'Comparative Law: A Theoretical Framework' (1974) 23(3) *ICLQ* 485

Karet I, 'Analysis: English Courts and the EPO: What Next?' (1997) 2 *IPQ* 244

Khuchua T, 'Different "Rules of the Game" – Impact of National Court Systems on Patent Litigation in the EU and the Need for New Perspectives' (2019) 10 *Journal of Intellectual Property, Information Technology and E-Commerce Law* 257

Koskenniemi M and Leino P, 'Fragmentation of International Law? Postmodern Anxieties' (2002) 15 *Leiden Journal of International Law* 553

Kreuder-Sonnen C and Zürn M, 'After Fragmentation: Norm Collisions, Interface Conflicts, and Conflict Management' (2020) 9(2) *Global Constitutionalism* 241

Kreuder-Sonnen C and Zürn M, 'Special Issue: After Fragmentation' (2020) 9(2) *Global Constitutionalism*

Krieger A, 'When Will the European Community Patent Finally Arrive?' (1998) 29(8) *IIC* 855

Laddie H, 'National IP Rights: A Moribund Anachronism in a Federal Europe?' (2001) 23(9) *EIPR* 402

LaFlame M, 'The European Patent System: An Overview and Critique' (2010) 32 *Houston Journal of International Law* 605

Lageza E, 'Mapping Judicial Dialogue across National Borders: An Exploratory Network Study of Learning from Lobbying among European Intellectual Property Judges' (2012) 8(2) *Utrecht Law Review* 115

Lamping M, 'Enhanced Cooperation – A Proper Approach to Market Integration in the Field of Unitary Patent Protection?' (2011) 42(8) *IIC* 879

Lamping M and Ullrich H, 'The Impact of Brexit on Unitary Patent Protection and its Court' [2018] *Max Planck Institute for Innovation and Competition Research Paper Series*

Larik J, 'From Speciality to a Constitutional Sense of Purpose: On the Changing Role of the Objectives of the European Union' (2014) 63(4) *ICLQ* 935

Laurie G, 'Intellectual Property Protection of Biotechnological Inventions and Related Materials' (2003) 4 *Innogen Working Paper*

—— 'Patenting Stem Cells of Human Origin' (2004) 26(2) *EIPR* 59

Lindroos A, 'Addressing Norm Conflicts in a Fragmented Legal System: The Doctrine of *Lex Specialis*' (2005) 74(1) *Nordic Journal of International Law* 27

Lock T, 'Taking National Courts More Seriously? Comment on Opinion 1/09' (2011) 36(4) *European Law Review* 576

Love J and Hubbard T, 'Prizes for Innovation of New Medicines and Vaccines' (2009) 18 *Annals of Health Law* 155

Luginbuehl S, 'A Stone's Throw Away from a European Patent Court: The European Patent Litigation Agreement' (2003) 25(6) *EIPR* 256

Machlup F, 'An Economic Review of the Patent System' [1958] Study of the Subcommittee of Patents, Trademarks and Copyrights of the Committee on the Judiciary

Mahalatchimy A, Rial-Sebbag E, Duguet A-M, Cambon-Thomsen A and Taboulet F, 'Exclusion of Patentability of Embryonic Stem Cells in Europe: Another Restriction by the European Patent Office' (2015) 37(1) *EIPR* 25

Majone G, 'Unity in Diversity: European Integration and the Enlargement Process' (2008) 33(4) *European Law Review* 457

McMahon A, 'An Institutional Examination of the Implications of the Unitary Patent Package for the Morality Provisions: A Fragmented Future Too Far?' (2017) 48(1) *IIC* 42

—— 'Brexit and the Unitary Patent Package: A Further Compromised Future?' (2018) 15(2) *SCRIPTed* 175

Meier-Beck P, 'The Scope of Patent Protection – The Test for Determining Equivalence' (2005) 36(3) *IIC* 339

Mejer M and van Pottlesberghe de la Potterie B, 'Economic Incongruities in the European Patent System' [2009] *Bruegel Working Paper*

Minssen T and Nordberg A, 'The Evolution of the CJEU's Case Law on Stem Cell Patents: Context, Outcome and Implications of Case C-364/13 *International Stem Cell Corporation*' (2015) 5 *Nordic Intellectual Property Law Review* 493

Moore S, 'Challenge to the Biotechnology Directive' (2002) 24(3) *EIPR* 149

Moore S and Wells A, 'Clarification of European Law Relating to Stem Cell Patents' (2015) 37(4) *EIPR* 258

Muller-Stoy T and Paschold F, 'European Patent with Unitary Effect as a Property Right' (2014) 9(10) *JIPLP* 848

Ng ES-K, 'Patent Trolling: Innovation at Risk' (2009) 31(12) *EIPR* 593

Nordberg A and Minssen T, 'A "Ray of Hope" for European Stem Cell Patents or "Out of the Smog into the Fog"? An Analysis of Recent European Case Law and How it Compares to the US' (2016) 47 *IIC* 138

Nott R, '"You Did It!": The European Biotechnology Directive At Last' (1998) 20(9) *EIPR* 347

O'Sullivan E, 'International Stem Cell Corp v Comptroller General of Patents: The Debate Regarding the Definition of the Human Embryo Continues' (2014) 36(3) *EIPR* 155
Odell-West A, 'Invention and the Human Embryo' (2020) 1 *IPQ* 1
Ohly A and Streinz R, 'Can the UK Stay in the UPC System after BREXIT?' (2017) 12(3) *JIPLP* 245
Parker S and England P, 'Where Now for Stem Cell Patents?' (2012) 7(10) *EIPR* 738
Paulus AL, 'Commentary to Andreas Fischer-Lescano and Gunther Teubner: The Legitimacy of International Law and the Role of the State' (2004) 25 *Michigan Journal of International Law* 1047
Peers S, 'The Constitutional Implications of the EU Patent' (2011) 7(2) *European Constitutional Law Review* 229
Pila J, 'Article 53(b) EPC: A Challenge to the *Novartis* Theory of European Patent History' (2009) 72 *MLR* 436
—— 'The European Patent: An Old and Vexing Problem' (2013) 62(4) *ICLQ* 917
—— 'Pluralism, Principles and Proportionality in Intellectual Property' (2014) 34(1) *Oxford Journal of Legal Studies* 181
Plomer A, 'A Unitary Patent for a (Dis)United Europe: The Long Shadow of History' (2015) 46(5) *IIC* 508
—— 'After *Brüstle*: EU Accession to the ECHR and the Future of European Patent Law' (2012) 2(2) *Queen Mary Journal of Intellectual Property* 110
—— 'The EPO as Patent Law-maker in Europe' (2019) 25(1) *European Law Journal* 57
Resnik D, 'A Pluralistic Account of Intellectual Property' (2003) 46(4) *Journal of Business Ethics* 319
Rowlandson M, 'WARF/Stem Cells (G2/06): The Ordre Public and Morality Exception and Its Impact on the Patentability of Human Embryonic Stem Cells' (2010) 32(2) *EIPR* 67
Rüting K, 'A New Scenario for Infringement of Second Medical Use Patents: Are Generics Liable when They Participate in Discount Contract Tenders?' (2016) 1 *epi Information* 25
Schade J, 'Is the Community (EU) Patent Behind the Times? – Globalisation Urges Multilateral Cooperation' (2010) 41(7) *IIC* 806
Schovsbo J, Riis T and Petersen CS, 'The Unified Patent Court: Pros and Cons of Specialization – Is There a Light at the End of the Tunnel (Vision)?' (2015) 46(3) *IIC* 271
Scott A, 'The Dutch Challenge to the Bio-Patenting Directive' (1999) 21(4) *EIPR* 212
Sherman B, 'Patent Claim Interpretation: The Impact of the Protocol on Interpretation' (1991) 54(4) *MLR* 499
Simma B, 'Fragmentation in a Positive Light' (2004) 25 *Michigan Journal of International* Law 845
Slaughter A-M, 'Judicial Globalization' (2000) 40 *Virginia Journal of International Law* 1103
Smyth D, 'Patent Law Decisions from Supreme Courts: How Can Non-specialist Judges Decide this Field of Law?' (2014) 9(1) *JIPLP* 31
—— 'Two Gaps Instead of One: The CJEU's Effect on Supplementary Protection Certificate Jurisprudence' (2014) 9(6) *JIPLP* 445
Stauder D, 'The History of Art. 69(1) EPC and Art. 8(3) Strasbourg Convention on the Extent of Patent Protection' [1992] *IIC* 311
Sterckx S, 'The European Patent Convention and the (Non-) Patentability of Human Embryonic Stem Cells – the WARF case' (2008) 4 *IPQ* 478
—— 'The WARF/Stem Cells Case before the EPO Enlarged Board of Appeal' (2008) 30(12) *EIPR* 535
Strath J and Jacob R, '*Actavis v Lilly*: The Madness Begins' (2018) 13(3) *JIPLP* 169
Tamanaha BZ, 'Understanding Legal Pluralism: Past to Present, Local to Global' (2008) 30 *Sydney Law Review* 375
Thambisetty S, 'Liza's Bucket: Intellectual Property and the Metamodern Impulse' [2020] *LSE Law, Society and Economy Working Papers* 19/2020
Tilmann W, 'The Compromise on the Uniform Protection for EU Patents' (2013) 8(1) *JIPLP* 78
—— 'Spain's Action Against the EU Patent Package – Arguments and Counter-arguments in Case C-146/13' (2014) 36(1) *EIPR* 4
—— 'The Transitional Period of the Agreement on a Unified Patent Court' (2014) 9(7) *JIPLP* 575

Treves T, 'Fragmentation of International Law: The Judicial Perspective' (2009) 16(27) *Agenda Internacional* 213
Trimble M, '*GAT*, *Solvay*, and the Centralization of Patent Litigation in Europe' (2012) 26 *Emory International Law Review* 515
Ullrich H, 'Patent Protection in Europe: Integrating Europe into the Community or the Community into Europe?' (2002) 8(4) *European Law Journal* 433
—— 'Harmonizing Patent Law: The Untamable Union Patent' [2012] *Max Planck Institute for Intellectual Property and Competition Law Research Paper* No 12-03
—— 'Enhanced Cooperation in the Area of Unitary Patent Protection and European Integration' (2013) 13 *ERA Forum* 589
—— 'The Property Aspects of the European Patent with Unitary Effect: A National Perspective for a European Prospect?' [2013] *Max Planck Institute for Intellectual Property and Competition Law Research Paper* No 13-17
—— 'The European Patent and Its Courts: An Uncertain Prospect and an Unfinished Agenda' (2015) 46(1) *IIC* 1
van Bentham JB, 'The European Patent System and European Integration' (1993) 24(4) *IIC* 435
Van Pottelsberghe B, 'Lost Property: The European Patent System and Why It Doesn't Work' (2009) IX *Bruegel Blueprint Series*
Wadlow C, 'Strasbourg, the Forgotten Patent Convention, and the Origins of the European Patents Jurisdiction' (2010) 41(2) *IIC* 123
Walsh K, 'Promoting Harmonisation across the European Patent System through Judicial Dialogue and Cooperation' (2019) 50(4) *IIC* 408
—— 'The Unitary Patent Package, the Court of Justice of the European Union, and Brexit: (Ir) reconcilable?' (2019) 2 *IPQ* 91
Warner S and Middlemiss S, 'Patent Litigation in Multiple Jurisdictions: An End to Cross Border Relief in Europe?' (2006) 28(11) *EIPR* 580
Weiler JHH, 'The Transformation of Europe' (1991) 100(8) *The Yale Law Journal* 2403
—— 'Europe After Maastricht – Do the New Clothes Have an Emperor?' [1995] *Jean Monnet Working Papers* No 12
—— '60 Years Since the first European Community – Reflections on Political Messianism' (2011) 22(2) *European Journal of International Law* 303
Widera P, 'Has *Pemetrexed* Revived the Doctrine of Equivalence?' (2018) 13(3) *JIPLP* 238
Willems J, 'The EPC: The Emperor's Phantom Clothes? A Blueprint Instead of a Green Paper' (1998) 1 *IPQ* 1
Wright B, 'The Economics of Invention Incentives: Patents, Prizes, and Research Contracts' (1983) 73(4) *The American Economic Review* 691
Xenos D, 'The European Unified Patent Court: Assessment and Implications of the Federalisation of the Patent System in Europe' (2013) 10(2) *SCRIPTed* 245
—— 'The Impact of the European Patent System on SMEs and National States and the Advent of Unitary Patent' (2020) 36(1) *Prometheus – Critical Studies in Innovation* 51
Zürn M and Faude B, 'On Fragmentation, Differentiation, and Coordination' (2013) 13(3) *Global Environmental Politics* 119

European Union Documents

Commission Notice on certain articles of Directive 98/44/EC of the European Parliament and of the Council on the legal protection of biotechnological inventions (2016/C 411/03)
Commission Paper (EU) on Promoting innovation through patents – Green Paper on the Community patent and the patent system in Europe [1997] COM (97) 314 final
Communication from the Commission to the European Parliament and the Council (EU) on Enhancing the patent system in Europe [2007] COM (2007) 165 final

Council Conclusions (EU) 17229/09 on the Enhanced Patent System in Europe [2009] PI 141 COUR 87

Council Decision (EU) 2011/167/EU of 10 March 2011 authorising enhanced cooperation in the area of the creation of unitary patent protection [2011] OJ L 76/53

Council Document (EU) 7159/03 of 7 March 2003 on the Community patent – Common political approach [2003] PI 24

Council Document (EU) 11622/07 of 12 July 2007 Towards an Enhanced Patent Litigation System and a Community Patent – How to Take Discussions Further [2007] PI 35

Council Document (EU) 9124/08 of 14 May 2008 on a Draft Agreement on the European Union Patent Judiciary [2008] PI 24 COUR 19

Council Document (EU) 13031/10 of 31 August 2010 on Reflection from the Spanish delegation on a possible model for the Regulation on translations [2010] LIMITE PI 94

Council General Approach (EU) 16113/09 ADD 1 on the Proposal for a Council Regulation on the Community patent [2009] PI 122

Council General Approach (EU) 11328/11 on the Proposal for a Regulation of the Council and the European Parliament implementing enhanced cooperation in the area of the creation of unitary patent protection and on the Proposal for a Council Regulation implementing enhanced cooperation in the area of unitary patent protection with regard to the applicable translation arrangements [2011] PI 67 CODEC 995

Council Orientation Debate (EU) 10630/11 creating a Unified Patent Litigation System [2011] PI 54 COUR 28

Opinion of the Legal Service (EU) 15856/11 on the compatibility of the draft agreement with the Opinion 1/09 [2011] PI 138 COUR 61

Presidency Text (EU) 11533/11 on a Draft agreement on a Unified Patent Court and draft Statute [2011] PI 68 COUR 32

Proposal for a Council Decision (EU) 2003/0324 (CNS) establishing the Community Patent Court and concerning appeals before the Court of First Instance [2003] COM (2003) 828 final

Proposal for a Council Decision (EU) 2003/0326 (CNS) conferring jurisdiction on the Court of Justice in disputes relating to the Community patent [2003] COM(2003) 827 final

Proposal for a Council Decision (EU) 2010/0384 (NLE) authorising enhanced cooperation in the area of the creation of unitary patent protection [2010] COM (2010) 790 final

Proposal for a Council Regulation (EU) 15086/03 of 21 November 2003 on the Community patent [2003] LIMITE PI 122

Proposal for a Council Regulation (EU) 2000/C 337 E/45 on the Community patent [2000] COM (2000) 412 final

Proposal for a Council Regulation (EU) 7119/04 on the Community patent [2004] LIMITE PI 28

Proposal for a Council Regulation (EU) 2010/0198 (CNS) on the translation arrangements for the European Union patent [2010] COM (2010) 350 final

Proposal for a Directive of the European Parliament and of the Council on the patentability of computer-implemented inventions (COM (2002) 92 final) [2002] OJ C 151 E/129

Revised Presidency Text (EU) 13751/11 on a Draft agreement on a Unified Patent Court and draft Statute [2011] PI 108 COUR 48

Press Releases, Memoranda, Reports and Statements

Deloitte, 'Analysis of prospective economic effects related to the implementation of the system of unitary patent protection in Poland' (1 October 2012)

European Commission Memo, 'Patent reform Package – frequently asked questions' (11 December 2011)

European Commission Memo, 'Commissioner Barnier welcomes the European Council's agreement on the seat of the Unified Patent Court – the final element in the patent package' (29 June 2012)

European Commission Memo, 'Results of the Competitiveness Council of Ministers' (MEMO/04/58, 12 March 2004)
European Commission Statement, 'Commissioner Barnier welcomes the conclusion of the first agreement on a regional division of the Unified Patent Court by Sweden, Lithuania, Latvia and Estonia' (4 March 2014)
European Parliament Press Release, 'Done deal on the EU patent?' (1 December 2011)
European Parliament Press Release, 'Parliament approves EU unitary patent rules' (11 December 2012)
German Federal Ministry of Justice and Consumer Protection Press Release, 'European patent reform is to be continued' (26 March 2020)
McDonagh L, 'Exploring Perspectives of the Unified Patent Court and Unitary Patent Within the Business and Legal Communities' (UKIPO, 2014)

Blogs

Barrett G and Rey-Alvite Villar M, 'Spanish government provides further reasons for not joining unitary patent and UPC system' (*Bristows*, 24 May 2018)
Bristows, 'Belgian UPC Case Dropped' (*Bristows*, 27 May 2015)
Dickinson T, 'Seven Organisations Assess the Impact of the EPC' (*Managing Intellectual Property, Europe IP Focus*, 2013)
ESOMA, 'Unitary Patent Challenged at the Belgian Constitutional Court' (*ESOMA*, 2015)
'FFII preparing constitutional complaint against Unified Patent Court Agreement' (*Kluwer Patent Blog*, 23 October 2020)
Lambers R, 'The Pemetrexed Pendulum Swings Back' (*Kluwer Patent Blog*, 21 June 2019)
Managing Intellectual Property, 'Analysing 40 years of the EPO: what has it done for us?' (*Managing Intellectual Property, European IP Focus*, 2013)
'Member States will sign Declaration to clear way for preparatory phase Unified Patent Court' (*Kluwer Patent Blog*, 28 October 2021)
Merelle Ward A, 'Recap & Update: the Unitary Patent System and Unified Patent Court' (*IPKat*, 20 December 2011)
—— 'UPC-ing is Believing: Preview of London's UPC location' (*IPKat*, 22 September 2015)
Sandys A, 'IP community losing appetite for Unified Patent Court' (*Juve Patent*, 17 April 2020)
—— 'Italian Government officially fields Milan for UPC central division' (*Juve Patent*, 11 September 2020)
Smyth D, 'Preparatory Committee launches consultation on the UPC Fees' (*IPKat*, 8 May 2015)
'Spain takes Parliament and Council to Court over Unitary Patent Package' (*IPKat*, 27 March 2013)
Vary R, 'Bifurcation: bad for business' (*Presentation to UKIPO*, 2012)

Miscellaneous

'A Programme for Partnership Government' [2016]
European Patent Office, Guidelines for Examination, March 2021
Intellectual Property Office, Manual of Patent Practice, October 2021 (UK)
Oral Hearing of the Preliminary set of provisions for the Rules of Procedure ('Rules') of the Unified Patent Court, 17th draft of 31 October 2014
Soloway A, Reply to the House of Lords EU Justice Sub-Committee, 'Unified Patent Court' (24 March 2020)

INDEX

Note: Alphabetical arrangement is word-by-word, where a group of letters followed by a space is filed before the same group of letters followed by a letter, eg 'patent offices will appear before 'patentees'. In determining alphabetical arrangement, initial articles and prepositions are ignored.

abstracts:
European patent applications, 28
international patent applications, 32
Academy, EPO, 137
access:
exclusivity within patent system and, balance between, 35
acknowledging fragmentation, 168
acknowledging inconsistencies, 97–98
active dialogue:
between national court judges, 142
Actavis v Eli Lilly, 133–35, 136, 137
Administrative Council:
European Patent Organisation, *see* European Patent Organisation
Aerotel/Macrossan, 116, 125, 158
Agreement on a Unified Patent Court, *see* **Unified Patent Court Agreement**
aims:
European Coal and Steel Community, 76
European Economic Community, 77
European Patent Convention, 28, 29–30, 80
Agreement on Trade-Related Aspects of Intellectual Property Rights (TRIPS):
EU patent law harmonisation lack due to, 10
intellectual property protection standards, 21
alternative language regimes, 56
Amsterdam Treaty, *see* **Treaty of Amsterdam**
analysis:
international legal systems, fragmentation in, 94–95
Angiotech Pharmaceuticals v Conor Medsystems Inc, 112
anticipatory prior art, 33
any hardware approach:
computer programs patentability, 115–16
appeals:
European patent system, 29
applicants:
advantages to, PCT, 33
careful consideration, 35
international patent applications
reports to, 33
applications:
European patent system, *see* European patent system
fees, 59
international patents, *see* international patent applications
appreciation of diversity, 12–13
Austria:
bifurcation, 68

Bayer/Carbonless copying paper, 113
Belgium:
Schuman Plan support, 75
UPCA ratification and challenge, 53
benefits:
diversity, 13
Benelux Court of Justice:
European and Community/Union Patent Court and, differences between, 41
bias towards certain viewpoints, 175
bifurcation:
Austria, 68
Court of Justice of the European Union, 27
Germany, 68
institutional fragmentation, 68–69
Poland, 68
Unified Patent Court, 68–69
UPCA, 68–69
Biogen v Medeva, 119
Biotech Directive, 9, 22–23, 103, 124–25
Boards of Appeal, EPO, 171
CJEU, 148, 171
EPC, 147, 148
EU implemented, 170–71

exclusions from patentability, 149–50
fundamental rights protection, 22–23
impact, 145–46
institutional addition, 148–49
legislative harmonisation, 146–48
national diversity consideration in, 172
transposed into EU Member States national law, 147
value pluralism consideration in, 172
biotechnological innovation, EPOrg, 147
biotechnological inventions:
interpretations relating to, Boards of Appeal, EPO, 148
substantive law, 148
boards:
Unified Patent Court dialogue with, 139
Boards of Appeal, *see* **European Patent Office**
Brexit, 50
Brussels Compromise, UPC, 65
Brussels Convention:
CJEU exclusive jurisdiction from, 25–26
***Brüstle*,** 151–52, 153–55, 156, 158

capacity of fragmentation to be harnessed, 173
case law:
European patent law shaping by, 138
cases:
European patent system, uploading and machine translation, 140
***Catnic v Hill & Smith*,** 127, 128, 129, 130, 137
Charter of Fundamental Rights for the EU, 86
civil law countries:
common law countries and, differences in practices, 141
CJEU, *see* **Court of Justice of the European Union**
claim construction, *see* **claims**
claimed invention obvious:
inventive step, EPO, 113
claims:
construction:
European patent system cooperation case study, *see* European patent system
Germany, 127
United Kingdom, 130
European patent applications, 28
international patent applications, 32
closest prior art:
inventive step, EPO, 113
coexistence:
European patent system, 49
coherence, judicial, 139
commercialisation:
inventions, 3
Committee of Experts on Patents:
Council of Europe, 78–79
common law countries:
civil law countries and, differences in practices, 141
common market:
consideration, ECSC, 77
communications, informal, 100
Community Patent Agreement (CPA):
Community Patent Convention redrafted as, 81
Community Patent Convention (CPC), 79, 103
Agreement of 1975/1989 (CPC/CPA), 20–21
drafting, 80
goals, 81
implementation intention, 81
redrafted as Community Patent Agreement (CPA), 81
unsuccessful, 82
Community Patent Court, 38
Community Patent Regulation, 37
Community Patents, 37
comparative reasoning and research:
between national court judges, 142
compensation scheme:
language translations, 60
competence, Unified Patent Court, 67
competing norms, 96
competition law, 104
competitors, 35
composition, UPC panels, 166
compromise, 56
political, 98
raising issue of legal uncertainty, UPP, 49
compulsory licensing, EPUE, 48
computer-implemented inventions, 9, 22
computer program patentability, 115–16
conceptualising fragmentation, 95
conflicts:
between distinct areas, fragmentation resulting from, 99
laws, 102
resulting from conflicting decisions, fragmentation resulting from, 99
consensus-building, 174
Constitutional Court:
Germany, *see* Germany

constitutionalism, 97, 98
contextual responsiveness, 95
continuation of divergence, 141
contract law, 104
Contracting States:
EPC provisions implemented into, 170
international patent applications by, 32
convergence:
attempts, UPC, 165
cooperation, 133–35
equivalents, 133–35
European patent system towards, 117–42
fragmentation, 12, 173
judicial cooperation progress towards, 168
judicial dialogue progress towards, 168
promotion, 176
cooperation:
enhanced, *see* enhanced cooperation
fragmentation risks reduction, 173
judges, 140, 41
coordinated international law fragmentation, 102
coordination, laws, 95
costs:
application fees, 59
European patent system, *see* European patent system
international patent applications, 34
language translations, 58, 60
national patent systems, 24
patent litigation, 59
potential disadvantage, national patent systems, 24
reduction, 59
renewal fees, 59
translations filing, 59
UPC, 59
UPP, 59
Council of Europe, 20
Committee of Experts on Patents, 78–79
establishment through Treaty of London, 74
Longchambon Proposal, 74–75
Strasbourg Patent Convention, 78–79
counterclaims:
revocation, for, UPC, 68
countries:
divergence within, 141
international conventions, considering, 102
national legal systems, considering, 102
national patent systems procedures depend on, 23
substantive patent law provisions interpretation, 103
see also individual countries
Court of Appeal (UPC):
language at, 61
UPC, 44, 64, 65
Court of First Instance (UPC):
language at, 61
UPC, 41, 44, 52, 64, 65
Court of Justice of the European Union (CJEU):
bifurcation, 27
Biotech Directive, 148, 171
Brüstle, 151–52, 153–55, 156, 158
cross-border enforcement, 24–26
decision-making, convergence as motivating factor, 145
decisions, Boards of Appeal considering, 124–25
doctrine of exhaustion, 21
EEUPC compatibility with EU law, Opinion 1/09, 38–41
enhanced cooperation, 55, 58
European patent system, 103
exclusive jurisdiction from Brussels Convention, 25–26
forum shopping, 26–27
generalist overview, 167
human embryos, defining for all EU Member States, 168, 174
institutional fragmentation, 26
language:
arrangements, 56
treatment differences, proportionality principle to be observed, 58
Netherlands case, 154
Omega case, 154
Regulation 1257:
designated national law applied, guaranteed, 47
legality challenged by Spain and Italy, 47
uniform protection guaranteed, 47
Regulation interpretation controversies, 22
substantive patent law:
interpretation role in relation to UPP, 46
involvement, 148–49
torpedoes, 26
United Kingdom staunch objection to, 51
UPC:
future relationships and, 166
role in relation to, 167
WARF, 157

courts:
divergent decisions producing institutional fragmentation, 2
multiple, negative consequences, 100
procedures:
differences in, 175
proliferation, international legal systems, fragmentation in, 93
see also Court of Appeal (UPC); Court of First Instance (UPC); Court of Justice of the European Union (CJEU); national courts; patent courts
CPC, *see* **Community Patent Convention**
Croatia:
not EU Member State, not interested in accession, 50
cross-border enforcement, 24–26
cross-border jurisdiction:
Unified Patent Court, 6
cultural differences:
remaining, fragmentation persisting, 168
cultural diversity, 5
cultural fragmentation, 5
cultures:
diversity, EU respecting, 86
European patent system, tension between, 166
current and future tribunals:
judicial dialogue between, 176

damages, 61
dates:
priority, *see* priority dates
international patent applications, 33
decision:
makers:
European patent system open dialogue among, 165
making:
CJEU, convergence as motivating factor, 145
deference, judicial, 100
designated priority dates:
international patent applications, 33
designs:
protection harmonised across EU, 8–9
unitary rights, 9
development, independent, 102
dialogue:
judges, 140, 141
regimes, between, 97
differentiation:
European patent system, 7
flexibility, 11
functional, 95
institutional, 95
'integration by parts', 11
integration mechanism, 11, 74, 83
Member State groups implementing new laws, enhanced cooperation allowing, 87
theory, 94–95
dignity, human, 22–23, 86
diminished fear of fragmentation, 173
disclosures:
patents promoting technological developments, 4
discrimination:
indirect, nationality grounds, EPUE, 48
dissenting opinions:
UPC panels, 166
divergence:
areas, 110–117
continuation of, 141
cooperation, 132–33
countries, within, 141
fragmentation, 173
international legal systems, fragmentation in, 93
national patent systems, 27
diversity:
appreciation of, 12–13
benefits, 13
considering when responding to fragmentation, 168
cultural, 5
ECSC, 76
EU traditions respecting, 86
European patent system, 5, 168
focus on, 12–13
fragmentation promotion of, 173
lack, judiciary, 141, 175
legal, 5
national, *see* national diversity
procedural, 5
division shopping, UPC, 66, 67
Document Security Systems v European Central Bank, 112
domestic law:
unitary patents governed by, 48–49
drawings:
European patent applications, 28
international patent applications, 32

duplicated litigation, 59
dysfunction:
bifurcation as, 68–69

economic activities:
harmonious development promotion, EEC, 77
economic perspectives:
patent law reform focused on, 5
ECSC (European Coal and Steel Community), 75–78
EEA (European Economic Area), 21
EEC, *see* **European Economic Community**
EEUPC (European and Community/Union Patent Court), 38–41
embryos, human:
industrial or commercial purposes, uses for, *see* patentability
enforcement:
costs, UPC, 59–60
European patent system, 30
minimal guidance on, European Patent Convention, 112
national patent systems, 35
proceedings, EPUE, 48
Enforcement Directive, 8, 9
enhanced cooperation, 39, 55–57, 58
authorised by UPP, 87
CJEU, 55, 58
EU, 11, 12
EU Member States, 87, 172
fragmentation may result, 87, 89
Italy exclusion:
use, 87–88
Spain exclusion:
use, 87–88
TEU, 42
Unitary Patent Package, 55–57
Enlarged Board of Appeal, *see* **European Patent Office**
enlargement, EU, 84
EPC, *see* **European Patent Convention**
EPLA (European Patent Litigation Agreement), 38
EPO, *see* **European Patent Office**
EPOrg, *see* **European Patent Organisation**
EPUE, *see* **European Patent with Unitary Effect**
equality, EU values, 86
equivalents:
convergence, 133–35
due account to be taken of, European Patent Convention, 129–30
treatment over Europe, 133
Espacenet, 30
essentially biological processes:
patentability exceptions interpretations, *see* patentability
EU law:
primacy, UPC respect for, ensuring, 166–67
UPC questions on referred to CJEU, 167
EU Member States:
Biotech Directive transposed into national law, 147
Croatia not interested in accession, 50
enhanced cooperation, 172
European Patent Convention transposed into national law, 147
interests, 85
groups implementing new laws, enhanced cooperation allowing, 87
human embryos defining for all, 168
laws:
divergence in, 172
fragmentation in, 172
national law referencing, uniform protection by, 46–47
Unified Patent Court agreement, 36–37
unitary patent for, UPP, 171
EU membership expansion, 84
EU Trade Mark, 58
EU unitary patent protection, 36–37
EU unitary patent system, 104, 73
implementation:
fragmentation increase, 175
main aim, 42
EURATOM, *see* **European Atomic Energy Community**
European and Community/Union Patent Court (EEUPC), 38–41
European Atomic Energy Community (EURATOM):
Merger Treaty, 79
Treaty establishing, 77
European Coal and Steel Community (ECSC), 75–78
European Commission:
Community Patent Regulation proposal, 37
products from essentially biological processes not patentable, 160–61, 164
European Council, 37, 38
European countries:
national patent laws retention, 103

European Economic Area (EEA), 21
European Economic Community (EEC):
aims, 77
approximation of laws, 83
common market establishment among Inner Six, 77–78
economic activities harmonious development promotion, 77
EPC and CPC, 79–81
European patent system:
impact on creation, 78
expansion:
continuous and balanced, 77
impact, 82
Merger Treaty, 79
peace, 77
prosperity, 77
stability increase, 77
States, closer relationship, 77
supranationalism, 77
Treaty establishing, 77
European (EPC) patents:
existence alongside EPUE, 49
protection route, 170
European harmonisation, 34, 149
European integration, 149
European Judges Forum, 138
European law-making, fragmentation in, 73–74
constructing Europe and European Patent System, 74
Council of Europe:
Longchambon Proposal, 74–75
Strasbourg Patent Convention, 78–79
European Coal and Steel Community, 75–78
European Economic Community, EPC and CPC, 79–81
Shifting Perspectives and Objectives, 81–82
expansion impact, 82–85
impact on patent system, 85–88
fragmentation as means of integration, 88–89
European law-making processes, 3
European Parliament:
Treaty of Amsterdam increasing powers of, 83
European patent attorneys, 30
European Patent Convention (EPC), 19, 79
aims, 28, 29–30, 80
Biotech Directive, 23, 147, 148
Contracting States:
autonomy retained, 10
Biotech Directive, 23
not members of EU, 7
provisions implemented into, 170
drafting, 80
EU patent law harmonisation lack due to, 10
European patent system:
governed by, 27–28
huge impact on, 82
fragmentation, 31
grant of patents through European Patent Office, 80
implementation of, 172
Implementing Regulations, 150, 174
Improver v Remington, infringement actions, differing results, 132
national judges, judicial internships for, 139
national law priority, 10
non-patentable subject matter listed in, 114
obtaining patents, 43
patent protection route, 1, 6
patentability requirements, harmonising, 86–87
equivalents, due account to be taken of, 129–30
minimal guidance on enforcement, 112
Protocol on the Interpretation of Article 69, 128, 134
search and examination standards balanced, 30
Strasbourg Patent Convention:
influence, 80
substantive law provisions incorporated, 20
streamlined procedure, 20
substantive patent law harmonised by, 142
European patent field:
harmonisation through international treaties and conventions, 9
European Patent Judges' Symposium, 138
European patent law:
case law, shaping by, 138
law-makers, 35
European Patent Litigation Agreement (EPLA), 38
European Patent Office (EPO), 1, 19, 28, 75
Academy, 137
applications to, *see* European patent system
Boards of Appeal, 29, 123–24
Biotech Directive, 171

conflicts between national regimes and CJEU, 104
European patent system and CJEU, conflicts between, 104
G2/13 and G2/12 *(Broccoli II and Tomatoes II)*, 160–61
interpretations relating to biotechnological inventions, 148
jurisprudence, aligning, 141–42
national judges of EPC contracting states at, judicial internships for, 139
T1063/18 *Extreme Dark Green, Blocky Peppers*, 161
T1441/13 *Embryonic stem cells, disclaimer/ ASTERIAS*, 158
T2221/10 *Culturing stem cells/ TECHNION*, 158
Vienna Convention use for interpretation of treaties, 173
decisions, CJEU considering, 124–25
Enlarged Board of Appeal, 113, 115, 123–24
Aerotel/Macrossan, 158
decision-making, convergence as motivating factor, 145
external members, appointment of, 138–39
G2/13 and G2/12 *(Broccoli II and Tomatoes II)*, 160–61
G3/19 *Pepper* (follow-up to '*Tomatoes II*' and '*Broccoli II*'), 162, 163
T1063/18 *Extreme Dark Green, Blocky Peppers*, 161
interpretations relating to biotechnological inventions, 148
WARF, 150–51, 157, 158–59
EPC grant of patents through, 80
European patent system, 103
Guidelines for Examination, 113
interpretation and consideration of national court decisions, 123–24
inventive step:
any hardware approach, 115–16
claimed invention obvious, 113
closest prior art, 113
objective technical problems, 113
problem and solution approach, 113
jurisprudence, Unified Patent Court consideration of, 166
official language of, 60
Vienna Convention rules on interpretation of treaties, use of, 142

European Patent Organisation (EPOrg):
Administrative Council, 1, 28
convergence on patentability of products resulting from essentially biological processes, push towards, 168
legislating in disguise, 163
pre-existing rule amended, 174
products from essentially biological processes not patentable, 161
biotechnological innovation, 147
European Patent Office (EPO), *see* European Patent Office
European patent system, 1, 5–7, 14
appeals:
fees, 29
notices, 29
applications, 43, 102–104
abstracts, 28
claims, 28
description of inventions, 28
drawings, 28
failed, appeals to EPO Boards of Appeal, 29
fees, 59
national translations, 29
procedural requirements, 28–29
requests for grant, 28
successful, resulting in bundle of national patents, 30–31
Boards of Appeal and CJEU, conflicts between, 104
cases:
uploading and machine translation, 140
CJEU, 103
coexistence and separate treatment, 49
convergence, towards, 117–42
cooperation case study, claim construction, 126
background, 126–27
convergence, 133–35
divergence, 132–33
impact, 136
of EPC, 128–31
literalism in, abandonment, 129–30
post-*Actavis v Eli Lilly*, 137
sign post approach, 126
strict literal approach, 129
costs, 59
reduction, 30
decision-making, 118
Boards of Appeal considering CJEU decisions, 124–25

CJEU considering Board of appeal decisions, 124–25
national courts
considering Board of Appeal decisions, 118–19
considering other national court decisions, 119–23
court referrals, 125–26
decisions, EPO interpretation and consideration of 123–24
open dialogue, 165
referrals by national courts, 125–26
differentiation, 7
divergence areas, 110–17
diversity, 5, 168
domestic courts and tribunals, 103
enforcement, 30
EPC impact on, 82
EPO, 103
EPUE existence alongside, 49
examiners, 28–29
fees:
appeals, 29
opposition, 29
renewals, 30
use, 30
flexibility:
current system, 7
fragmentation, 144–45, 176
addressing, 173
considering diversity and value pluralism when responding to fragmentation, 168
current system, 7
fears in, 103
increase by UPP expected, 7
inherent aspect of European patent system, as, 109–10, 117–18, 142–43, 169
inherent part as, 15
minimising, 171
perceptions of, 173
responses, 15–16, 104, 173, 175
Unitary Patent Package, *see* Unitary Patent Package
harmonisation:
approximation rather than assimilation of laws, 8
efforts, 7
rather than unification, 8
impact of Unitary Patent Package, 139–40
infringement claims, national level, 31
institutions:
independent development, 102
integration efforts, 7
international legal system interpretation rules introduced into, 175
international patent applications and, 35
interpretation rules introduced into, 175
judges duty to cooperate with one another, 122–23
judicial cooperation, 117–18
judicial dialogue, 117–18, 140
judicial meetings and appointments, 137–39
laws:
independent development, 102
limitations of judicial dialogue and cooperation, 140–42
multiplicity of institutions, 109
national diversity consideration in, 172
national patent systems and, 35
national regimes, conflicts between, 104
norms:
independent development, 102
open dialogue system, 140
opposition proceedings, 29
opting out of UPC jurisdiction, 49, 62
partial unification attempt, Unitary Patent Package, 36
partial unification efforts, 8
pluralism, 7
prosperity aim, 82
reforms:
integration promotion aims, 10
tension between cultures in, 166
territorial fragmentation, 2
time taken to reach agreement, 166
translations, 29, 30
unification efforts, 7, 8, 81
value pluralism consideration in, 172
validity claims, national level, 31
European Patent with Unitary Effect (EPUE):
coexistence and separate treatment, 49
compulsory licensing, 48
enforcement proceedings, 48
existence alongside European patent system, 49
fees, 59, 60
indirect discrimination on nationality grounds, 48
insolvency, 48
language arrangements, 56
licensing, 48

national law applicable to, same across all Member States, 49
national patents:
existence alongside, 49
participation of, Member States, treated as, 48
object of property, as, 46, 48
participating Member States, equal effect in, 45–46
prohibited acts not included, 46
proprietors' rights, UPCA provisions on, 44
protective rights applications, 48
Regulation 1257 established, 42, 45–46
rights in *rem*, 48
scope of right and limitations, 46
transfer of rights, 48
translation requirements, 54–55
uniform protection, 45
unitary character, 45
unitary effect requests, 43
UPCA settlement of disputes relating to, 43–44
European policy-makers, 35
European states:
nationalistic attitudes, 76
European substantive patent law, 20
European Union, 74
Biotech Directive, 22–23
Charter of Fundamental Rights for the EU, 86
computer-implemented inventions, 22
creation, 83
cross-border enforcement, 24–26
cultures, diversity respecting, 86
designs protection harmonised across, 8–9
enhanced cooperation procedure, 11, 12
enlargement, 84
fundamental rights interests, 85
institutional structure reformed, 84
internal market, 84
law-making methods, 172
law primacy, UPC, 44
Member States, *see* EU Member States
membership expansion, 84
public policy interests, 85
social policy interests, 85
subsidiarity principle, 83
Supplementary Protection Certificate (SPC) Regulations, 22
TEU created, 83
trade mark protection harmonised, 8–9
traditions, diversity respecting, 86
unitary intellectual property rights, 85–86
unitary patent system, 14
values:
appearance before objectives, 84–85
equality, 86
freedom, 86
human dignity, 86
promotion, 83
solidarity, 86
Europeanisation, 27, 34
examination standards:
search standards and, EPC balanced, 30
examination systems:
national patent systems, 23
examiners:
European patent system, 28–29
exclusive rights:
patentees, 20-years, 4
exclusivity:
access within patent system and, balance between, 35
exhaustion doctrine, 21
existing fragmentation, 34–35
existing routes to patent protection in Europe, 19
European (EPC) patent system, 27–31
existing fragmentation, 34–35
international patent application, 31–34
national patent systems, 19–27
expected fragmentation, 95

failed applications:
appeals to EPO Boards of Appeal, 29
fair protection:
affording inventions, 34
fear of fragmentation:
diminished, 173
fear to acceptance:
international legal systems, fragmentation in, 101–102
fees:
application, 59
EPUE, 59, 60
European patent system, *see* European patent system
renewal, *see* renewal fees
search, 59
UPC, 60
filing:
international patent applications, 32

financial provisions, UPC, 44
Finland:
post-*Actavis v Eli Lilly*, 137
flexibility:
differentiation, 11
European patent system:
current system, 7
international legal systems, 95
focus on diversity, 12–13
Formstein, 130
forum shopping, 98, 100
CJEU, 26–27
national patent systems, 24, 26
UPC, 66, 67
fragmentation:
acknowledging, 168
capacity to be harnessed, 173
conceptualising, 95
convergence, 12, 173
cooperation:
fragmentation risks reduction, 173
current system, 7
divergence, 173
diversity, 168, 173
enhanced cooperation, 87, 89
EU Member State laws, 172
EU unitary patent system, 175
European law-making, in, 73–74
means of integration, as, 88–89
European Patent Convention (EPC), 31
European patent system, *see* European patent system
fear of, diminished, 173
inherent, 95, 168
institutional, *see* institutional fragmentation
integration, as means of, 88–89
international law, *see* international law
International Law Commission, 91–94
treatment methods, 95–96
international legal system, *see* international legal system
judicial dialogue, 173
law:
EU Member States in, 172
legal, 5
legal systems inherent aspect, 105
national patent systems, 20, 27, 31
negative effects, 94, 97
patent protection in Europe, 34–35
perceptions of, 173
persistence of, 168
perspectives on, 12–13
procedural, *see* procedural fragmentation
regimes, within, 173
responding to, *see* responding to fragmentation
substantive, *see* substantive fragmentation
territorial, *see* territorial fragmentation
Unified Patent Court Agreement (UPCA), increase, 69–70
UPP, 69–70
value pluralism, 168, 173, 174
France:
equivalents, 132
inventive step:
problem and solution approach, 113
proceedings from other courts increasingly considered, 122
Schuman Plan support, 75
freedom, EU values, 86
Fujitsu, 115
functional differentiation, 95, 101
fundamental rights:
EU interests, 85
protection, Biotech Directive, 22–23
further fragmentation:
UPP, 69–70
future and current tribunals:
judicial dialogue between, 176

G2/13 and G2/12 *(Broccoli II and Tomatoes II)*, 160–61, 162
G3/19 *Pepper* (follow-up to '*Tomatoes II*' and '*Broccoli II*'), 162, 163, 164
Gale's Application, 115
GAT v LUK, 24–25, 26
Genentech's Patent, 115, 118
generalist overview, CJEU, 167
Generics (UK) Ltd v Daiichi Pharmaceutical Co Ltd, 114
Germany:
bifurcation, 68
claim construction:
general innovative ideas, 127
signpost method, 127
technical teaching of inventions, 127
Constitutional Court:
complaints against EPO, 53
equivalents, 132–33
expertise of Courts in patent field, 140–41
Formstein, 130
inventive step:
problem and solution approach, 113

national courts considering other national court decisions, 121–22
Patents Act, 130
post-*Actavis v Eli Lilly*, 137
Schneidmesser, 130–31, 132
Schuman Plan support, 75
Supreme Court:
invention requiring technical teaching, 121
national courts considering Board of Appeal decisions, 121–22
national courts considering other national court decisions, 121
Walzenformgebungsmaschine case, 122
Zahnkranzfräser case, 121
UPCA:
compatibility with Constitution, 52
ratification, 52–53
goals:
Community Patent Convention, 81
governance, multi-level, 139
granted international patent applications:
enforcement at national level, 34
grants:
requests for:
European patent applications, 28
validated by relevant European patent system Contracting States, 29
Grimme v Scott, 120, 121
Guidelines for Examination, EPO, 113

harmonious interpretation of law, 97
harmonisation:
approximation rather than assimilation of laws, European patent system, 8
attempts, 174
efforts, 7
European, 34, 149
intellectual property law concept familiarity, 8–10
international, 34
judges, 140
judicial cooperation leading to, 133, 173
judicial dialogue leading to, 133
legislative, 146–48
progress towards, 12
rather than unification, European patent system, 8
harmonised interpretation, 97
harmonising patentability requirements, EPC, 86–87
hierarchical coordination:
absence of fragmentation in international legal systems, 93
High Authority, ECSC, 76
human dignity, 22–23, 86
human embryos:
defining for all EU Member States, 168, 174
industrial or commercial purposes, uses for, *see* patentability
Human Genome Science v Eli Lilly, 119
human rights:
concepts being heard in patent law cases, 104
humanitarian law and, divergence risks, 98
Hungary:
UPCA ratification not compatible with Fundamental Law, 53–54

ICJ (International Court of Justice), 100, 141
ILC, *see* **International Law Commission**
impact:
cooperation, 128–31, 136
implementation of European Patent Convention, 172
Implementing Regulations, EPC, 150, 174
Improver v Remington, 31, 112, 128–129, 131, 132, 124, 135, 137, 170
inconsistencies:
acknowledging, 97–98
increased innovation:
societal benefits of, 4
independent development:
European patent system institutions, 102
indirect discrimination:
nationality grounds, EPUE, 48
indirect infringement, UPCA, 44
individual investors:
applications, national patent systems, 23
industrial property:
Paris Convention, 20
informal communication, 100
informal search for prior art, 33
infringement:
actions, national courts, different outcomes, 132
claims, national level, European patent system, 31
non-discrimination principle, 57
inherent aspect:
European patent system fragmentation, 169
inherent fragmentation, 95, 168
Inner Six, ECSC, 75
innovation, 4

institutional addition:
Biotech Directive, 148–49
institutional differentiation, 95
institutional fragmentation, 2, 13, 35, 63, 96, 109, 141, 170
bifurcation, 68–69
CJEU, 26
courts, divergent decisions producing, 2
ICJ response role, 141
internal structure of UPC, 64–67
jurisdiction and competence of UPC and the transitional period, 67–68
national patent systems, 24, 31
offices, divergent decisions producing, 2
UPC response role, 141
institutional structure of EU, 84
institutions:
critically considering own precedents:
responding to fragmentation, 168
interactions between, 139, 168
multiple, 3
multiplicity of, European patent system, 109
integration:
differentiated, 11, 74, 83
ECSC attempts, 76
efforts, European patent system, 7
European, 149
fragmentation as means of, 88–89
mechanism:
differentiation, 11
patent system to advance, promotion of, 34
progress towards, 12
promotion aims:
European patent system reforms, 10
regime interaction and, 100
substantial progress towards, 11
systemic, 94, 96
integrative effects:
limiting Unitary Patent Package to certain patentees, 62
intellectual property:
exhaustion doctrine:
rights holders' rights of first marketing in EEA, 21
law:
Enforcement Directive, 8
harmonisation concept familiarity, 8–10
protection in international law, 13
protection standards, TRIPS, 21
rights:
protection, 86
unitary, TFEU, 85–86
interaction, 100
institutions, between, 139, 168
regimes, 97
promoting coordination in multiple areas of fragmentation, 99
internal market, 81–82, 84
internal structure of UPC:
institutional fragmentation, 64–67
international agreements:
UPC basing decisions on, 44
International Bureau of WIPO:
international patent applications to, 32, 33
international community:
states' predetermined obligations to, 96
international conventions:
countries considering, 102
International Court of Justice (ICJ), 100, 141
international harmonisation, 34
international law:
fragmentation in, 13
coordinated, 102
discussion on, 102
fear of, 101
functional differentiation increase, 101
specialised regimes introduction, 101
intellectual property law protection in, 13
see also international legal system
International Law Commission (ILC):
fragmentation, 91–94
treatment methods, 95–96
international legal system:
application to European patent system, 102–104
contextual responsiveness, 95
flexibility, 95
fragmentation as inherent aspect of legal systems, 105
fragmentation in, 3, 90–94
absence of hierarchical coordination, 93
addressing in, 173
analysis, 94–95
divergence, 93
inherent part of, 12, 15
multiplicity of international regulations, 93
overview, 92–93
perceived in, 173
powerful states' calculated strategies, result of, 101
proliferation of courts or tribunals, 93
responses to, 95–99, 104
judicial dialogue and cooperation, 99–101

fear to acceptance, 101–102
specialisation of international regulations, 93
interpretation rules introduced into European patent system, 175
methods used in, 175
proper functioning, 97
scholarship:
fragmentation focus, 12
see also international law
international order based on rule of law, 95
international patent applications, 19, 31
abstracts, 32
administered by WIPO, 32
claims, 32
Contracting States, by, 32
cost, 34
descriptions, 32
designated priority dates, 33
drawings, 32
European patent system and, 35
filing, 32
granted:
enforcement at national level, 34
International Bureau of WIPO, to, 32
international priority filing dates, 33
International Search Authority, copies to, 32
national patent systems and, 35
PATENTSCOPE, published on, 33–34
prescribed languages of PCT, filing in, 32
prior art:
additional, supplementary searches of, 32
anticipatory, 33
informal searching for, 33
international searches of, 32
Receiving Offices:
applications through, 32
checks, 32
reports:
applicants, to, 33
International Bureau of WIPO, to, 33
PATENTSCOPE, published on, 33–34
PCT, 33
requests, 32
searches:
fees, 34
prior art, of, 32
international priority filing dates:
Patent Cooperation Treaty, 33
international regulations:
international legal systems, fragmentation in, 93
International Search Authority (ISA):
international patent applications copies to, 32
international searches of prior art, 32
International Stem Cell Corporation (ISCC), 152, 155
international treaties and conventions:
European patent field harmonisation through, 9
interpretation:
European patent system, introduced into, 175
harmonised, 97
inventions:
biotechnological, *see* biotechnological inventions
commercialisation, 3
computer-implemented, *see* computer-implemented inventions
description:
European patent applications, 28
fair protection, affording, 34
patentees' exclusive rights, 3–4
protection across Europe fragmented, 23
supplementary protection certificates, 9
inventive step, EPO:
any hardware approach, 115–16
closest prior art, 113
objective technical problems, 113
problem and solution approach, 113
Ireland:
UPCA ratification, referendum required, 54
ISCC, *see* ***International Stem Cell Corporation***
Italy:
exclusion:
enhanced cooperation use, 87–88
negotiations, from, 55
language, 55, 58
opposition to Regulations, 47
post-*Actavis v Eli Lilly*, 137
Schuman Plan support, 75
unitary patents, 55
UPCA ratification, 51

judges:
coming together, 175
confidential online links to judges in other jurisdictions, 140
cooperation, 140, 41
dialogue, 140, 141
duty to cooperate with one another, European patent system, 122–23

European Patent Judges' Symposium, 138
final written decisions departing from status quo, 140
harmonisation, 140
taking each others' judgments into account, 173
Unified Patent Court, 6, 44, 64
different Member States, from, on same UPC panels, 166
regular meetings, 139
retaining positions as judges in national courts, 166
judicial bodies, 35
judicial borrowing, 99
judicial coherence, 139
judicial cooperation, 102
fragmentation responses, 173
harmonisation, leading to, 133, 173
point of, 175
progress towards convergence, promotion, 168
judicial deference, 100
judicial dialogue and cooperation, 99, 102
current and future tribunals, between, 176
European patent system, 117–18, 140–42
fragmentation responses, 173
harmonisation, leading to, 133
international legal systems, fragmentation in, 99–101
point of, 175
progress towards convergence, promotion, 168
judicial integration, 99
judicial internships:
national judges, for, 139
judicial law-making, 175
judicial meetings and appointments:
European patent system, 137–39
judicial panels, 175
judiciaries:
diversity lack, 141, 175
Unified Patent Court dialogue with, 139
jurisdiction:
shared:
Unitary Patent Package, 171
Unified Patent Court, 67–68
jurisprudence:
differing, erosion of international law unity, 100
EPO Boards of Appeal, aligning, 141–42
Unitary Patent Package, 175–76
UPC, critical consideration, 176
national, UPC consideration of, 166
jus cogens, 96

Kirin-Amgen v Hoechst Marion, 129, 134–35

languages:
arrangements:
CJEU, 56, 58
EPUE, 56
TFEU, unanimity, 55
alternative regimes, 56
choice reduction, 61
Court of Appeal (UPC), at, 61
Court of First Instance (UPC), at, 61
EU Trade Mark, 58
Italy, 55, 58
official, *see* official languages
official, of EPO, 60
patent granted in, 61
proceedings, of, 61
regime:
appropriate, 58
too narrowly considered, 57
restrictions, patents availability, 57
Rules of Procedure, 61
Spain, 55, 57, 58
translations:
compensation scheme, 60
costs, 58, 60
lack of, 57
machine, 58, 59
last resort condition, 56
law:
approximation, EEC, 83
conflict, 102
coordination, 95
domestic, *see* domestic law
EU Member States:
divergence in, 172
fragmentation in, 172
European patent system, 102
harmonious interpretation, 97
intellectual property law, *see* intellectual property law
international law, *see* international law
making:
European, fragmentation in, *see* European law-making
fragmentation ensured, 169
methods, EU, 172
processes, European, 3
national, *see* national laws
overlapping, interpretation, 35
patchwork of, 171
patent, *see* patent law

rule of, *see* rule of law
sources:
considering all, 175
Unified Patent Court, 175
substantive, 148
unification, 95
legal basis:
regarding legal uncertainty, UPP, 47
legal fragmentation, 5
legal pluralism, 11–12, 97
legal systems:
fragmentation as inherent aspect of, 105
pluralist, 97
legal uncertainty:
compromise raising issue of, UPP, 49
legally qualified judges:
judicial panels, 175
legislative harmonisation:
Biotech Directive, 146–48
legitimacy:
issues impacting UPP, 70
***lex posterior*,** 94, 96
***lex specialis*,** 94, 96
licensing:
compulsory, EPUE, 48
limited membership:
ratification, UPP, 49
Lisbon Treaty, 38–39, 84
litigation, 59
litigators, 35
local divisions of Court of First Instance (UPC), 64
London Agreement (2000), 30
Luxembourg:
Schuman Plan support, 75

machine translations, 58, 59
manipulative behaviour, 98
market, internal, 81–82, 84
market operations, 34
Mediation and Arbitration Centres, UPCA, 60
Member States:
EU, *see* EU Member States
individual decisions to become bound by UPP, 54
national law, UPC applying, 44
membership:
EU, expansion, 84
UPCA, 50–54
Merger Treaty:
ECSC, 79
EURATOM, 79
European Economic Community, 79
***Merrell Dow v Norton*,** 118, 119
***Merrill Lynch*,** 115
minimising European patent system fragmentation, 171
***Muller v Hilti*,** 112
multi-level governance, 139
multi-sourced equivalent norms, 98
multi-speed Europe, 11
multifaceted approach to fragmentation, 12, 16, 102, 172
multinational composition:
judicial panels, 175
multiple courts and tribunals:
negative consequences, 100
multiple institutions, 3
multiple patents, 3
multiplicity of international regulations:
international legal systems, fragmentation in, 93

national courts:
decisions:
Board of Appeal considering, 118–19
EPO interpretation and consideration of, 123–24
other national court decisions considering, 119–23
infringement actions:
different outcomes, 132
judges:
active dialogue between, 142
comparative reasoning and research between, 142
UPC, retaining position, 166
national patent systems, 23
new precedent filtering into, UPC panels, 176
referrals by, 125–26
rulings, 25
substantive patent law interpretation differences, 170
national diversity, 169
allowance for, 168
Biotech Directive, consideration in, 172
European patent system, consideration in, 172
fragmentation consideration in, 173, 174

national judges:
EPO Boards of Appeal, *see* European Patent Office
European Patent Convention, judicial internships for, 139
national jurisprudence:
UPC consideration of, 166
national languages:
translations, European patent applications, 29
national laws, 102
priority:
European Patent Convention (EPC), 10
referencing:
uniform protection by EU Member States, 46–47
national legal systems:
countries considering, 102
national parliaments:
ratification or refusal, UPCA, 54
national patent laws:
retention, European countries, 103
national patent offices, 19, 30
national patent rights:
bundle of, successful European patent applications resulting in, 30–31
granted by application to national patent offices, 19
territorial, 20
validated and enforced at national level, 1–2
national patent systems, 1, 19–20, 170
aim, 20
coexistence and separate treatment, 49
costs, 24
cross-border enforcement lack, 24
divergence, 27
enforcement, 35
EPUEs' existence alongside, 49
European patent system and, 35
examination systems, 23
forum shopping, 24, 26
fragmented nature, 20, 27, 31
individual investors' applications, 23
institutional fragmentation, 24, 31
international patent applications and, 35
national courts, 23
new challenges, 20
patent priority systems, 23
patent protection route, 6
potential cost disadvantage, 24
prior art searches, 23
priority dates, 23–24
procedural fragmentation, 24
registration systems, 23
relevant national law, 26
small and medium-sized enterprises (SME) applications, 23, 27
tactical filing strategies, fragmentation use, 24
territorial fragmentation, 24
territoriality, 35
torpedoes, 26
national property laws:
plethora of applying to different patents, EPUE, 48
national regimes:
European patent system, conflicts between, 104
national route, patent protection, 170
national sovereignty, ECSC, 76
nationalistic attitudes:
European states, 76
necessity for fragmentation, 168
negative effects of fragmentation, 94, 97
negotiations:
Italy and Spain exclusion from, 55
Netherlands:
Improver v Remington, 132, 132
inventive step:
problem and solution approach, 113
Schuman Plan support, 75
***Netherlands* case,** 154
Nice Treaty, *see* **Treaty of Nice**
non-discrimination principle, 57
non-patentable subject matter, 114
normative parallelism, 98
norms:
competing, 96
European patent system:
independent development, 102
multi-sourced equivalent, 98
peremptory, 96
***Novartis AG and Cibavision AG v Johnson & Johnson Medical Ltd and others*,** 112

objective technical problem:
inventive step, EPO, 113
***obligations erga omnes*,** 96
offices:
divergent decisions producing institutional fragmentation, 2
official languages:
EPO, 60
European patent system, 28
UPP, 43

Omega case, 154
open dialogue system:
European patent system, 140
open-endedness of fragmentation, 95
opinions, dissenting, UPC panels, 166
opposition:
fees, European patent system, 29
opting in, UPC, 62, 63
opting out, UPC, 62, 63
over-protection curtailment, 34
overlapping laws:
interpretation, 35

panels:
judicial, 175
UPC, *see* Unified Patent Court
parallel proceedings:
divergence areas, 112
procedural fragmentation, 141
parallelism, normative, 98
Paris Convention, 10, 20, 32, 102–103
partial unification efforts:
European patent system, 8
participating Member States:
equal effect of EPUE, 45–46
patchwork of laws, 171
patent assertion entities, UPC, 66–67
patent attorneys, 30
Patent Cooperation Treaty (PCT), 1
advantages to applicants, 33
EU patent law harmonisation lack due to, 10
international patent applications reports, 33
international priority filing dates, 33
patent protection route, 6
prescribed languages:
international patent applications filing in, 32
reports, 33
World Intellectual Property Office introduced by, 1
patent courts:
European law-makers, 35
judiciary, UPC, 139
property aspects lack of harmonisation, 48
public policy issues, 167
relevant, UPC taking into consideration, 175
unified, 35
US system, 66
patent law:
cases, human rights concepts being heard in, 104
property aspects of:
lack of harmonisation, 48
public policy issues, 167
reforms, 5
UPC judiciary, 139
patent offices, 35
patent priority systems:
national patent systems, 23
patent protection:
current routes:
criticisms of, 170
fragmented nature, 170
European Patent Convention (EPC), 1, 6
national route, 170
Patent Cooperation Treaty, 6
PCT route, 170
patentability, 75
approaches, 111–12
inventive step, 113–14
patentable subject matter, 114–17
Biotech Directive exclusions from, 149–50
exceptions interpretations, 149
essentially biological processes, 160
conclusion, 164–65
evaluation, 162–65
fragmentation and, 173–74
G2/13 and G2/12 *(Broccoli II and Tomatoes II)*, 160–61
G3/19 *Pepper* (follow-up to '*Tomatoes II*' and '*Broccoli II*'), 162, 164
institutional interactions and convergence overreach, 162–63
specialist institution perspective, 164
T1063/18 *Extreme Dark Green, Blocky Peppers*, 161
uses of human embryos for industrial or commercial purposes, 149–50, 174
conclusion, 159–60
convergence overextended, 153–56
Brüstle, 151–52, 153–55, 156
evaluation, 152–60
generalist v specialist decision-making, 156–57
institutional interactions, 157–59
ISCC, 152, 155
WARF, 150–51
responding to fragmentation in relation to, 15–16
substantive patent law exceptions to, 174
patented technology:
downstream accessibility, 34–35

patentees:
inventions, exclusive rights, 3–4
patents, national, *see* **national patent systems and national patent rights**
PATENTSCOPE:
international patent applications published on, 33–34
PBS PARTNERSHIP/Controlling pension benefits system, 115–16
PCT, *see* **Patent Cooperation Treaty**
peace:
European Economic Community, 77
promotion, ECSC, 76
peremptory norms, 96
persistence of fragmentation, 168
pluralism, 11–12
European patent system, 7
legal, 97
recognising, 97
response, 98
value, *see* value pluralism
plurality of values, 169
Poland:
bifurcation, 68
decision not to sign UPCA, 50
policy-makers:
European, 35
political compromise, 98
potential users, 49
powerful states:
calculated strategies, result of:
international legal systems, fragmentation in, 101
Pozzoli v BDMO SA, 112
precedent:
Unified Patent Court, 166
prior art:
additional, supplementary searches of, 32
anticipatory, 33
closest, inventive step, EPO, 113
informal searching for, 33
international searches of, 32
searches:
national patent systems, 23
see also international patent applications
priority dates:
designated:
international patent applications, 33
national patent systems, 23–24
problem and solution approach:
inventive step, EPO, 113
procedural aspects:
UPC considering, 165
procedural diversity, 5
procedural fragmentation, 2, 5, 35, 109, 170
judicial dialogue limiting, 141
national patent systems, 24
parallel proceedings, 141
progress towards integration, 12
prohibited acts:
not included, EPUE, 46
promotion:
EU values, 83
proper functioning:
international legal systems, 97
property:
aspects of patent laws:
lack of harmonisation, 48
object of, EPUE as, 46, 48, 49
laws:
national, *see* national property laws
rights:
unitary intellectual, EU, 85–86
proprietors' rights, EPC:
UPCA provisions on, 44
prosperity:
ECSC, 76
EEC, 77
European patent system aim, 82
protection:
costs of, European patent system, 30
intellectual property rights, 86
Protocol on the Interpretation of Article 69:
European Patent Convention, 128, 134
Protocol on Privileges and Immunities, UPC, 6, 50
Protocol on Provisional Application, UPCA, 50
public policy:
EU interests, 85
patent law, issues, 167

qualified majority:
changes by rather than by unanimity, 168

ratification:
UPCA, 49, 50–54
Re Symbian's Application, 116
Receiving Offices, *see* **international patent applications**
reciprocity, 100
***Red Dove* case,** 115

reduction of costs:
European patent system, 30
referrals to CJEU:
no provision for, 159
reforms:
integration promotion aims, European patent system, 10
patent law:
focused on economic perspectives, 5
societal considerations, 5
regimes:
dialogue between, 97
fragmentation within, 173
interaction, 97, 102
integration and, 100
productive friction, 97
unions of rules laying down particular rights, duties and powers, 93
weaker, co-opting of, 100
regional divisions of Court of First Instance (UPC), 64
registration systems:
national patent systems, 23
Registry, UPC, 44
Regulation:
interpretation controversies, CJEU, 22
regulations, international, 93
relevant national law:
national patent systems, 26
renewal fees:
European patent system, 30
unitary patent, 59
reports:
international patent applications, *see* international patent applications
Patent Cooperation Treaty, 33
requests:
international patent applications, 32
responding to fragmentation, 168, 173–74
diversity considering, 168
European patent system, 173, 175
institutions critically considering own precedents, 168
understanding and, 172
value pluralism considering, 168
revocation:
European patent system, 29
rights:
exclusive, patentees, 4
fundamental, *see* fundamental rights
in *rem*, EPUE, 48
national patents, territorial, 20
transfer, EPUE, 48
unitary, 9
risks:
judicial law-making, 175
reduction, substantive fragmentation, CJEU and, 167
***Roche v Primus*,** 24, 25–26
rule of law:
international order based on, 95
understanding, 95
Rules and Procedure:
Unified Patent Court, 6, 62
Rules of Procedure:
language, 61
UPC, 62

***Schneidmesser*,** 130–31
scholarship:
international legal system:
fragmentation focus, 12
Schuman Declaration, ECSC, 75–76
***Schütz v Werit*,** 121
search standards:
examination standards and, EPC balanced, 30
searches:
international patent applications:
fees, 34
prior art, of, 32
secondary rules, 99
separate treatment:
European patent system, 49
shifting perspectives and objectives, 81–82
sign post approach, cooperation, 126
Single European Act, 82
small and medium-sized enterprises (SME):
applications, national patent systems, 23, 27
search fees, 34
UPCA language of proceedings, 60
UPP concerns, 60, 176
SME, *see* **small and medium-sized enterprises**
social policy interests, EU, 85
societal benefits, 4
societal considerations:
patent law reform, 5
societal differences:
remaining, fragmentation persisting, 168
societal issues, 5
society:
confusion caused by patent protection complexity, 35

solidarity, EU values, 86
sources of law, *see* **law**
sovereignty:
  national, ECSC, 76
Spain:
  exclusion:
    enhanced cooperation use, 87–88
    negotiations, 55
  language, 55, 57, 58
  opposition to Regulations, 47
  refusal to sign UPCA, 50
  unitary patents, 55
  UPP rejection, 55
SPC, *see* **Supplementary Protection Certificate (SPC) Regulations**
specialised court, UPCA, 43–44
specialised regimes:
  international law fragmentation introduction, 101
stability, increase, EEC, 77
standard of living:
  accelerated raising of, EEC, 77
states:
  predetermined obligations to international community, 96
Statute, UPC, 44
Strasbourg Patent Convention, 10, 20–21, 28, 78–80, 82, 103
streamlined procedure:
  European Patent Convention, 20
strict literal approach, cooperation, 129
subsidiarity principle, EU, 83
substantial progress towards integration, 11
substantive aspects:
  UPC considering, 165
substantive fragmentation, 2, 104, 109, 170
  potential increased for, 174
  risk reduction, CJEU and, 167
substantive law:
  biotechnological inventions, 148
substantive patent law:
  CJEU:
    interpretation role in relation to UPP, 46
    involvement, 148–49
  countries interpretation, 103
  exceptions to patentability, 174
  harmonised, Strasbourg Patent Convention, 82
  interpretation:
    current, 173
    differences, 170
  provisions, UPCA, 44
  harmonised across Europe, 2
  harmonised by EPC, 142
  interpretation, 2
    divergence areas, 112
  national courts interpretation differences, 170
  UPC interpretations:
    tribunals' jurisprudence and, bringing closer together, 175
sunrise periods, UPC, 62–63
Supplementary Protection Certificate (SPC) Regulations, EU, 22
  inventions, 9
  UPCA settlement of disputes relating to, 43–44
supplementary searches:
  additional prior art, 32
supranational agreement, UPCA, 43–44
supranational legal systems:
  fragmentation as inherent aspect of, 173
supranationalism:
  ECSC, 76
  EEC, 77
  European patent system aim, 82
Sweden:
  post-*Actavis v Eli Lilly*, 137
Switzerland:
  post-*Actavis v Eli Lilly*, 137
Symbian v Comptroller General of Patents, Designs and Trademarks, 116
systemic integration, 94, 96, 173

T1063/18 ***Extreme Dark Green, Blocky Peppers***, 161
T1441/13 ***Embryonic stem cells, disclaimer/ ASTERIAS***, 158
T2221/10 ***Culturing stem cells/TECHNION***, 158
tactical filing strategies:
  fragmentation use, national patent systems, 24
technical character approach:
  EPO, 115–117
technical contribution approach:
  EPO, 115, 116–17
technical problems, objective, 113
technically qualified judges, 175
technological developments, 4
technology:
  enormous changes in, 34
  patented, downstream accessibility, 34–35

terminology, 7–12
territorial fragmentation, 35, 49, 109, 170, 171
European patent system, 2
national patent systems, 24
participation in unitary patent, 54–59
ratification and membership of UPCA, 50–54
translation requirements, 54–59
users of UPP, 59–63
territorial national patent rights, 20
territoriality:
national patents, 35
TEU, *see* **Treaty on European Union**
TFEU, *see* **Treaty on the Functioning of the European Union**
torpedoes, 26
trade marks, 8–9
traditions:
diversity respecting, EU, 86
transfer of rights, EPUE, 48
transitional period, UPC, 67
transitional provisions, UPC, 44
translation:
European patent system, 29, 30
filing costs, 59
languages, *see* languages
regime, 38, 39
requirements, EPUE, 54–55
UPP arrangements, 42, 43
transnational cooperation, 82
treaties, interpretation:
Vienna Convention on the Law of Treaties, 95–96
Treaty establishing EEC, 77
Treaty of Amsterdam:
TEU amended by, 83
Treaty of Lisbon, 38–39, 84
Treaty of London:
Council of Europe establishment through, 74
Treaty of Nice:
TEU amended by, 83–84
Treaty of Paris (1951), ECSC, 75
Treaty on European Union (TEU)
enhanced cooperation procedure, 42
EU created, 83
Lisbon Treaty changes, 84
Treaty of Amsterdam, amended by, 83
Treaty of Nice, amended by, 83–84
Treaty on the Functioning of the European Union (TFEU), 84
language arrangements, unanimity, 55
unitary intellectual property rights, 85–86
UPP legal basis in, 6
tribunals:
multiple, negative consequences, 100
proliferation, international legal systems, fragmentation in, 93
TRIPS, *see* **Agreement on Trade-Related Aspects of Intellectual Property Rights**

unanimity:
changes by qualified majority rather than by, 168
understanding:
rule of law, 95
unification, 10
efforts, European patent system, 7, 8
European patent system aim, 81
laws, 95
partial efforts, 8
Unified Patent Court (UPC):
Agreement, 6
agreement, EU Member States, 36–37
aims, 7
bifurcation, 68–69
Brussels Compromise, 65
central division of Court of First Instance (UPC), 64, 65
CJEU:
cooperation, 44
future relationships, 166
competence, 67
convergence attempts, 165
costs, 59
counterclaims for revocation, 68
Court of Appeal (UPC), 44, 64, 65
Court of First Instance (UPC), 44, 52, 64, 65
cross-border jurisdiction, 6
dialogue with judiciaries and boards, 139
dysfunction, bifurcation as, 68–69
division shopping, 66, 67
enforcement, costs, 59–60
EPC, basing decisions on, 44
EPO jurisprudence, consideration of, 166
EU law:
primacy, respect for, ensuring, 44, 166–67
questions on referred to CJEU, 167
fees, 60
financial provisions, 44
first budget adoption, 6
forum shopping, 66, 67
fragmentation increase expected, 7
fragmentation within, possibility, 64
hybrid court, seen as, 167

institutional fragmentation response role, 141
internal structure, 64–67
international agreements, basing decisions on, 44
judges, 44, 64
  appointment, 6
  regular meetings, 139
  retaining positions as judges in national courts, 166
jurisdiction:
  European patent system opting out of, 49, 62
  institutional fragmentation and transitional period, 67–68
jurisprudence, critical consideration, 176
local divisions of Court of First Instance (UPC), 64
national jurisprudence, consideration of, 166
national law of Member States, applying, 44
opting in, 62, 63
opting out, 62, 63
panels:
  composition, 166
  dissenting opinions, 166
  judges from different Member States on same panels, 166
  judicial, 175
  national courts, new precedent filtering into, 176
  specialist nature could lead to very closed legal culture, 166
patent assertion entities, 66–67
patent laws:
  judiciary, 139
precedent, 166
procedural aspects, considering, 165
procedure, 44
Protocol on Privileges and Immunities, 6, 50
provisions and structure, 44
regional divisions of Court of First Instance (UPC), 64
Registry, 44
Rules of Procedure, 6, 62
sources of law, 175
Statute, 44
structure, 44
substantive aspects, considering, 165
substantive patent law interpretations:
  tribunals' jurisprudence and, bringing closer together, 175
sunrise periods, 62–63
transitional period, 67
transitional provisions, 44
Union law, basing decisions on, 44
UPCA, basing decisions on, 44
value pluralism, consideration of, 166
Unified Patent Court Agreement (UPCA), 6
  Articles 25–27 transferred from Regulation 1257, 46
  Belgium ratification and challenge, 53
  bifurcation, 68–69
  dialogue between national courts, Boards of Appeal, CJEU and UPC divisions, 175
  EPUE proprietors' rights, provisions on, 44
  finalised, 41
  fragmentation increase, 69–70
  Germany:
    compatibility with Constitution, 52
    ratification, 52–53
  Hungary ratification not compatible with Fundamental Law, 53–54
  indirect infringement, 44
  Ireland ratification, referendum required, 54
  Italy ratification, 51
  language of proceedings:
    small and medium-sized enterprises, 60
  Mediation and Arbitration Centres, 60
  membership, 50–54
    territorial fragmentation, 50–54
  national parliaments ratification or refusal, 54
  Poland decision not to sign, 50
  Protocol on the Provisional Application, 6, 50
  ratification, 49, 50–54
    territorial fragmentation, 50–54
  settlement of disputes relating to EPC, 43–44
  settlement of disputes relating to EPUE, 43–44
  Spain refusal to sign, 50
  specialised court, 43–44
  substantive patent law provisions, 44
  supranational agreement, 43–44
  United Kingdom ratification, later withdrawn, 51
  UPC basing decisions on, 44
  UPC provisions and structure, 44
  UPC respect for EU law primacy ensuring, 166–67
  UPC sources of law, 175
unified patent courts, 35
uniform protection, EPUE, 45
Union law:
  UPC basing decisions on, 44

unitary character, EPUE, 45
unitary effect requests, EPUE, 43
unitary intellectual property rights, EU, 85–86
Unitary Patent Package: (UPP):
aims, 45
background, 37–42
coexistence and separate treatment, 49
compromise not ideal, 49
concerns, 45, 176
institutional fragmentation, 63
bifurcation, 68–69
internal structure of UPC, 64–67
jurisdiction and competence of UPC and the transitional period, 67–68
substantive issues, 45–49
territorial fragmentation, 49
participation in the Unitary Patent, 54–59
ratification and membership of the UPCA, 50–54
users of the UPP, 59–63
costs, 59
enhanced cooperation, 55–57, 87
EU Member States, unitary patent for, 171
EU unitary patent system established, 6
European patent system:
additional institution with numerous divisions, introducing, 171
establishing, 171
impact on, 139–40
European (EPC) patents inside:
coexistence and separate treatment, 49
European (EPC) patents outside:
coexistence and separate treatment, 49
fragmentation:
central feature, as, 172
increases, 7, 69, 70
negative consequence, 172
functioning, issues impacting, 70
further fragmentation, 69–70
impact, 139–40
fragmentation, accepting as necessary aspect of, 165–67
inadequate for small and medium-sized enterprises, 60
integrative effects, limiting to certain patentees, 62
jurisdiction, shared, 171
jurisprudence, 175–76
legal uncertainty:
compromise raising issue of, 49
regarding legal basis, 47
legitimacy, issues impacting, 70
limited membership, ratification, 49
Member States' individual decisions to become bound by, 54
official languages, 43
partial unification attempt, European patent system, 36
patchwork of laws, deriving substance from, 171
Regulation 1257, 45
Regulation 1260, 6, 36, 42, 43, 55, 57, 59, 60, 61
scope limited, 54
Spain rejection, 55
translation arrangements, 42, 43
UK decision not to participate, 60
unitary patents governed by domestic law, 48–49
United Kingdom participation willingness, 50–51
users of, territorial fragmentation, 59–63
unitary patents, 35
general:
EU system and, distinction between, 7
Italy, 55
participation in, territorial fragmentation, 54–59
protection Regulations, 36–37
renewal fees, 59
Spain, 55
systems, 1, 2
EU, 14, 104
European Council, 37, 38
Unified Patent Court cross-border jurisdiction, 6
unitary rights, 9
unitary systems, 56
United Kingdom:
Brexit, 50
CJEU, staunch objection to, 51
claim construction, 130
claim interpretation:
Actavis v Eli Lilly, 133–35, 137
Catnic v Hill & Smith, 127, 128, 129, 130, 137
Improver v Remington, 31, 112, 128–129, 131, 132, 135
Kirin-Amgen v Hoechst Marion, 129, 134–35
pith and marrow approach, 126–27
Court of Appeal reference to EPO Enlarged Board of Appeal, 125–26

decision not to participate in UPP, 60
divergence, 111
ECSC High Authority, refusal to accept, 75–76
equivalents, 132
Actavis v Eli Lilly, 133–35, 137
European Patent Convention, commitment to, 136
expertise of Courts in patent field, 140–41
inventive step:
obvious to try test, 114
Windsurfing/Pozzoli approach, 114
judicial cooperation, 136
national courts considering Board of Appeal decisions:
Biogen v Medeva, 119
Boards of Appeal decisions as persuasive authority, 119
EPC provisions interpretation, 118
Genentech Inc's Patent, 118
Human Genome Science v Eli Lilly, 119
Merrell Dow v Norton, 118, 119
national courts considering other national court decisions, 119
Court of Appeal emphasised, 120–21
Grimme v Scott, 120, 121
Supreme Court, 121
patentable subject matter:
Aerotel/Macrossan, 116, 125
any hardware approach rejected, 116
common law rules of precedence, 116
Symbian v Comptroller General of Patents, Designs and Trademarks, 116
technical character approach criticised, 117
technical contribution approach, 115, 116
Patents Act 1977, 111, 113
EPC provisions:
implementation into national law, 128
interpretation, 118
non-patentable subject matter listed in, 114–15
Protocol Questions, 129
Supreme Court:
approximations, 132
considering other national court decisions, 119
convergence, 124–35
doctrine of equivalents, 136
judicial cooperation, 136
Kirin-Amgen v Hoechst Marion, 134–35
promoting consistent approach to interpretation, 119
Schütz v Werit, 121
Warner-Lambert v Generics, 121
technical contribution approach, 115
UPCA ratification, later withdrawn, 51
UPP participation willingness, 50–51
United States:
patent court system, 66
UPC, *see* **Unified Patent Court**
UPCA, *see* **Unified Patent Court Agreement**
UPP, *see* **Unitary Patent Package**

validity claims:
national level, European patent system, 31
value pluralism, 83, 85, 86, 168
Biotech Directive, consideration in, 172
consideration in European patent system, 172
considering when responding to fragmentation, 168
disagreement reasons based on, 87
fragmentation consideration in, 173, 174
importance, 88–89
UPC consideration of, 166
values:
EU, *see* European Union
importance, 88–89
plurality of, 169
VICOM/Computer-related invention, 115
Vienna Convention on the Law of Treaties:
interpretation rules in:
fragmentation and, 173
introduced into European patent system, 175
interpretation of treaties, 95–96, 142
European Patent Office use of, 142
use for interpretation of treaties:
Boards of Appeal, EPO, 173
viewpoints:
bias towards, 175

Walzenformgebungsmaschine **case,** 122
WARF, 150–51, 157, 158–59
Warner-Lambert v Generics, 121
Windsurfing International v Tabur Marine, 113
World Intellectual Property Office (WIPO):
International Bureau:
international patent applications to, 32
international patent applications, 19, 32
introduced by Patent Cooperation Treaty, 1

Zahnkranzfräser **case,** 121

Lightning Source UK Ltd.
Milton Keynes UK
UKHW020914290922
409627UK00002B/29

9 781509 939312